Orville's Aviators

San Diego Christian College
2100 Greenfield Drive
El Cajon, CA 92019

629.13092
E260

40.50
Avi

Orville's Aviators

Outstanding Alumni of the Wright Flying School, 1910–1916

JOHN CARVER EDWARDS

McFarland & Company, Inc., Publishers

Jefferson, North Carolina, and London

LIBRARY OF CONGRESS CATALOGUING-IN-PUBLICATION DATA

Edwards, John Carver.
Orville's aviators : outstanding alumni of the Wright
Flying School, 1910–1916 / John Carver Edwards.
p.   cm.
Includes bibliographical references and index.

ISBN 978-0-7864-4227-0
softcover: 50# alkaline paper ∞

1. Air pilots — United States — Biography.
2. Wright Flying School — Alumni and alumnae.
I. Title.
TL539.E39   2009
629.13092' 273 — dc22   2009006340

British Library cataloguing data are available

©2009 John Carver Edwards. All rights reserved

*No part of this book may be reproduced or transmitted in any form
or by any means, electronic or mechanical, including photocopying
or recording, or by any information storage and retrieval system,
without permission in writing from the publisher.*

Cover image: Photograph from a series of flights from May through
July, 1910, just after the opening of the Wright Flying School,
probably with Orville acting as instructor;
Simms Station, Dayton, Ohio, Library of Congress.

Manufactured in the United States of America

*McFarland & Company, Inc., Publishers
Box 611, Jefferson, North Carolina 28640
www.mcfarlandpub.com*

CONTENTS

For Judy

PREFACE

During the heyday of the Wright Company, the Wright-Martin Aircraft Company, and the Dayton-Wright Aircraft Company (1909–1923), Dayton, Ohio, was the nation's Cradle of Aviation and fairly teemed with skilled craftsmen and daring pilots, the former who constructed the Wrights' gossamer planes at their spartan work stations and the latter who flew these craft on a daily basis as exhibition, instructional, test, and acceptance flyers for their respective companies, all of whose names have since dipped below history's radar screen. By today's standards their labor may seem hopelessly rudimentary and their machines downright primitive; but for them, every day dawned as a learning experience and, more important, as an adventure.

It was at this critical stage in aviation history, when early laboratory and on-site experimentation was giving way to the equally challenging realities of aircraft refinement and more sophisticated line production, that the individuals who appear in my book made their mark. For nearly a decade, while the Wrights searched for markets at home and overseas for their aircraft and defended their patent rights against a bevy of perceived interlopers, these aerial pioneers, as former Wright students and, in several instances, subsequent employees, worked tirelessly to spread the gospel of flight. Their active involvement in numerous air-minded organizations, publications, and national and international competitive meets would bring home the possibilities of aviation to many of their countrymen and a phalanx of enthusiasts abroad. Fortunately, several of them would survive near fatal crashes during their incipient careers to witness remarkable changes in aeronautical advancement such as the transition of aircraft control from the wing warping process to the use of ailerons, the adoption of improved power plants, research into new engine fuels, the introduction of retractable landing gear and ground-to-air communication, and many additional improvements too numerous to mention here.

The six unsung individuals I have chosen to profile in this study are more than representative of the entire Wright student body in terms of biographical interest and aeronautical accomplishment. These colorful Simms Station alumni include Russian immigrant Arthur L. Welsh for his fine work as an early flight instructor and a promoter not only of Wright machines but of the public's understanding and acceptance of flight as a practical everyday phenomenon; Howard W. Gill, the beneficiary of wealth and social position, whose reputation as pioneer aviation's devoted patron, publicist, and pilot has been sadly overlooked; New York native Archibald Freeman, who made headlines as this country's early architect and demonstrator of strategic bombing; Grover C. Bergdoll, whose brilliant early career as America's leading amateur flyer presented such a shining prologue to an otherwise tragic life; George Alphonso Gray, whose multifaceted career as a skilled exhibition flyer, test pilot, and flight instructor only begins to describe his amazing contributions to aviation; and Howard Max Rinehart, a true twentieth century adventurer whose exploits beggar the imagination, ranging from his Dayton days as barnstormer and test pilot for Orville — with a foray into revolutionary Mexico as flyer-of-choice in Pancho Villa's pathetic air force — to his time in Brazil as an explorer and a consultant to the Roosevelt administration's Rubber Development Corporation during World War II.

The Wright Flying School Brochure (Wilbur & Orville Wright Collection, Library of Congress, Washington, D.C.).

Without question, the selection process was difficult, and my attempts at tracing careers and major flying records — which were seemingly set and broken on a routine basis — were even more daunting. As stated earlier, despite the fact that the half dozen pioneer flyers profiled in this book came from dissimilar backgrounds, taken collectively they, in my judgment, fairly represented their 113 fellow alumni in so many ways and were therefore my picks. Their common characteristics as pilots included an all-consuming love of flying; a superior intelligence coupled with a near genius for mechanical innovation; overweening self-confidence; obsessive-compulsive behavior; a superb knowledge of the aircraft of the day; a dash of sardonic fatalism in their otherwise optimistic outlook on life; restlessness; a gritty persistence; a somewhat irascible temperament (varying in degree) which did not suffer fools lightly; and an absolute devotion to their instructors and the Wrights.

In the preparation of this book I discovered that the contemporary primary sources and the rich store of secondary works were barely sufficient to keep abreast of the nomadic and often irregular lifestyles of these engaging personalities. A few of the Wright airmen, aside from their commitments to the firm, moonlighted on the side in various enterprises, and even flew random exhibition dates on their own, risking violation of the brothers' patent infringement policies, which not only limited their use of Wright aircraft to company purposes but also forbade them contractually from flying competitive machines as well.

There were other research hurdles to overcome. Since flying school operators and the exhibition team coexisted during 1910–1911, what few instructors there were often filled one capacity or the other. The "road pilots," as Orville referred to his exhibition performers, were constantly fulfilling engagements across America, and what we know about them is limited to select sources, such as correspondence between the Wrights' manager, Roy Knabenshue, and his itinerant birdmen concerning flying dates, aircraft malfunctions and crashes, hotel bookings, and personnel complaints. Back in Dayton, documentation is equally circumscribed regarding some of these same individuals who also flew as instructors, test pilots, or demonstration and acceptance flyers. Tattered instructional logbooks are great artifacts and acceptable predictors of an early flyer's potential, but they reveal little about the personality, character, or motivations behind the subject's decision to make the pilgrimage to Simms Station.

Conversely, scrapbooks, reminiscences, memoirs, and especially hometown and national newspapers afforded me a peek into the private lives of my subjects. These sources answered many questions I had about the formative years of these early flyers and, more important for the focus of this work, their crowded lives following Simms Station. The issues of a flyer's youth, parental and spousal support or opposition, divorces and breaches of promise legal filings resulting from divorce, and other low points in one's flying career such as poor pay, few benefits, the inability to keep one's own winnings, and the loss of compatriots, all factored into what it meant to be not only a pioneer flyer, but a Wright flyer as well.

Many friends and colleagues read versions of this book in manuscript form, and I am grateful for their suggestions and support. In particular, special thanks to Dr. Mary Anne Whelan, daughter of Bernard L. Whelan, for her invaluable advice, for the use of her father's wonderful diary, and for her family's extraordinary pictures of Howard Rinehart and Arch Freeman. My new Aussie friend (American by birth), Rob Grant, has afforded me much welcome material on, and photographs of, his greatuncle, Howard Rinehart, and his beautiful wife, Miriam Dove Rinehart. I am also indebted to the archival staffs of the Smithsonian Institution, National Air and Space Museum, Washington, D.C.; the Special Services Division, Research Branch, Wright-Patterson AFB, Ohio; Special Collections and Archives, Dunbar Library, Wright State University, Dayton, Ohio; the Historical Collection, Kettering University; University Archives, Roesch Library, the University of Dayton; the Manuscripts Division of the Library of Congress, Washington, D.C.; Catherine Allen and William Herndon, College Park Aviation Museum, College Park, Maryland; Jean Doherty, Glenn H. Curtiss Museum, Hammondsport, New York; and Joan and Bill Hannan, Hannan's Runway, Magalia, California. For her unflagging faith in this book and her efforts on its behalf, I must thank my wife, Judith Task Edwards, for her suggestions in the areas of substance, style, and format.

INTRODUCTION

Aviation came into its own in Dayton, Ohio, on November 22, 1909, with the incorporation of the Wright Company, Wilbur serving as its president and younger brother Orville as one of two vice presidents. Enjoying a $1 million stock capitalization, a corporate office in New York City, and a projected manufacturing complex, the organization's future seemed bright. Already, Wright-built and licensed machines were being offered for sale by British, German, and French subsidiaries. In scarcely a year's time the first of two factory buildings would be erected, with the company's output running at two airplanes a month.

A new two-plane hangar on Huffman Prairie signified that after a protracted hiatus the Wrights had returned to fly once again. Always a beehive of activity, the crude shed represented two separate divisions of the Wright enterprise: its exhibition company and its school of aviation, which lasted from 1910 through 1916. In addition to the Simms Station instructional site, by the close of 1911 there would be other flying fields established at Montgomery, Alabama (terminated in late May 1910), Augusta, Georgia, and Belmont Park, New York.

The school noted in its brochure that "four hours of actual practice in the air" would be afforded the candidate, as well as "such instruction in the principles of flying machines as is necessary to prepare the pupil to become a competent and expert operator." Attention to the aforementioned principles consumed the students' time for most of their customary ten days of training, with usually a maximum of fifteen minutes in the air each day. A great deal of time was spent on the ground waiting, making the pilots, in one wag's words, "aviwaiters." A wind of much more than ten miles an hour kept the planes on terra firma, and a cross-country flight of eight miles was enough to warrant a column in the local press.

Tuition rose to $500 per pupil in 1912, payable at the beginning of the course, and reduced by half for the aspiring flyer who agreed to purchase a Wright craft in the bargain. Any damage inflicted on the trainers was covered in the initial fee, an eventuality largely mitigated by the fact that the aircraft were equipped with dual controls so that the instructor could immediately take charge in cases of mechanical failure or pilot error.

All students soon acquired a thorough knowledge of the machines they would fly: how to service, mend, and modify their planes in record time. Wright training commenced with a tour of the factory and included instruction in how the planes were made. Trainees were required to witness the reassembly of planes after shipping and rebuilding after crashes, and to perform flight inspections before every takeoff. In a back room of the factory these rookies spent hours on a primitive flight simulator preparing for their first venture aloft.

The Wrights' control system was involved, so there was little opportunity to consider the next move. One lever managed the elevator, and that worked in the anticipated way: push it forward to dive, pull it back to climb. The other lever consisted of two parts, activating both the rudder and the wing warping. The Wright wing was controlled by warping, the trailing edge of the wing flexed, comparable to the tips of a bird's wing. To veer right, for example, the pilot had to pull the lever back to lift the left wing, while also turning the top of the lever the correct number of degrees to move the rudder. By comparison, archrival Glenn Curtiss had devised more up-to-date controls — pull a wheel back to make the plane climb, and push it forward to dive. A right turn was achieved by leaning to the right in a harness. "The Wright control system," according to then novice Lieutenant Henry H. Arnold, "was the most difficult."

This is where the flight simulator came to the rescue of many baffled pupils. "It [a retired Flyer] was probably taken out of commission due to its age and need of general overhauling," recollected Grover C. Bergdoll, a member of the class of 1912. "The motor was taken out, but the propellers were still in place. It was mounted on a kind of wooden trestle which permitted it to tip over from side to side, and would not remain in a horizontal position if left to itself." This contrivance made an indelible impression on Lieutenant Arnold:

> The lateral controls were connected with small clutches at the wingtips, and grabbed a moving belt running over a pulley. A forward motion, and the clutch would snatch the belt, and down would go the left wing. A backward pull, and the reverse would happen. The jolts and teetering were so violent that the student was kept busy just moving the lever back and forth just to keep on an even keel. That was primary training, and it lasted for a few days.

In order to make the exercise challenging, Orville Wright would slip up behind students from time to time and yank down on a wing to test their reaction.

Although many would-be pilots showed up at Simms Station and the other Wright fields nattily attired, their instructors quickly had them without boaters, ties, and coats, their sleeves rolled up above their elbows, their bodies reeking of perspiration and gasoline, and covered from head to shoe with dirt, engine oil, and grease. The Wrights' promotional literature understandably made no mention of the ruts, hummocks, cow patties, and rattlesnakes to be found on the Simms Station flying site; nor, for that matter, of the daily grind of removing the flimsy biplanes from their hangar each morning and late afternoon for a takeoff, and the backbreaking task of dragging or carting them back from their landing spot to the hangar when flying was done. Completely exhausted classmates spent their "free" moments tuning engines

Wilbur (left) and Orville Wright, June 1909 (Wilbur & Orville Wright Collection, Library of Congress, Washington, D.C. Correspondence File: Family Papers).

and repairing worn or damaged airframes. With such a grueling regimen from dawn to dusk, it was small wonder that pupils were known to collapse on cots inside the Wright hangar at day's end without a thought about supper. And yet, as if by magic, these determined apprentices always seemed to find time for pranks, bull sessions, and poker marathons—usually on Sunday, as the brothers forbade Sabbath flying.

Horseplay and pranks, in fact, proved to be the perfect anecdote against the fatigue, frustration, and tension associated with the beginning flyer's obsessive desire to perform well. When Boston native Harry Nelson Atwood enrolled in the Wright School in the summer of 1911, his fellow students soon took advantage of his overly serious nature and mind-boggling gullibility. Wright plant manager Grover Loening indicted Lieutenant "Hap" Arnold as Harry's chief tormentor, who "picked on his [Atwood's] zeal to do everything to be a perfect aviator as a swell chance for some first-class kidding." Ringleader Arnold and others explained in-depth to their victim how important it was to master a sense of balance, and that the "Wright" way of achieving this skill was by climbing atop a two-wheeled handling cart and, standing astride the vehicle at its center with a long plank across one's shoulders, proceeding to balance the board and himself on the two wheels. "Hap's" dupe immediately tackled this hopeless feat with a fellow conspirator seated at a table before the hangar entrance checking Atwood's performance on a phony score pad, tallying numbers which would determine whether Harry possessed good enough balance to fly. In another instance, his chums confided to him that to be an outstanding pilot he had to learn to fly in a straight line and, moreover, that Orville required every new pupil to make his or her own line to practice on. As a favor, Arnold and company presented Atwood with his personal whitewash pail and brush to paint a white line several hundred feet long on Simms Station's grassy field. Harry took to the task with the earnestness of a convert. The Wrights ultimately put a stop to these practical jokes.

Despite the pressures, hard work, and random hazing associated with student flying, Bernard Leonard Whelan looked back at his time at Simms Station with great fondness.

> I must say that the summer of 1913 spent learning to fly at Simms Station was one of the happiest periods of my life. Flying was so new and original and, if you will, romantic in a sense. The Wright "B" was as controllable as any plane I piloted in subsequent years. Very light pressure was required for response in each of the three elements of control— vertical, horizontal and directional and flying in itself gave one a feeling of exhilaration, especially in a Wright "B" of that vintage where you sat entirely exposed to the elements on a seat near the leading edge of the wing. A surprise when you had your first flight was the fact that there was no feeling of height, something hard to understand except that you were in or on a moving vehicle and not stationary above anything reflecting a vertical dimension.

Authorized breaks from Orville's arduous routine did occur on occasion in the guise of "hangar flying" sessions between instructors and their charges, an informal conference amounting to a critique of each student's aerial transgressions. The Wrights would drop by periodically and quietly monitor these confabs, offering no opinion unless asked by a chastened student seeking an expert referee. Lieutenant Arnold called to mind one such incident.

> One, I remember well, a loud argument was in progress about just how the loop would be accomplished — a time we hoped was not far off. Opinions differed as to whether it would be done from "the inside" or the "outside.".…The Wright brothers listened with interest, never saying a word. Then, as everyone was laying down the law about this or that approach, Wilbur quietly attracted our attention and pointed overhead. In the slightly windy air far above the shed, a lark was fighting hard to fly straight upward, and as we watched the bird struggled over on its back and curved down again, coming out in level flight from a crude but indisputable loop.

Having graduated from the simulator, trainees flew with an instructor, initially as passengers, then little by little taking over the controls. No more than four or five pupils drew a single instructor, and the lessons were given on a rotating basis. Mentor and protégé sat side by side, and the Wright system produced some pilots who flew from the left and others who flew from the right, depending on how they were trained. For example, Harry Atwood and Thomas DeWitt Milling were southpaw flyers.

After nearly two dozen flights and two or three hours in the air, a pupil soloed. But even following graduation, the proud aviator or aviatrix was warned against flying in the wind too quickly or seeking appreciable altitude without additional experience, as well as of the pitfalls of up-trends and down-trends, thin-air, holes-in-the-air, and back drafts.

Howard Rinehart (left), aviatrix Marjorie Stinson, and Griffith Brewer (in duster) take a break during flying lessons in Dayton with unidentified students (courtesy Dr. Mary Anne Whelan).

Few graduates displayed the same instincts or the same skills for various aspects of flying. Some managed to land their machines with precision in record time, but needed repeated coaching in their training before they learned to take off correctly; some were quick studies, while others who were exceedingly slow to learn at the outset caught on suddenly to the proper handling of the machine. Also, a difference evolved between those who displayed early brilliance as pilots, and others who developed into steady flyers, both categories, nevertheless, exhibiting an equal measure of skill. There were graduates who went through back-to-back courses in order to both refine their techniques and extend their enjoyment of flying among worthy peers.

According to historian Howard Mansfield, the students' emotional state generally correlated with their flying progress over the period of instruction at Simms Station, fluctuating from abject despondency to vaulting self-confidence. A lot had to do with the temperament and patience of one's instructor. Following her enrollment on June 26, 1914, Marjorie Stinson recalled that her greatest dread was being chewed out by her instructor, Howard Rinehart, always within earshot of her peers. She found this dressing down more "humiliating than being a minor." On the afternoon of August 4, Stinson endured one flight with Rinehart, then a two-minute flight alone which included a set of figure eights. It was a liberating experience to be without Howard: "I knew exactly who was flying then, and I could almost hear the other students' sighs of relief when I stepped out of the plane leaving it all in one piece, that they might later fly in it." Andrew Drew, a former St. Louis balloonist who took his lessons in August of 1911, described his personal mood swing as rather dramatic.

> When you enter the Wright School of Aviation here, they first warn you of two things — a dismal feeling that comes in the beginning of the course that you don't really want to fly so much after all, and the belief that comes after you make your first trip alone that you can fly from New York to San Francisco immediately.... After my twelfth lesson, when I had flown the machine around the field several times without any assistance, I ceased calling my instructor "Mr. [J. Clifford] Turpin," and said, "Well, Turpi, I guess I am a birdman."

Despite Harry Atwood's repeated early threats made to his instructor about leaving Orville's program in the summer of 1911, he stuck to his flying and became one of the Wrights' most spectacular pilots. After two weeks of training he graduated, having completed eighteen lessons and flown for a total of one hour and fifty-five minutes. Some years later Atwood recounted the particulars of his unofficial solo.

> Orville had gone to town one day and I decided I'd fly the machine. I had never been up but one time and then it was only for a few feet. But this time I got the thing off the ground and into the air. I had to learn how to maneuver the stick and make the airplane fly. I simply got the thing into the air and didn't know how to get it down. It took about two hours for me to get the feel of it and know just how to make it do what I wanted. After that it was easy and I landed and found that I'd been in the air longer than any other person. Everybody thought I was a hero.

Whether Harry's claim was true or not is subject to discussion, as his alleged solo flight would have constituted his entire time in the air, not taking into account his recorded eighteen lessons. His claim notwithstanding, Atwood did conquer the air, flying from Boston to Washington, D.C., a few weeks later, and more important, setting a new American long-distance record by summers' end, winging his way from St. Louis to New York in twelve days with but a single extended layover for repairs along the way.

The ultimate attainment of a student's initial level of proficiency following the instruction at Dayton — what is generally referred to as the pilot's license, which was but the first step in flying and becoming the possessor of a license — made them a pilot capable of flying a machine; the student was not considered an "expert" until more experience had been gained under extraordinary circumstances. Another accolade was awarded by the International Aeronautical Federation. This was known as the Expert Aviator's Certificate, which could be earned by licensed aviators, but only after demonstrating uncommon ability in difficult landings and takeoffs, cross-country flights, the indisputable exhibition of competence in the air, and sound judgment. A select number of Wright birdmen went on to win this rating; many others did not.

Altogether, 119 civilian and military students of every stripe migrated to Simms Station alone, among the other Wright fields: society blue bloods, or their progeny, with a thirst for flying and the cash to purchase one of the Wrights' sky chariots; ordinary citizens who could barely afford the price of their lessons; army officers slated for instructorships at Signal Corps aviation schools such as the one at College Park, Maryland; transplanted Canadians (41) whose wartime tutelage was mandated under contract between Montreal and Washington; and last but not least, three daring young women who thumbed their noses at convention: Marjorie Stinson, Leda Richberg-Hornsby, and Rose Dougan (Dugan).

Of the three aviatrixes, Marjorie Stinson and Leda Richberg-Hornsby seem to have captured most of the headlines. Inspired by sister Katherine's exhibition flying around the country, Marjorie enrolled in the Wright flying academy at the tender age of eighteen, soloed on August 4, 1914, and received her license eight days later. After a fruitless effort to create an airmail route in Texas, she joined her family in establishing a flight school in San Antonio. Marjorie and Katherine became instructors; their brother Edward worked as chief mechanician; and their mother rounded out the family enterprise as business manager. Inducted into the U.S. Aviation Reserve Corps in 1915, Marjorie began instructing Royal Canadian Flying Corps cadets the following year. She soon earned the affectionate moniker the "Flying Schoolmarm," and her broods were known as the "Texas Escadrille." The Stinson training facility closed at war's end, and Marjorie barnstormed county fairs until the late twenties. When she finally left active flying, Stinson moved to Washington, D.C., in 1930, where she worked as a draftsman with the aeronautical division of the U.S. Navy. Following her death in April 1975, Stinson was cremated and her ashes scattered over San Antonio Airport, the site where she initially learned to fly prior to Dayton.

A 1913 Simms Station matriculate, Chicago socialite Leda Richberg-Hornsby spent her postgraduate time in assorted pursuits. She became involved in the suffrage movement, working closely with Carrie Chapman Catt. Leda specialized in dropping campaign leaflets over metropolitan centers from her Model B. Owning membership in the Aero Club of America and the United States Aviation Reserve of St. Louis, Richberg-Hornsby attempted to join the U.S. flying corps in France in 1916, but the Paris government refused her service, despite the twenty-six-year-old's record of having made over one thousand flights. Shaking off this rebuff, Leda gamely charged ahead, offering the press her future projects in aviation.

> I am now planning to attempt a 1000-mile flight and when I have accomplished that I will cross the Continent from ocean to ocean. And if all goes well you will find me among the pioneers to attempt a trans-Atlantic flight.
>
> My own experience has shown me that flying can be made just as wholesome for my sex as any other sport — golf, tennis, motoring. I am going to start an aviation school in Florida — not like the ugly things the men have created, but having the aspect of a country club.
>
> We will have tea served and find what we can't get at any of the hangars now dressing rooms. There will be a special course to teach women and girls military observation, and I shall ask for the appointment of an Army and Navy officer to instruct us.

Following America's declaration of war on the Central Powers, Richberg-Hornsby again tried to enlist as a combat pilot in France, and again her overture was rejected. From this point on she seemingly took leave from the world of aviation. Leda Richberg (she divorced her husband in 1915) passed away on August 25, 1939, of a heart condition at the age of 47, her grandiose dreams unrealized.

When Wright instructors signed off on each member of this diverse fraternity, the graduates left Dayton or remained as employees of the company, with the confidence of knowing that they had conquered a new and exciting endeavor — the art of flying. Perhaps more important than teaching them the nuts and bolts of flight, Wilbur and Orville had inculcated in their freshman aviators an unswerving conviction that they were more than equal to any challenge, not only in the realm of flying, but in the totality of one's life as well. Five-star general of the air force "Hap" Arnold later wrote in his 1949 autobiography, *Global Mission*, that "more than anyone I have ever known or read about, the Wright brothers gave me the sense that nothing is impossible. I like to think — and during World War II often did — that the Air Force has rooted its traditions in that spirit."

As civilian orders for their pusher-type aircraft began to wane by the summer of 1912, a situation brought on by growing domestic and foreign competition and a string of fatal crashes later attributable to design flaws, Orville began to rely ever more on his relationship with the Army Aviation Corps for business, serving as consultant and teacher of both military pilots and instructors. Following Wilbur's death from typhoid fever on May 30, 1912, Orville succeeded his brother as president of the Wright Company, now finding himself saddled with not only oversight of the Wright School of Aviation (the exhibition team having been cancelled in November 1911 due to the excessive loss of life among its pilots), but also the direction of the firm's patent infringement litigation and its development and research operation.

"Orv's" personal flying career lasted less than two years beyond the close of his once famous school. On May 13, 1918, he took up a Model B one last time, cruising alongside a Wright modified prototype of the British deHavilland DH-4, newly minted at the Moraine City plant, south of Dayton. Today one can review the names of the brothers' 119 graduates, which are embossed on one of the commemorative plaques surrounding the Wright Memorial at Wright-Patterson Air Force Base. The memorial is situated in a 27-acre wooded park called Wright Brothers Hill in Area B of Wright-Patterson and is located atop a 100-foot bluff which overlooks Huffman Prairie and Simms Station.

Research suggests that for many of the Wrights' students the field at Simms Station symbolized much more than simply a geographical location on the outskirts of Dayton. For those who pursued their dream of flying and succeeded, the site represented a transformative crucible wherein instruction and friendships reforged and redirected their lives. Whether these candidates were civilians chasing an exciting new sport or preparing for a serious flying profession, or junior military officers seeking to further their careers as pilots, for a brief period they all shared a common passion. It is comforting to imagine that the memories of those with whom these pioneer aerialists flew, and from whom they learned, sustained them in their latter years, their mellowed recollections undiminished by time and the painful loss of classmates from long ago who had perished in their vintage machines doing what they, too, loved best.

One

ARTHUR L. WELSH

The Wrights' Peerless Salesman of Flight

Arthur L. Welsh was born Laibel Wellcher or Willcher in a small village near Kiev, Russia, to Abraham and Dvora (Dora) on August 14, 1881. His family came to the United States in 1890, settling in Philadelphia, Pennsylvania. He attended public school but failed to graduate, subsequently receiving the balance of his elementary education from a retired teacher who resided with the family. Young Laibel also attended a cheder where he learned the basics of prayer and Jewish religious service. Records indicate that Laibel was especially adept at mathematics, languages, and pen and pencil etching. Stocky and athletically inclined, he also became an expert swimmer and accomplished oarsman. His father died in 1894 and his mother soon remarried, to Frank Silverman. The stepfather worked in a tailor shop on 4½ Street and Dvora opened a grocery store in the basement of the family home, as well as rented out rooms, to make ends meet. His stepfather, known as Uncle Frum to the children, taught Laibel to play the zither and imitate bird calls, and he even encouraged the boy to perform strenuous exercises to help lengthen his short stature. Laibel was eventually dispatched to Washington, D.C., to stay with relatives — perhaps due to friction between the boy and his new stepfather — until his parents followed in 1898. After becoming a naturalized citizen, Welsh enlisted in the navy in April 1901 at twenty years of age. As a means of protecting himself from discrimination or worse because of his faith, Laibel changed his name to Arthur L. Welsh, and was known to his friends as Al.

Welsh served from 1901 to 1905 on the U.S.S. *Hancock* and U.S.S. *Monongahela* and drew shore duty for a time in Guantánamo, Cuba. He was honorably discharged as a seaman in April 1905. The following month he contracted typhoid fever and was hospitalized for four months. During his long period of recovery Welsh became infatuated with flying machines and the mechanics of flight, his interest going back to the earliest reports of man's ability to fly. With his health restored Al took two jobs, one as a bookkeeper for a local gas company and the second as a boys' physical education instructor, all the while retaining his interest in aviation.

During this juncture Welsh joined several youth organizations connected with

Adas Israel Congregation in Washington, where his stepfather was an active member. At one such meeting he met his future wife, Anna Harmel, a daughter of Paul Harmel, an immigrant from Liepaja, Latvia. Mr. Harmel was a member of the board of managers of the congregation and an early leader in the Zionist movement of Washington, the United Hebrew Charities, HIAS, and other area and national Jewish groups. Al Welsh married Anna on October 10, 1907, the Rabbi Gedaliah Silverstone of the Adas Israel Congregation presiding.

Welsh attended Orville Wright's first public aerial demonstrations before War Department military brass and government officials at Fort Myer, Virginia, in September 1908. He was there again when both Orville and Wilbur completed these tests the next year. In the fall of 1909 Welsh began corresponding with the Wrights about employment opportunities, but received little encouragement. He next appeared before them in Dayton to apply for admittance to their planned flying school. At first, the brothers refused his requests due to his lack of background in engine mechanics — he had never even driven an automobile. In order to rid themselves of him, he was told to go to New York and make his case to the Wrights' representative in that city. This rebuff only served to occasion yet another pilgrimage to Ohio. This time his earnestness and self-confidence won the day and he was tentatively accepted, but only when conditions permitted.

Meanwhile the Wrights elected to launch an exhibition flying program and employed the celebrated balloonist Roy Knabenshue to manage the business. Naturally, for such an undertaking Orville and Wilbur required a stable of young pilots, and in the midst of their planning phase the brothers kept their word and wired Welsh that they would accept him as one of this group. Despite his mother's determined opposition, Al jumped at this opportunity and arrived in Dayton in the spring of 1910 to undergo flight training.

Desirous of launching their plans as early as possible in warmer climes, the Wrights went South to establish their first civilian flying school at Montgomery, Alabama, in March 1910. Wilbur had earlier engaged a field, and on March 19 Walter Brookins, a West Side Dayton native, James W. Davis of Colorado Springs, Colorado, and Wright mechanician Charles Taylor showed up in Montgomery to assemble the plane and get operations underway. Five days later Orville and student Spencer Crane from Dayton made their appearance and instruction began, with Brookins, Davis, and Crane as pupils. Within the week, Welsh and automobile enthusiast Arch Hoxsey from Pasadena, California, arrived, thereby rounding out the class. Perhaps all five students took special pride in the knowledge that the trainer they flew was the same machine Wilbur had used the previous fall when he made the famous flight for the Hudson-Fulton Celebration in New York.

The solitary airplane shipped to Montgomery for use at the school was also the 10th or 11th machine built in America by the Wrights, five of the preceding planes having been sent to Europe for exhibition purposes. The plane topped out at 902 pounds with gasoline and water and carried a four-cylinder motor weighing 190 pounds capable of developing from 25 to 35 hp. Orville's machine was launched from a monorail, 192 feet long, built in 6-foot sections, so that it could readily be shifted to provide for a takeoff into the wind. The entire length was seldom needed. Flights were of short duration in the beginning, but after a few days, altitude and duration were extended until a ceiling of 2,000 feet was attained in a flight of 30 minutes on May 2.

On May 10, Welsh returned to Ohio with Orville, who left Brookins in charge at the Montgomery field. Back in Dayton everything was in readiness to open the larger Simms Station summer school. By now, Al was flying alone, and the quality of his performance was such that Orville both invited him into the Wright organization as an instructor and decided to personally groom him for that role. Brookins returned to Dayton toward the end of May and was tapped by Orville as chief instructor, with Welsh as his assistant. Working together with Orville, the trio began the training of Ralph Johnstone, a native of Kansas City, Missouri, who had earned his living as a trick bicycle rider since the age of fifteen, Duval LaChapelle, a Parisian who had worked as Wilbur's mechanician, and Frank Coffyn, an affluent New Yorker who joined Orville's select group through the influence of his banker father.

An accelerated training program was rushed forward to prepare the exhibition team for public appearances. During the final three weeks of May and the first ten days of June, 260 instructional flights were conducted by Orville, Al, and Walter Brookins. The Model B Flyer made its debut in early July, and further tests were carried on with wheeled machines later that month.

The first Wright exhibition date was scheduled to be held at the Indianapolis Motor Speedway between June 13 and 18, and Welsh scrambled to be as prepared as possible for the event. Orville's aerial ensemble had five machines for their opening show. With scarcely a scintilla of flying experience beyond Orville's instructorship, Welsh, Brookins, Hoxsey, Johnstone, Coffyn, and LaChapelle performed acceptably well, for novices. To begin with, Welsh and Brookins went aloft together with passengers and remained airborne for 12 minutes. Unfortunately, the team's inexperience resulted in most of the flying at Indianapolis consisting of humdrum laps around the track. Having overbilled the event, the promoters were disappointed. "The age is one of speed and competition," groaned an attending official, "and I want to see a flock of airships fighting for first place under the wire." Over 30 flights were made without incident, however, and "Orv" bestirred the galleries by performing several flights with distinguished guests.

From July 2 to July 7 Al flew alone at Aurora, Illinois. On July 5, in the midst of a 20-minute flight, he experienced a forced landing in an oat field. Following his adjustment of the engine, the starting track was brought near the plane; but on leaving the rail one wing hit the ground with minor damage to the machine. Welsh's best showing came on the last scheduled day of the date when he accomplished an extraordinary 55 minute flight. Intermittent bad weather forced Al to remain in Aurora for two extra days as a sop to his patient fans. When not on the exhibition circuit that summer, Al instructed Phil O. Parmelee and J. Clifford Turpin back in Dayton.

Welsh came to Minneapolis, Minnesota, on September 5 for a five-day engagement. There he encountered a challenging assignment of flying out of a confined area inside a racetrack surrounded by obstructions. Al gamely attempted to honor the contract; but after a bit of flying he suffered a smashup on landing which put his craft out of commission and landed him in bed with strains and bruises. Arch Hoxsey arrived from Lincoln, Nebraska, with another Flyer to complete Welsh's engagement.

All the while, Glenn Curtiss was assembling his own exhibition outfit at Hammondsport, New York, with the intention of taking on the Wright flyers at every meet. Operating under the lax direction of manager Jerome Fanciulli, Curtiss' crew was handsomely paid, receiving 50 percent of the gate. Since the Wrights were suing Curtiss for patent infringement at this time, there should have been considerable animosity between the competing aviators. "We were taught by the Wrights that the Curtiss crowd was just no good at all," Frank Coffyn recollected. "We turned our noses up at them. But we found out later on, by flying at the same meets, that they were a pretty nice bunch of fellows."

Wright pilots, by comparison, sometimes chafed under the brothers' family values. The sins of drinking, gambling and Sabbath flying were strictly forbidden. Worse still, the pay — a set fee of $20 per week and $50 for every day a man flew — scarcely compensated for their employers' bluenose regulations. In contrast, the Wrights demanded $1,000 for each day that their people flew at an event. The company received $6,000 per pilot for a standard one-week meet, plus any prize money earned; the flyer received $320. In 1910 the company's exhibition profits topped $100,000, half of which went to the brothers themselves.

Since everyone knew that the Wrights and Curtiss were feuding in the courts, many spectators took sides, regarding any particular meet as a de facto field of honor. Consequently, risk-takers on each tour played to the grandstands. Hoxey and Johnstone took on the competition and each other as the "Stardust Twins" in duels of aerial aerobatics and high jinks — and danger. The first accident occurred on August 10 at Asbury Park, New Jersey, when Brookins suffered a broken nose, a broken ankle, and the loss of several teeth in a crash while attempting to avoid a bevy of reporters. With Brookins' Model A out of commission, Orville ordered the new B type with wheels sent to Asbury Park. Unused to the Model B's long landing roll due to its wheels, pilot Johnstone misjudged his set down and collided with a line of parked cars. In early September Hoxsey's machine, during a dangerously low pass before a packed grandstand, suddenly fell to earth at the Wisconsin State Fair in Milwaukee, injuring a number of spectators. Arch's mishap elicited a stern written rebuke from Wilbur to both Hoxsey and Johnstone.

From October 8 to October 18 Al flew at Kinloch Park, St. Louis, Missouri. Appearing with him were Wright airmen Brookins, Hoxsey, Turpin, Parmelee, and Johnstone. At this venue Johnstone lost control of his plane in a turn and set down so hard that his engine separated from its mount and rocketed forward, narrowly missing him. Unfazed, former President Theodore Roosevelt went up with Hoxsey the following day. Overall, Welsh posted an enviable performance, remaining aloft a total of 16 hours and 13 minutes during the ten-day competition. On October 11 he won the James A. Blair Cup when he set a new United States endurance record of 3 hours, 11 minutes and 55 seconds, covering 120 miles during the flight. Al stayed behind at Kinloch for several days to obtain his F.A.I. pilot's license, no. 23, dated October 23, 1910.

After St. Louis Welsh journeyed to New York to enter the 1910 Belmont Park competition running from October 22 through the 30th of the month. This was a huge international event held at a Long Island racetrack, and Wilbur and Orville were there along with Brookins, Hoxsey, Welsh, Johnstone, Parmelee, and Turpin. Six Curtiss flyers were also entered, as well as a number of the leading aviators of Great Britain and France. Finally, there were seven independent American competitors, including Clifford B. Harmon in his Farman machine; Earl Ovington piloting his American-built Blériot monoplane; John Moisant, who had only recently crossed the English Channel in his Blériot; and millionaire Harry Harkness in his Antoinette.

Welsh was drawn to Belmont by the lure of $72,300 in prize money. The contest would end with the second running of the James Gordon Bennett speed classic, which archrival Curtiss had captured at Reims the previous year. The Wright team banked on a special Model R machine called the Baby Grand. The plane had a shortened wingspan of just 21 feet and a more powerful engine that produced upwards of 60 hp. Orville, who had flown the craft at 70 mph, expected real results from it. Further inducements included a $10,000 race around the Statue of Liberty and an array of altitude, speed, and duration events.

The contest began on a positive note when Johnstone set a new world altitude record of over 9,200 feet. Regrettably, Brookins smashed the Baby Grand four days later on a trial run, thereby nullifying Wright hopes of winning the Gordon Bennett. Englishman Claude Grahame-White, the subject of one of the Wrights' patent infringement suits, took the 1910 Gordon Bennett trophy. Independent aviator John Moisant won the Statue of Liberty race. Only Johnstone's recording of another altitude record on October 30, which raised the brothers' total earning to $15,000, together with the $20,000 paid them for sanctioning the Belmont, saved the day. As Wright scholar Tom Crouch has observed, "It was clear that they [Wilbur and Orville] had lost their technological edge. After Belmont, the inventors of the airplane resigned themselves to a position back in the middle of the pack." Welsh's name scarcely surfaced with regard to the Long Island contest, a circumstance not altogether surprising in that Al's forte lay in instruction rather than competition. Returning to Dayton, Welsh continued his instructional work for the remainder of the season, and on December 24 took his stepsister, Clara Wiseman, for an aerial spin. On June 28, 1957, Clara recalled that flight for the flyer's nephew:

> I made my first flight with Uncle Arthur at the controls at Wright Field, Dayton, Ohio, when he took his machine up 1,250 feet, which lasted all of nine minutes during which time he made a number of figure 8s. He looked at me to see what my feelings were also if I was frightened. Having had complete confidence in his ability, it left me completely fearless.

While Welsh tended to his flock of aspiring birdmen back in Dayton, the "Stardust Twins" continued on the exhibition circuit. Hoxsey performed at Baltimore, Maryland, on November 2, after which he, Johnstone, and Brookins were scheduled to fly at a Denver air meet beginning November 16. Johnstone flew first, climbing high and winging over into a spiraling volplane. He went straight into the ground. Also in the air, Arch was unable to prevent his partner's mangled body and demolished machine from being picked clean by a souvenir-hunting mob. Six days after Welsh took his half-sister on a joyride over Wright Field, Hoxey and Brookins took off from Dominguez Field, Los Angeles, California. Arch soared to 7,000 feet hoping to set a new altitude record, called it quits, and dipped into a hurtling dive from which he, like Johnstone, never recovered. The Wrights persevered in the exhibition business for another eleven months following Hoxsey's death, but with profits falling and bad publicity rising regarding the questionable reliability of their machines, the brothers dissolved the team in November 1911.

On January 1, 1911, The *Washington Post* carried a "no-holds-barred" interview with Welsh regarding the loss of his colleagues:

> Hoxsey's death is a direct result of the dangers confronting all aviators attempting the spiral dip or dive. When he tried this vaudeville stunt it was in violation of a precaution urged by both Orville and Wilbur Wright. Johnstone met his death last November in a similar attempt to thrill the crowds. Instead of trying to astonish spectators, aviators should spend their efforts in a practical use of the flying machine. Their [Hoxsey and Johnstone] familiarity with the machines seems to breed a contempt for danger. Any aviator who attempts the spiral dive is simply flirting with death.

Addressing Arch's fearlessness, Welsh recollected that when in Grand Forks, North Dakota, the preceding July, Hoxsey could not bring his craft down without crashing into a grandstand filled with people. To prevent this catastrophe, continued Al, the aviator drove his plane downward at terrific speed, but escaped injury, and with the satisfaction of not causing a loss of life. Probing further into Hoxsey's indomitable spirit, Welsh alluded to a recent incident when he was making flights in Minneapolis, Minnesota, and Arch was flying in Lincoln, Nebraska. Welsh recalled that Arch was badly bruised in an accident which kept him bedridden for several months. The same day, in Lincoln, Hoxsey flew into a barn and was also badly shaken up. Despite Arch's painful condition, he entrained for Minneapolis and made flights for three days in Welsh's stead to avoid disappointing the crowds.

In explaining the dangers of the spiral dive, Welsh told the reporter that the more daring aviators would tilt their ships to such an extreme angle that a gust of wind, in striking either the upper or lower wing, would upset the machine before the pilot could right the aircraft. Despite the deaths of his daring but reckless friends, Al concluded that these tragedies would not dampen the future of aviation. Scarcely two months later, Welsh endorsed a plan to erect a monument in Washington to the memories of Hoxsey and Johnstone, together with fellow aerial victims Lieutenant Thomas E. Selfridge and John B. Moisant. Speaking for the project's sponsor, the New York Aeronautical Society, Major Henry T. Allen told reporters, "These men will be to aviation what Robert Fulton was to the steamboat. They are the men who have given their lives that men may learn to fly." Al's ideas for a lasting commemorative tribute to his old pals included "an aviation school, a building [possibly a hangar] of some sort, or a monument to their memory.... It should be erected in any park in the District which is suitable."

During the brief life of the Wright exhibition team Welsh was well received by its members, with the possible exception of Frank Coffyn, who gave him a mixed review. In a May 1939 article for the *Sportsman Pilot*, Coffyn recalled:

> Al Welsh was short, stocky, with a peculiar quirk to his mouth giving him the expression of a constant sneer. Actually he was amiable and a hard and willing worker, but lacking in more than rudimentary education. Of the five of us who qualified as pilots in the first exhibition team he was the hardest to teach, yet Orville Wright displayed the greatest patience.

Oddly enough, one could infer that Frank's feelings toward Al stemmed from his relationship with Orville. Coffyn favored Wilbur over his younger brother, whom he regarded as aloof and distant:

> The man [Wilbur] who always will be my hero shook hands with me [on our first meeting]. You felt about Wilbur, from the first, that you had known him a long time; no matter how long you knew Orville, you had an uneasy feeling each time you met him that you had never been introduced. Wilbur was no more talkative or friendlier outwardly, than Orville; but he was charged with reticent affections.

When the Wrights finally disbanded the exhibition team, Welsh was kept on as a valued instructor, a questionable decision Coffyn obviously placed with Orville rather than with Wilbur. Finally, the shaky association between Frank and "Orv" turned sour in December 1932 when Wright gave offense to Coffyn by correcting Frank's statement to a potential biographer that he himself had taught Coffyn to fly, a detail, according to the biographer, that would greatly enhance book sales. Going further, Orville denied that he had ever been aloft with him, stating that Walter Brookins was Coffyn's instructor of record. The contemplated biography went nowhere. Did Coffyn's animus toward Orville spill over into his condescending 1939 profile of Al, whom he perhaps regarded as the unmerited benefactor of Orville's patronage while other "road pilots" were sent packing in 1911? Who can say?

On January 5 the *Washington Post* ran an article announcing that Welsh would serve as chief instructor of the newly minted National Aviation Company (NAC) located at College Park, Maryland. Nowhere in the piece was a reason given as to why he had decided to leave the Wrights and return home. The notice did reveal that just prior to his relocation, Al had joined the Washington station of the United States Aeronautical Reserve with the rank of lieutenant. There was even speculation that he would be assigned to the Mexican border to fly reconnaissance in search of revolutionaries and gun smugglers. His contract with the NAC carried a clause reserving for him a month off during the summer of 1912, when he planned to attempt a cross-continent flight for which more than $100,000 in prizes had been offered.

Ostensibly, the NAC was formed to provide instruction in Curtiss, Blériot, and Wright aircraft and to make available repairs for these ships, while acting as the sole licensed agency for Curtiss machines in the Washington-Maryland-Virginia area. Aside from chief instructor Welsh, the organization's flying staff would include Georges Legagneux who had recently flown a Blériot to an altitude record at Pau, France; Bessica Raiche, first among America's pioneer aviatrixes; and Bernhard Levey, a respected Long Island flyer.

The NAC site would also have a quasi-military component, serving as an aerial combat training field, a testing/demonstration reserve, and a supply depot for assorted fighting planes. In addition, private exhibition flights were to be provided for the entertainment and instruction of delegates to the many conventions held in the district annually. Finally, this multifaceted enterprise would assist its civilian and army sponsors in lobbying for the creation of a Washington-based aerodynamics laboratory.

In order to secure employment with the NAC, Al first had to contact the Wrights to properly secure his release from their company. The following exchange of correspondence gave him some anxious moments:

My Dear Mr. [Wilbur] Wright: December 14, 1910

The National Aviation Company of this city having offered me a position as instructor, I would be glad to have you advise me if I may accept this position or if you will exercise the clause in our contract which states that I am not to fly for pleasure or profit in any aeroplane not owned by the Wright Company. I am withholding my signature to a contract with the above company pending a statement from you that you will not exercise the clause above mentioned.

In this connection, I wish you would quote me price and terms on one of your machines, and the earliest possible date delivery can be made; also kindly advise me as to whether we can make some arrangements whereby I would be able to serve in the capacity of instructor to those who will purchase your machines during the coming year.

Appreciating an early reply from you,

I am,

Very sincerely yours,
A.L. Welsh

Wilbur responded by return mail:

Dear Mr. Welsh: December 16, 1910

It is impossible for us to give a definite answer to your question without knowing just what kind of business the National Aviation Company intends to engage in.

We could not consent if it is the intention to have you fly a Wright machine for exhibition purposes.

Neither could we consent that you should fly any machine that infringes our patents unless the company pays license on all the infringing machines it uses. We naturally could not consent to have you give the benefit of the training obtained from us to assist a pirate company to compete with us. It would compromise our rights if we gave consent to anyone to fly a pirate machine. If the machines of the National Aviation Company should be free from infringement and this is made clear to us, we will consider further the question of waiving the provision of our contract referred to by you. We would be glad to help you in any work you may wish to engage in provided it does not compromise our patent rights.

Yours truly,
Wilbur Wright

My dear Mr. Wright: December 20, 1910

Yours of the 16th instant to hand, and I beg to state in reply that the National Aviation Company is an organization which intends to open up an aviation school and to act as an agency for the sale of the Curtis[s], Blériot, and other makes of flying machines, including the Wright, provided they can secure the agency for your machine.

The company does not want to do anything that will antagonize the Wright patents, and is entirely willing to pay a royalty for any machine other than the Wright that they may sell and to operate under a license from you.

The National Aviation Company desires my services as teacher on the Wright machine and to take part in exhibition flights around Washington with the understanding that a percentage of the receipts from such flights is to go to your company providing a percentage basis can be arranged between the National Aviation Company and yourself. In case, however, such arrangement cannot be made, the exhibition end of the matter will be dropped.

Do I understand correctly from your letter that I will be allowed to make flights in other machines that are an infringement on the Wright patents provided the makers of such machines pay a royalty to you or operate under your license?

I will thank you to kindly let me know your charges for a license to operate a machine which is an infringement on your patents; also upon what percentage basis you would permit me to participate in exhibition flights in one of your machines.

Very truly yours,
A.L. Welsh

P.S. The reason for my telegraphing for your address was because Mr. [Major Charles J.] Fox, a member of the National Aviation Co., and myself, had intended to go to Dayton to see you on Thursday, but have postponed our trip until next week.

A.L. Welsh

The following week a date was set after which Welsh and Fox went to Canossa, in this case, Dayton, to plead their cause before the Wrights. Evidently an understanding was effected, as Al assumed his new post on March 1, 1911.

On his second day at work, Al barely avoided a fatal accident at the Washington Speedway. District officials had issued a permit to the NAC allowing week-long trial runs of the Overland "Wind Wagon." Army and navy officers were well represented; there were also several congressmen present to assess the possible military application of the contraption. As expected, Welsh was tapped to perform the demonstrations.

To be sure, the "Wind Wagon" resembled more of an experimental vehicle than a conventional car, even though its sales were reportedly quite brisk at various automobile dealerships across the country. Everything was removed from the chassis back of the clutch on the speedster; and instead of an ordinary rear axle with a differential, a plain, straight axle was substituted. A wooden propeller eight feet long was mounted in position. The drive shaft, instead of running back to the differential on the rear axle, was extended straight back until it protruded about six inches beyond

the seat. Here a silent chain, which ran upward about two and one-half feet, connected it with another short driving shaft, the upper driving shaft extending back in
the rear of the car and holding the propeller. The propeller made 750 revolutions per
minute. Its pitch and diameter were nearly nine feet. The weight of the car was 1,800
pounds, with a 40 horsepower motor. It could be equipped with floats for water
travel, or skis for use on ice. Regrettably, there was only a six-inch clearance between
the tip of the propeller and the ground, largely limiting the "Wagon" to track racing. Horror stories abounded of drivers and passengers unconsciously walking into
the whirling rear propeller after alighting from the racer. Despite its hazardous nature,
"Wagons" were frequently placed in competition against flying machines at scores of
local air meets.

On the morning of March 2, Al climbed into his "Wagon" and took several laps
at a 55-mile-an-hour clip. Suddenly, a tire on one of the front wheels tore loose, and
as his machine passed over the wheel it became entangled in the propeller on the rear
of the converted automobile. The propeller splintered, and the test vehicle, gradu-
ally gaining in speed, was sent spinning to the roadside. Incredibly, Welsh managed
to keep his "Wagon" from overturning, while avoiding several large obstructions in
his path. He must have noticed that his stripped-down chariot lacked a rollbar. Al
later confided to a reporter that he did not get the shakes until after viewing the carnage his conveyance left on the track. "It's all right up in the air, where you can pick
your landing place when your machine breaks down," he nervously concluded, " but
on the ground you generally land before you realize what has happened."

It remains unclear why Welsh stayed with the NAC for only a month. Could it
have been his harrowing introduction to the "Wind Wagon," problems with management, an earlier understanding that he would simply be "on loan "to the NAC,
or that perhaps he felt more comfortable as part of the Wright family? For whatever
reason, he returned to Ohio in early April for the spring flying season.

Once back in Dayton, Al discovered an unexpected lull in exhibition flying by
his old teammates and an upsurge in flight training out at Simms Station. The year
1911 evolved into the largest training period in the history of the Wright School, and
a flood of students kept Welsh and Cliff Turpin hopping as instructors. Among the

The Windwagon (Washington Post).

many applicants Al taught
that year were individuals
whose names would illumi-
nate the history of early
aviation — Lieutenants
Henry "Hap" Arnold and
Thomas DeWitt Milling,
U.S. Army; Lt. John
Rodgers, U.S. Navy, Cal-
braith P. Rodgers, Oscar
Brindley, Harry Atwood,
Howard Gill, and Andrew

Drew. On every flyable morning and late afternoon the Simms Station facility was a beehive of activity, with novices aloft with their teachers and the more advanced students practicing short flights, landings and takeoffs.

Lieutenants Arnold and Milling arrived at Simms Station in late April. "Hap" was assigned there from the 23rd Infantry Division, and Al undertook his instruction beginning May 3. Arnold's course was completed ten days later after 28 lessons, with 3 hours, 48 minutes total flying time. The lieutenant would remain in the military for the duration of his life, eventually rising to the rank of five-star general of the air force during World War II. At the beginning of his lessons, Arnold asked Welsh about the man with the black derby sitting on the wagon at the edge of the field at Simms Station. "That's the local undertaker," Welsh replied. "He comes out every day and drives back empty. Let's keep it that way." In his 1949 memoir, *Global Mission*, Arnold wrote:

> I still have the official summary which Al Welsh turned in to the Wright Company on my training. The first date is May 3, 1911. The number of the machine was "B2." "Time of Flight" and "Wind Dircn Victy" are not filled in, but in the line reporting lesson No. 1, Al notes that the flight lasted seven minutes, and that he carried Lt. Arnold as a pupil. "Rough," he says under "Remarks," "just rode as passenger."
>
> The next lesson lasted only five minutes; the "Remarks" were the same. But the day following, with twelve minutes in the air, my first operational experience was described, "Hard on elevator." Lesson No. 4, and I "had charge of elevator part of the time." Then four more tries, each lasting from seven to fourteen minutes, and Welsh could report that during Lesson No. 9, I "Had charge of warping lever part of the time." After flight

Al Welsh's performance report on Lt. Henry H. Arnold (The Wilbur & Orville Wright Papers, Library of Congress).

No. 10—really two hops lasting fourteen and three minutes each—there is the notation, "To Shed." I had taxied the plane myself.

Beginning with Lesson No. 12, Al was "teaching landing." And after being charged with his first aerial mission—"To get photos of two machines in air," Lt. Arnold at Lesson No. 19, "landed without assistance" and "To shed." The flights that day were four minutes and one minute long, respectively. Thereafter, it went rapidly. Following five minutes in the air on Lesson No. 26, I "landed without assistance." At the end of Lesson No. 27, I "landed without assistance," and as we came in from Lesson No. 28, I again triumphantly "landed without assistance." I could fly! I was an aviator! Al wrote at the bottom of my report, "Number of flights, 28. Total time in air 3 hours 48 minutes. First lesson 3 May, finished 13 May—10 days learning. Average 8 minutes." Without filling in the blanks for "Gasoline and Oil used," Al signed it "A.L. Welsh, Teacher," and turned it in. He had taught me all he knew. Or rather, he had taught me all he could teach. He knew much more.

During the second week in May, Welsh took Harry Nelson Atwood under his wing, a precocious student who later garnered notoriety for his cross-country flights and his heralded first landing ever on the White House lawn in Washington, D.C., on July 14, 1911, to pay his respects to President William Howard Taft. Surprisingly, Atwood became so depressed by his lack of progress during the early phase of his training that only Al's constant encouragement kept him in the air. In early June Welsh joined Turpin to instruct Cal Rodgers, whose subsequent transcontinental flights from September 17 through December 10, 1911, captured the imagination of a nation.

The Wrights dispatched Welsh to Belmont Park, Long Island, New York, in mid–June to demonstrate their machines, open a flying school, and carry paying customers. Al's pupils were already in place and Orville had shipped three new planes for his use. One machine was for William C. Beers of New Haven, Connecticut, the other for Alex C. Cochran, an affluent New York yachtsman. Welsh supervised the assembly of the aircraft and gave all three a preflight check before commencing the instruction of Cochran, Beers, George W. Beatty, W. Redmond Cross, and E.F. Gallaudet.

In an admirable display of goodwill and aerial camaraderie, Welsh and fellow aviators from Nassau Boulevard and the Moisant Aviation School at Mineola, Long Island, took the time to stage, on July 16, an exhibition benefit for a local resident, the widow of Marcel Penot, a French flyer who was killed in Havana, Cuba, the previous year. A throng of 3,000 onlookers came afoot, in trains, and by automobile to see Al, Tom Sopwith, and other pilots of note carry passengers between the fields.

At this time Nassau Boulevard was the official flying field for both the Aero Club of America and the Aero Club of New York, and on Saturday, July 22, both organizations cosponsored their first weekly air meet for local aviators to impress the spectators and pique public awareness of flying. Al entered the first event and won the George Campbell Wood trophy by setting a new U.S. 2-man altitude flight of 2,648 feet, carrying his student George W. Beatty. Later that afternoon he took the Aero Club of New York Cup for achieving the quickest start, but trailed Tom Sopwith in both the bomb-throwing and speed cross-country events, settling for second place.

In the final contest for combined time in the air, Al placed ahead of all others with 35 minutes, 4 seconds. Unfortunately, Welsh's fifteen minutes of glory ended on August 4 when pupil Beatty broke his mentor's 2-man altitude mark by reaching a height of 3,080 feet, above his beaming teacher. On the following day, Al reported that all of his charges had finished their training and had obtained their pilot's license except Cochran, who dropped out.

While stationed at Nassau Boulevard, Welsh provided numerous excursions to friends of the fourth estate as an effective public relations service, particularly Jimmy H. Hare, famous photojournalist for *Collier's* magazine. Hare's employer, Robert J. Collier, also loved flying and earlier ordered a machine along with Welsh's tutelage from the Wrights for his own edification. In early 1911 Collier lent his Flyer to the military, and it was used by army pilots when General John Pershing crossed into Mexico to apprehend the revolutionary leader Francisco Villa.

Al was always well received within Collier's social circle and, indeed, throughout the entire Northeast's Brahmin community. Prospective buyers of Wright models appreciated his flying skills, Al's understated approach as a salesman, teacher, and demonstrator, and his dry humor. Welsh liked to recount a humorous incident which occurred during one of his dinner appearances at the Collier estate, this time on a Friday evening. In observance of Jewish dietary law (which outlaws pork and forbids the combining of beef and poultry with dairy), the Orthodox Welsh shunned meat, contenting himself with fish and the other side dishes. Following the meal, a priest who had shared his table approached Al and blurted out, "Welsh, you're a good Irishman and a very good Catholic."

On August 8 the Wrights interrupted Welsh's Long Island posting temporarily and ordered him to Chicago, where he was to compete in the International Aviation Meet at Grant Park, an eight-day event beginning on August 12. Before his Grant Park date, however, Welsh dropped by College Park on July 10 to congratulate Lieutenant Roy C. Kirtland on being the government's first flyer to receive his pilot's license. After the ceremony Al was invited onto the field by former students Arnold and Milling as a gesture of respect, and during this reunion several flyovers were performed by army aviators in appreciation of Welsh's many contributions to their program. The press observed that Al was much delighted with the tribute paid him.

The Wright Company sent seven machines to Chicago, along with all of their available pilots. Al was one of the first pilots in the air, and he flew daily except once when windy conditions kept nearly all thirty-nine competitors grounded. Welsh, Oscar Brindley, Cal Rodgers, and George W. Beatty routinely spent three hours aloft every afternoon. During the nine-day contest, flyers William R. Badger and St. Croix Johnstone were killed; and Arthur Stone, Howard Gill, Cal Rodgers, Oscar Brindley, and even Welsh, himself, barely escaped injury in crashes and hard landings. In the end Al won several prizes for duration records, and recorded an impressive two-man altitude mark. Ironically, the only flyer to again eclipse Welsh's performances was his own pupil, George Beatty.

After winning $3,500 in prize money, Al returned to Dayton where he taught

Robert Elton and gave degrees of instruction to Cliff Webster, Philip Page, and George Gray. During this interim, aviator Bob Fowler took delivery of the Wright craft he would fly on his west-east transcontinental flight, and on August 31 he took it aloft at Dayton, following some instruction from Welsh. Already an accomplished pilot with other types of aircraft, Fowler only needed Al's help to familiarize himself with the Flyer's controls. Elton had also purchased a plane and, following his instruction, wanted to fly it to his home in Youngstown, Ohio. Welsh agreed to accompany him as a passenger, and on September 2 they took off, winging their way to Columbus, a distance of 70 miles, where they stayed overnight. The next day they expected to reach their destination, but became lost and again spent the night at Tinway after stopping three times to orient themselves. Finally, on September 4, the twosome did reach Youngstown after setting down at Canton and Salem. The 247 mile roundabout trip came perilously close to establishing a new cross-country record.

As Welsh's work was completed in Dayton, Orville returned him to Nassau Boulevard and matriculating classes there. First on his schedule were near-graduates George Gray, Philip Page, and Clifford Webster, who had received earlier instruction from him at Dayton. There was also Harold H. Brown's final flights, the young man having begun his courses with Frank Coffyn at the Augusta, Georgia, school earlier in the year. In need of a break, Welsh flew for three days, starting September 28 at the Lake Aerodrome at Bridgeport, Connecticut. Sponsored by the Aero Club of Connecticut, he carried passengers, including a number of women, on brief flights at 200 to 300 feet in what was basically a Wright goodwill venue. Scarcely back at the Long Island base, Al found yet another class awaiting his attention that included Arch Freeman and George Norton.

Al left his Long Island duties in mid–October, with pupil Arch Freeman in tow, for a three-day private social gathering and air meet at Rest Hill, the Collier estate located near Wickatunk, New Jersey. Flying there also were British aviator Tom Sopwith and the publicist's mechanician and unlicensed pilot, Oliver G. Simmons, who was flying Collier's Wright Model B. On October 14 Welsh and Simmons carried cameraman Jimmie Hare intermittently on flights to Freehold, New Jersey, where the photographer made aerial photos of a fox hunt and polo match in progress. A special to the *New York Times* reported:

> The hunting party ... left East Freehold at noon. Hare and Simmons in the aeroplane went into the air soon after and flew low over the ground. By circling they were able to keep near the hunters most of the time. The meet ended at the polo grounds, and about 300 guests had been invited to be in at the [fox's] death. A long string of automobiles followed in the main road from East Freehold and reached the grounds about the time the hunters appeared.
>
> During the polo match Al Welsh flew in a Blériot, frightening the ponies. One threw Mr. [Réné] la Montaigne, but without seriously injuring him.... The flights were witnessed by thousands, and the personal guests of Mr. Collier were numbered by the hundred.

Hare's photographs would appear in the October 28 issue of *Town and Country*, along with commentary from a preceding installment of the same magazine which portrayed the significance of Collier's Roman holiday as a natural symbiosis between wealthy, socially and politically connected sportsmen and the burgeoning aviation industry.

> Mr. Walter Damrosch went for a spin with Welsh in Mr. R.J. Collier's Wright flyer, which did such good work down in Texas with the Army. After breakfast next morning Mr. Collier with Welsh, and Mr. Richard Harding Davis with Sopwith, flew from Mr. Collier's house to Mr. Lewis Thompson's place five or six miles away. The Wright machines took hardly more time to tune up than it takes to crank an automobile, and they were very much faster once they got started.... After that, thirty or forty guests of the two house parties made ascensions with Welsh and Sopwith, the young Englishman using his Wright and his Blériot alternately. Of course there was nothing wonderful in this. Thousands of people have ridden as passengers in aeroplanes. But the ease and simplicity with which one could pay visit to a neighbor several miles away was fascinating.... It is perfectly certain that the number of amateur aviators will increase rapidly next year. It only requires one or two pioneers to lead the way. And as soon as the amateur begins to fly, the aeroplane industry will increase by leaps and bounds, and the manufacturers will have capital at their disposal to make all sorts of improvements. In the meantime let us keep our eye on the Wrights, who are practicing with their new glider down among the sand dunes of North Carolina.

Clearly, Wilbur and Orville understood the vital importance of the well-heeled patron to their company, as witnessed by Welsh's presence at the Rest Hill event.

Returning to Nassau Boulevard, Al carried passengers and worked with his students through October. Then, on October 27, he flew from Nassau to Belmont Park Terminal, carrying socialite Mrs. Richard (May) Corcoran as a passenger, to attend the United Hunts Races where they met a thunderous ovation and were royally welcomed by New York financier and Wright Company stockholder August Belmont. In a trailing Model B, Welsh understudy Philip W. Page transported aviatrix Blanche Stuart Scott. Society reporters for *Town and Country* magazine and the *New York Times* caught the ambience of the moment. The *Town and Country* piece read as follows:

> On Saturday, just as the crowds were eagerly watching the third race, a buzzing sound overhead drew all eyes skyward. There were two airships, each with a feminine passenger. What chance did any horse have to finish with a burst of glory? None at all. The ships came lightly to rest in the center of the open field and men and women burst through the fences to study the visitors at close range...It was probably the first time that a horse race has been interrupted by an airship race, for the two machines were really racing.

According to the *Times*:

> With the dropping of the two biplanes ... society for a moment lost all interest in the thoroughbreds and bubbled over with interest concerning the novel means of invasion, many speculating as to just when it would be as ordinary as by motor car or other conveyance.
>
> To Mrs. Richard Corcoran is given the credit of being the first woman to choose this method of racetrack visitation, she having engaged A.L. Welsh of the Wright aviation forces to biplane her to the track from the aviation grounds at Nassau Boulevard. They made the trip of over three miles in a trifle less than six minutes, being shortly followed by Philip W. Page and Miss Blanche S. Scott.

The first named used the Curtiss-Wright machine which did such good service in recent Nassau Boulevard flights for Lieut. Milling, while the other machine was the plane driven by Lieut. Arnold at the same meeting. There was a general stampede for the midfield as soon as the machines dropped safely to earth, which they did after circling the field several times.

On November 18 Welsh oversaw the seasonal closing of the Wright facility at Nassau Boulevard and the return of planes and equipment to Dayton. At this juncture, Wilbur and Orville abandoned exhibition work and released all of their "road pilots" except Al, retaining him as their instructor and test pilot. Once back in Dayton, he taught Californian Farnum T. Fish and assisted both Fish and Arch Freeman in obtaining their pilot's license. By year's end, Welsh had trained over 30 students for the Wright Company.

Despite the prevailing notion among aviation historians that the Wright Company's experimentation with water-based aircraft began in 1913, Welsh's trials with such ships documents not only earlier attempts at producing a hydroplane, but also that Orville was willing to market such a machine as early as the winter of 1911–1912. The earliest prototype used was a Wright Model B, outfitted with a pair of wooden floats and a water rudder, which was attached to the air rudder and hung under it.

On January 2, 1912, Al requested Orville's permission to go to publisher A. Holland Forbes's New Haven, Connecticut, home and carry prominent members of that state's Aero Club. He wrote that Robert Collier's biplane would be used, but that state law forbade his personal aviator, who lacked a pilot's license, from flying. Orville acceded to Welsh's proposal with the understanding that the cost of his services would be comparable to those charged Collier at his housewarming shindig the previous October.

While in New Haven, Welsh took an order for a Wright hydroplane, which was, amazingly, still in development. Fast forward to May 28, when Al notified Orville of problems with the same hydro, an issue temporarily overshadowed by Wilbur's impending death from typhoid fever. A week later Welsh wrote his boss again from Washington, announcing that he had discontinued further tests on the New Haven water craft, citing problems associated with poorly designed and leaking floats, aircraft instability during water takeoffs, an underpowered engine, and a faulty starting device. There was no mention of proposed compensation to the disappointed buyer. In the end, it was left to Wright pilot Charles Wald to advance Welsh's premature work with hydroplanes.

Welsh was booked to fly at the annual meeting and banquet of the Aero Club of Connecticut at Bridgeport on January 11, 1912. His sometimes patron Robert Collier had again shipped his Wright craft there for the occasion, but bad weather forestalled the event. Instead, Collier made abrupt plans to send his Wright biplane and photographer Hare to Panama to shoot aerial photos of the canal for a feature item in *Colliers'*. Then, too, there was a $3,000 purse offered by the City of Panama to the first airman to fly Panamanian skies.

In addition to Hare, Collier stuck to his old team of Welsh as principal pilot and Simmons as mechanician and fill-in aviator. Collier told reporters that he had picked Al because of his rich aeronautical experience and the fact that he was one of the lightest aeroplanists around, weighing in at little more than one hundred pounds. He shipped his Model B along with Welsh, Simmons, and Hare on the United Fruit Company steamer, S.S. *Turrialba*. The publisher himself traveled to New Orleans in late January by rail, then boarded a vessel to Panama.

The canal was then under construction and Collier wanted to fly over the entire route and get clear aerial views of the dams, docks, and cuts being made along the course. Upon their arrival, the team took a trip across the isthmus aboard a train, which paralleled canal operations, in order to assess the project's challenges. The findings were none too promising. Hare was expected to use a fifty pound moving picture machine in flight with a capacity for 400 feet of film, which when in action moved at a rate of a foot per second. Maps showed that the terrain was level over the Gatun Dam, and there were suitable places to land around the canal. Unfortunately, about ten miles from Colon the mountains presented problems on either side of the waterway, and the most dangerous part of the trip would be met in the district of the divide between the Atlantic and Pacific oceans, or between the cities of Culebra and Pariso. Welsh's concerns focused on the probability of swift and irregular air currents in this region, not to mention atmospheric disturbances caused by repeated dynamite blasts; and, both threats were exacerbated by the necessity of frequent landings each time Hare's bulky machine required reloading with new film reels. Al also noticed what the hot humid weather was doing to Collier's machine; the wing fabric began to sag, making the craft resistant to lift, and the laminated propellers showed signs of separation. What's more, Simmons informed Welsh that under these tropical conditions the engine could provide no more than fifteen minutes of continuous running time. The deciding factor was Chief Engineer George Goethal's overall pessimistic appraisal of Collier's fool's errand. After further investigation and careful consideration, Welsh and company packed up and returned to New York City on April 3.

In less than three weeks following Welsh's departure, one Clarence DeGiers flew before 4,000 spectators at Juan Franco Field in La Cabana, thus winning the $3,000 purse offered by the City of Panama. One year later, Robert G. Fowler, one of Al's best students, took off from Bella Vista Beach in a pontoon-equipped aircraft and, with a motion picture cameraman aboard, successfully transited the isthmus from ocean to ocean on April 27, 1913, setting down in Cristobal. When Fowler's much awaited movie film began to be shown in North American theaters, government agents seized every reel they could find, claiming that shots of the canal and its fortifications presented a danger to national security.

Al returned to Dayton posthaste and opened the spring 1912 training season with a sizeable class that included Pennsylvanian Grover Cleveland Bergdoll, Brooklynite Charles Wald, Ohioan John Klockler, Wisconsinite William Kabitzke, and Minnesotan Fred J. Southard. Of the lot, poor Southard exhibited the least talent for flying, and his mistakes drove Welsh near to distraction. Fellow trainee Bergdoll

Al Welsh (left) instructs student George Beatty on the fine art of flying (George Grantham Bain Collection, Library of Congress).

recalled that Fred used to sit in Orville's nonflying trainer for hours and "practiced so long that he could finally read a newspaper and keep the wings level without any thought of same." Nevertheless, every time Southard went aloft with Welsh he always pushed or pulled the wing warping lever in the wrong direction. Once down on the ground, Al patiently lectured the forty-year-old about his miscues, but to no effect. Southard, during one such exchange, sarcastically replied to Welsh, "Oh, I just wanted to see if you would notice it." Al retorted, "You sure will notice it when you get up there alone, sometime."

Despite Welsh's best efforts and much time in the air, Southard could not learn to balance his machine. Totally exasperated, Al told Orville that his pupil was a hopeless case and that he would waste no more time on him. Despite Welsh's misgivings, however, Wright sold Fred an airplane with the understanding that Southard could not fly until he had received more lessons and had met Orville's standards of excellence. On May 21 the impetuous Minneapolis native violated his promise and, while everyone was away, broke the lock off his ship's hangar door, wheeled his new Model B out, and took off alone. He rose no more than 50 feet when the biplane rolled over on one side and skidded to the ground, killing Southard instantly. For a final time he had pulled the warping lever in the wrong direction.

By January 1912 the U.S. Army had come full circle from its earlier lukewarm acceptance of aviation as a viable component of the military. There were even congressional proposals for fixed officer appointments in the flying corps, increased pay and benefits, and, of course, more airplanes. Just prior to his participation in Collier's Panama fiasco, Welsh had called at the War Department as a representative of the Wrights to confer with chief signal officer Brigadier General James Allen. He allowed that his firm was in position to deliver a new machine to the government, a variant of the popular Model B, which would revolutionize its air arm. The new features of the Model C, according to Al, included automatic lateral stability, a muffled engine; portable wings that allowed for quick disassembly and assembly; and a 6-cylinder, 50-horsepower engine, instead of the standard 4-cylinder, 30-horsepower power plant.

Evidently Welsh made the sale, for in February the government ordered ten of these planes, to be refigured somewhat for military deployment. Dubbed the CM-1 Wright Military Scout, the craft was slightly larger and more durable than its predecessor, designed to carry two people with a dual control system, capable of climbing 2,000 feet in ten minutes with a 450 pound load, have fuel capacity for a four hour flight, and boast a minimum speed of 45 miles per hour.

In May the prototype of these military versions was ready for delivery to College Park, and Welsh and Orville migrated there from different destinations on the 17th to begin the official trials. "Orv" was somewhat upset because Al had dallied at the Grover Bergdoll estate in Philadelphia from the 10th through the 14th, acquainting his recently graduated pupil with the finer points of Bergdoll's newly purchased Flyer B and thereby postponing the "C" trials. Wright met with army and government officials to discuss matters pertaining to the impending tests and then returned to Dayton, leaving Al to conduct the demonstrations.

The following day, Welsh made his first of sixteen official and countless unofficial flights before his fatal crash. All army standards had been met except the load climb test of 2,000 feet in ten minutes. In unofficial attempts, those in attendance noted that even under ideal conditions it was barely possible to meet this requirement. On nearly all of his official flights, Welsh had taken along some officer or enlisted man, and among them was Lieutenant Leighton W. Hazelhurst, Jr., who had asked permission to fly with Welsh as much as possible in hopes of acquiring more air experience. Whenever the weight carrying tests were conducted, shot-log ballast was secured to the center section of the craft.

In the midst of these grueling tests, Welsh learned that former fellow Wright pilot Phil Parmelee had lost his life while giving an exhibition flight at North Yakima, Washington, when his plane was overturned by a gust of wind. His only comment was, "Poor Phil, he was one of the best ones. I hope I won't go the same way."

On June 10 Welsh made an official climbing test carrying Captain F.B. Hennessy, but only reached 1,500 feet in ten minutes. The following day, June 11, they tried again, attaining 1,827 feet. Later that afternoon, Al announced that he wanted to try again. He impatiently insisted to Hazelhurst that the Model C was capable of passing the final hurdle, for the feat had been accomplished by Orville back at Dayton before the plane's shipment to College Park. "I'm going to make that climb tonight or know the reason why," he groused as he began to tune up the motor. "I'm tired fooling," he added.

At twenty-six years of age, Lieutenant Hazelhurst stood at the threshold of a promising military career. Born in Brunswick, Georgia, on June 25, 1886, he had been appointed to the U.S. Military Academy on June 16, 1904, and graduated from West Point on February 14, 1908. Assigned to the 17th Infantry as a second lieutenant, he joined his regiment in Camaguey, Cuba, on April 18, 1908, before returning stateside to Fort McPherson, Georgia, with his outfit. For the first half of 1910 he was stationed at New Orleans, Louisiana, involved in cartography work. At his request, Hazelhurst was finally sent to the Signal Corps Aviation School at College Park on March 1, 1912.

A few minutes past six o'clock, Al yelled that he was ready, and Lieutenant Hazelhurst followed him into the machine, taking the passenger's seat. Welsh took off and flew the length of the field, rising 200 feet. As the plane turned toward the group of army officers standing in front of the hangars, Al dived abruptly to signal that he was ready for the anticipated test climb. The dip carried the Model C to within seventy-five feet of the ground, and it then leveled out sharply — too quickly, those on hand later observed. Suddenly, the craft's aluminum wings collapsed upward, so that they nearly touched above the engine. The plane stalled, then turned its nose toward the earth and plummeted downward.

The crash occurred about 1,000 feet from the hangars, but when those present reached the site everyone knew that both men were dead. Welsh was buried in the debris, but the body of Hazelhurst had been catapulted nearly twenty feet from the point of impact. Al's clothing was nearly gone, revealing a bruised and battered body. The lieutenant's skull was badly disfigured. Both corpses were rushed by army ambulances to Walter Reed Hospital. Meanwhile, the army lost little time in arranging for Welsh pupil George Beatty to resume the trials.

Captain Charles DeForest Chandler, commanding the Army Aviation Corps, immediately convened a board of inquiry, consisting of seven officers who had witnessed the crash. Those officers included Captain F.B. Hennessey, president; Captain Paul W. Beck; and Lieutenants Harry Graham, R.C. Kirtland, Thomas DeWitt Milling, William C. Sheeman, and Benjamin D. Foulois.

The board found that no airplane, no matter how strongly built, could have sustained the terrible strain put upon it, when Welsh dived from a height of about 150 feet and at an angle of 45 degrees, and then tried to turn suddenly upward. In sum, the pilot had tried the impossible and forfeited his life and another's in the process. Military witnesses recalled the statement of Lieutenant Hazelhurst just prior to his stepping into the Model C for his last flight, that he did not want to go up with Al because he objected to "those dips" that Welsh was in the habit of making. Although the subsequent army report found Wright's civilian pilot at fault, this finding did not mean to imply that he was greatly in error. Several officers observed that the manipulation of an aircraft was largely a question of judgment, and that it was extremely difficult for one aviator to tell what he would do under certain circumstances.

Perhaps such an ambiguous finding resulted from glaring discrepancies offered in eyewitness testimony as opposed to the same accounts reported in the press. On June 14 Wright troubleshooter Arthur A. Gaible arrived first on the scene at College Park:

My Dear Mr. Wright:

Have instructed men at field reference loading of wrecked machine.

Did you understand that Corporal Adams was in the vicinity of the hangars when the accident occurred?

In a conversation this afternoon he stated that from this position he saw the machine start downward at angle of approx. 45°, but that it never did straighten out, to the contrary, when the aeroplane was about 30 feet from the ground it assumed an even greater angle of about 65° and maintained it until striking the ground.

Did you understand the accident occurring as above stated?

I did not.

From this it would appear that the elevator never operated.

Adams is positive on these points.

According to Gaible's conversation with Corporal Adams, pilot error resulted from Welsh's delayed response in controlling the Model C. However, on the preceding day *The Washington* reported:

That Mr. Welsh made a desperate effort to drive his machine upward was shown by the testimony of Corporal Adams, who said that he had seen the elevation planes turn upward just before the fatal crash, but that the aeroplane did not respond, and that the wings immediately afterward collapsed.

The *Washington Post* also corroborated its sister paper's story, referencing Al's "frantic efforts" to reverse the direction of an unresponsive aircraft.

Anna Welsh was playing with her two-year-old daughter, Aline, at the Harmel home at 466 H Street SW, when called to the telephone to hear that her husband had been killed. Shocked, she dropped the receiver and fainted. The family summoned two physicians to attend her. When Anna revived, she paced the floor, sobbing uncontrollably. At points she stood with outstretched arms before a picture of Al, pleading for him to return to her. "Mama, Mama, don't cry," called little Aline, who wandered behind Anna.

Mother and child had come to Washington for the government trials. Al had been anxious for them to be concluded, looking forward to taking his family to New York where other tests were scheduled. When Wilbur died on May 30, Welsh had gone to the funeral, and returned to the District on the eve of the Model C demonstrations completely exhausted. On the evening of June 10 the Welshes and several friends had gone to the theater and afterward to a supper party in one of Washington's more upscale cafes. The next day, the day of Al's death, he and Anna talked about Aline's future. "We'll send her to the best girls' school in the country," he told his wife. "Then I'll quit the aviation game, and live at home."

Welsh's funeral was held on June 13, postponed until 2:00 P.M. so that Orville
and Katharine Wright would have time to arrive from Dayton. The coffin was draped
in a silken tallis, and Cantor Samuel Glushak of Adas Israel Congregation delivered
the eulogy, selecting words from the Psalms: "What is man that he shall be remembered." The Yiddish publication *Forward* reported, "All present were in tears, including Mr. Orville Wright and his sister, who were doing all they could to console the
mother and wife of the deceased."

Welsh was buried in the Alabama Street Cemetery of the Adas Israel Congregation of Washington, D.C. Today his grave is marked by a small flat memorial bear-
ing only the words "Arthur L. Welsh: Father."

Several days after Al's service, Katharine wrote Milton Wright:

> June 15, 1912
>
> Dear Grandpa Wright:
>
> We arrived Thursday morning about nine and were met by Mr. [Arthur] Gaible. We all
> went right out to see what we could do for Mrs. Welsh. Mr. Gaible found that she didn't
> have a cent of money and has found since that there are some debts — besides funeral
> expenses.
>
>   They had a regular Jewish ceremony and burial. All of his family and his wife's family
> show their Jewish traits much more than Mr. Welsh did.... Yesterday morning we went
> to Lieut. Hazelhurst's funeral....
>
> Affectionately,
> Tochter [daughter]

Lieutenant Hazelhurst was laid to rest in Arlington National Cemetery on June
14 beside the grave of Lieutenant Thomas E. Selfridge, the first army officer to forfeit his life in the pursuit of flying, on September 17, 1908, when both he and Orville
crashed at Fort Myer, Virginia. Although army regulations required only a platoon
of infantry for an officer of his grade, the entire garrison of Fort Myer, including the
first squadron of the Fifteen Cavalry, the second battalion of the Third Field Artillery,
the cavalry band, and every officer and enlisted man of the aviation corps was turned
out for the occasion.

In a June 26 letter to Wright Company stockholder Russell A. Alger, Orville
wrote:

> I went down to Washington to attend Mr. Welsh's funeral and from there to New York
> where we had a meeting of the Board of Directors. The Board left it to me to arrange for
> an annuity for Mrs. Welsh, similar to the annuities given Mrs. Hoxsey [Arch's mother] and
> Mrs. Johnstone [Ralph's wife]. Of course, this will require the consent of the stockholders
> before it can be put through, but I think there will be no trouble in getting consent.

Alger responded to Wright in a July 1 letter:

> Welsh's death, of course, was a very serious and sad blow to us. It will have a very
> decided detrimental effect on aviation this year. I think whoever gave out the notices
> that the Wright Company's Directors were persuading you not to risk your life in test
> flying this year was a very foolish individual. That in itself made us conspicuous as it
> was, and had about as detrimental an effect upon amateur flying as anything I have seen.

Alger again replied to an intervening missive from Orville on the 13th of July:

> I absolutely agree with you that what we will have to do is to produce a machine that
> will inspire some confidence in the public in its safety. The Company is nicely financed
> now and I think that all our energies and time should be spent in the next year in our
> development work and that you should associate with yourself a corps of experienced
> engineers or an experienced engineer, who would relieve you of the tedious details and
> would, in turn, aid in minor suggestions....
>
> In reference to a pension for Mrs. Welsh,— of course of this I highly approve. I am
> glad to hear that her parents are well-to-do. I believe in the case of Johnstone and others
> we have put a certain sum out of our capital account aside (as I remember $10,000)
> sufficient to insure them an income. This, of course, was very generous, but is it quite
> just to the Company? It seems to me we should pay them directly from our treasury a
> pension so long as we are able to and so long as they need it for their support. I would
> suggest therefore she [Anna Welsh] be advised of this and that the sum be paid directly
> from the treasury.

On July 22, Orville reported to Alger his dealings with the Wright Board:

> When I brought up before the Directors the matter of some help to Mrs. Welsh several
> of the directors, Mr. [Andrew] Freedman and Mr. [August] Belmont particularly
> expressed the opinion that the annuity should be paid for so that the Company would
> never have any further connection or responsibility concerning it. After receiving your
> letter I took up the matter with Mr. [Alpheus] Barnes [Company treasurer], but he said
> that the New York directors preferred to dispose of the matter now in such as a way as to
> have no future responsibility in it. In the resolution of the Board, I was authorized to
> negotiate for an annuity like those given to Mrs. Johnstone and Mrs. Hoxsey but I am
> inclined to think as you do, that these were more than sufficient in this case. I have,
> therefore, asked Mr. Barnes to see what can be done with some of the New York insur-
> ance companies on a sum one-half of what was paid for the Johnstone and Hoxsey annu-
> ities.

One might possibly conclude from the foregoing correspondence that Orville
regarded the charge of pilot error against his most trusted flyer, the plummeting reputation of his Model C, and the downturn of his company's fortunes as inextricably
linked. If so, did his distress over Al's perceived failure in judgment work to the detri-
ment of his widow?

On October 26, Wright confessed to Alger:

> The series of accidents which occurred in the early part of the summer had a very
> depressing effect on the business this year. We had a number of sales practically com-
> pleted which were lost as a result of the accidents. We have been doing a pretty good
> business with the Government, however, so that Mr. Barnes reports that the Company
> will be able to declare a dividend, though not as large a one as in the past two seasons. I
> think it quite probable that for the next year or two, we will have to depend almost
> entirely on the Government business.

Wright's hopes for a reversal of the Model C's reputation were misplaced. On
September 4, 1913, Lieutenant Moss Love was killed in a Model C at the army's North
Island training facility at San Diego, California. Then, on November 14, Lieutenant
Perry Rich plunged into Manila Bay, Philippines, and perished. And within the

month, Lieutenant Hugh Kelly and Chief Instructor Eric Ellington were killed in
another crash at North Island. For some time Ellington, a splendid pilot, had been
in correspondence with Grover Loening, Orville's plant manager, concerning the
deficiencies of the Model C. The army aviator had written Loening that the machine
was tail heavy and impossible to control. Loening, a 1910 engineering graduate of
Columbia University, now took Ellington's dire appeals to heart in a widening professional feud with his boss. Orville, as in Welsh's case, insisted that the problems
with the Model C centered around pilot error, not the craft's design, claiming that
the machine's more powerful engine caused stalls because its pilots misjudged their
angle of attack. Orville's plans to rectify the Model C's problems with two innova-
tions — an angle-of-incidence indicator that alerted pilots when their climb or dive
was too steep, and an automatic pilot — failed to end the deaths. On February 9, 1914,
Lieutenant Henry Post's fatal crash at North Island caught the army's attention. The
brass complained that six of the men killed in flying accidents were piloting the Model
C, a tally representing one half of all military flyers lost in air mishaps. A subsequent
board of investigation condemned the plane's elevator as woefully weak and damned
the C as "dynamically unsuited for flying."

Orville participated in the inquiry, even though he stubbornly refused to
acknowledge its finding. He ordered his chief instructor, Oscar Brindley, to conduct
a company probe at North Field. Brindley concluded that aircraft maintenance had
accounted for many of the C's problems, whereupon the army advertised for an aeronautical engineer to insure the viability of its machines and to promote development.

Loening applied for and secured the position. Wasting no time, he declared all
Wright and Curtiss pusher type aircraft as unsafe, condemning their tendency to stall
and the dangerous mounting of their engines, which were apt to break free in a crash
and crush the pilot. Attempts by Loening to maintain friendly contact with Wright
failed. In time, he grew to believe that his former employer never forgave him for
denouncing his planes.

Meantime, President Wright was absorbed in battling patent infringers in the
courts and formulating a way to sell his company. The latter objective he consum-
mated on October 15, 1915. The revamped Wright organization introduced two new
designs to supplant the Model C. Its Model K was designed for the navy, and the
army's Model L served as a reconnaissance machine. Both were tractor types and
employed ailerons instead of wing-warping for the first time.

Anna and Aline Welsh continued living at the Harmel family home in southwest Washington until Anna's death in 1925. Aline moved to England at the outset
of World War II, changed her Christian name to Abigail, married, and later became
a British citizen, working at the American Embassy in London. From last report
(2006), she was 92 years of age. Abigail's cousin, Grace Berlowe, who took up residence in Israel, recalled that Anna always felt that the War Department pushed Al
too hard for tests which were sure to fail.

Clara Wiseman, Welsh's half sister, wrote Orville on February 21, 1928, seeking
his support in the creation of a lasting memorial to her brother, citing the fact that

an airfield had been named for his army escort that fateful day. Wright declined to respond. On January 14, 1930, Wiseman contacted Frank H. Russell, former factory manager for the Wrights and Loening's predecessor, with a similar letter, ending:

> I am sending you attached hereto, a copy of a letter which I wrote to Mr. Orville Wright on February 21, 1928. This letter was ignored for I have never heard from them. I am certain that they have received it, because of the fact that on the envelope there was the return address, and this leads us to believe that while the letter was of some importance to us, yet the contents of the letter was of little or no importance to the firm of Wright Brothers.... Her [Anna Welsh] loss was an irreparable one, but she never forgot the sting that her husband's memory was ignored and left out of the picture entirely, and now, with her daughter left all alone, with neither father nor mother to comfort and cheer her, she too feels that a great injustice has been done.

A bust of Arthur L. Welsh, together with the trophies he won at various meets across the United States are now part of the collection of the Smithsonian National Air and Space Museum in Washington, D.C. Of course, there is no mention as to how he spent his competition winnings, which went to the Wrights so long ago.

Two

HOWARD GILL

Baltimore's Privileged Birdman

Howard Warfield Gill was neither the first, nor the most talented, nor the most daring of the pioneer aerialists — such as Arch Hoxsey, Ralph Johnstone, and Lincoln Beachey — although he could bring screaming crowds to their feet on occasion as a Wright exhibition pilot. The paradoxical nature of his strengths, by comparison, were manifested as examples of solid airmanship performed by a highly ambitious and innovative aviator of uncommon modesty, who was genuinely liked by all who knew him, a rare combination of competing character traits in the highly mercenary atmosphere surrounding aviation's infancy. In fairness to Gill's more blatantly competitive peers, a substantial family inheritance allowed the Baltimore native to engage his muse on a less materialistic level.

Unlike such contemporaries as the seemingly glum Glenn Curtiss and the standoffish Wright brothers of Dayton, Gill exhibited a welcoming affability toward his hangar mates and fans and, in the beginning, an infectious enthusiasm for flying which proved to be his trademark at airfields from coast to coast. During two brief years, Howard's contributions to the aeronautical advances of his time as patron, aircraft designer and engineer, publicist and writer, and flyer were noteworthy. And yet, despite his promising future in aviation, Gill's record betrayed a serious weakness — he was accident prone — and fickle Lady Luck was bound to collect her due.

Howard Gill was born on May 13, 1883, with a silver spoon in his mouth. His father, Martin Gillet Gill, as a youth of 18, first traveled to Paris and England aboard the ship of a tobacco trader, subsequently undertaking three round-the-world trips over the course of his 69 years. The elder Gill rose through the ranks of his grandfather's tea importing firm, which was established in 1811. As a representative of the company, Gill Sr. went to China and Japan in the capacity of tea-taster and remained in the Orient for seven years. During his stay in Japan it was reported that Martin traded arms to the Mikado in his struggle with the Tycoon government, and amidst this turmoil he conceived the idea of the teabag — a product later sold as He-No tea.

A Democrat with independent leanings and a staunch Episcopalian, Gill Sr. was to become affiliated with several other businesses in the Baltimore area while serving as a senior officer in his country's oldest tea company. He also sat as a charter member of the Automobile Club of America and he possessed the first car locally as well as founding Baltimore's earliest garage, an enterprise which Howard would eventually take over as president following his private schooling.

In 1875 Martin Gill married Alice Warfield, sister of governor-to-be Edwin Warfield (1904–1908). The wedding, held at the ancestral estate of the Warfields in Howard County, amounted to the major social event of the year.

Gill Sr.'s civic involvement ran the gamut. At 38, as a lieutenant in the Maryland militia, he was conspicuous in quelling the 1877 riot of striking Baltimore and Ohio Railroad workers. The owner of fine Japanese bronzes, which filled his home in the city's exclusive Roland Park district, Gill Sr. held sway in the Municipal Art League and his neighborhood's prestigious Oakdale Club — an association of wealthy art lovers.

Following the death of Martin Gill in September 1908, Howard's six figure inheritance and his now thriving car dealership allowed the twenty-five-year-old bachelor the means to pursue his passion for speed. He would evolve to heavier-than-air flight by way of motorcycle and auto competition, as well as ballooning.

Gill's impressive showings along the Eastern Seaboard's automobile circuit brought him to Long Island's internationally renowned Vanderbilt Cup Race on October 24, 1908. The *Atlanta Constitution* proffered a warm welcome to the young Baltimore sportsman:

> The Vanderbilt cup race is bringing out many ambitious drivers, some who have gone the route, but have never driven in so important an event as the Vanderbilt; others are of the promising but painfully lacking variety who try, but never make good.
>
> Howard W. Gill, a prominent young society man of Baltimore, is one of the first class, winning twenty-six out of thirty-one events in which he started. He has been in competition in track events against some of the best racing drivers alive; making good in almost every case. Endowed with a large fortune, well up in the six figures, he is so enthusiastic about the racing game that he has entered this race purely as an amateur, paying his own and his mechanics' expenses.
>
> Born in the city of Baltimore twenty-six years ago, he started in the racing game when the motorcycle was the speed merchant of the cycle path, and from the motorcycle to the auto racer was but a step.
>
> Gill is well known in Philadelphia and Washington where he has the reputation of being a daredevil track driver, willing and very apt to take long chances with his neck to put his machine through a winner.
>
> To look at the man or boy, for he is but a boy, one would hardly imagine that he was capable of some of the stunts credited to him. Imagine a tall, slender chap with light, curly hair and blue eyes, with the manner of a divinity student during his first year in preparatory school, retiring and unwilling to talk about himself or what he has done.
>
> The E.R. Thomas Motor Car Company, of Buffalo, will have two of its famous Vanderbilt auto racers entered in the Vanderbilt cup race of October 24th. One will be driven by George Salzman, the veteran race driver, known the world over, and the other by Mr. Gill.
>
> Both men will bear watching. The word has been passed along the line that there would be something doing on October 24th, and as neither man has the slightest indication of a yellow streak, there is very apt to be some [smashed] pumpkins.

Unfortunately, despite the *Constitution's* top billing, Howard suffered a disabled clutch and failed to complete the contest.

The period 1908-1909 was a time of trial for Howard. The strain associated with his father's passing coupled with the demands of business drained his frail constitution. Public rumors that Gill suffered from tuberculosis were always discounted by family and friends. During this demanding phase of his life, Howard took refuge in the sport of ballooning. His new airship, which contained 22,000 cubic feet of gas, represented a junior version of the larger capacity spheres used by the army. Nevertheless, there was always enough room in his gondola for relatives and chums when he went aloft.

A Baltimore society editor outlined in vivid reportage the local enthusiasm for Howard's new distraction:

> Friends of Mr. Howard W. Gill ... will be interested to learn that Mr. Gill is in the Adirondacks in the neighborhood of Saranac Lake to recuperate from a rather run-down condition. During his absence the big balloon is stored away very carefully.... His brother ... said this morning that the various rumors that the young aeronaut has been threatened with lung trouble are false.
>
> With the absence of Mr. Gill from the city the spring ballooning season here has come to an end.... In the latter part of April [1908] Mr. Gill made a very successful ascension from Washington [D.C.], staying up in the air 70 minutes and landing at Brandywine, MD.... The ascension was witnessed by relatives and friends of the air captain. Mr. Gill made the ascent alone, but the others tried unsuccessfully to follow the flight of the balloon in an automobile. The balloon followed the course of the Potomac for a short distance, then crossed the Anacostia River and headed in a southerly course for Oxon Hill, Fort Washington and Port Tobacco. The balloon traveled at the rate of about 18 miles an hour, but after half an hour Mr. Gill found the big bag was losing gas and after clearing a dense fog ... he alighted without harm at Brandywine and took a train back to Washington.

Howard's reputation as a balloonist attracted the attention of fellow enthusiast Hillery Beachey in the early spring of 1908. The elder brother of legendary flyer-to-be Lincoln Beachey, Hillery had spent his formative years in San Francisco, California, before an eight-year hitch in the United States Navy. Following his discharge he went into the ballooning business, teaming with Lincoln, who worked for aerial showman Captain Thomas S. Baldwin.

Hillery profited from his service-acquired knowledge of rope work, and with Lincoln as its operator, he served as rigger and winchman, allowing Baldwin's captive balloon to take up sightseers to a height of 1,000 feet at a dollar per customer. In 1906 Lincoln started his own balloon venture, with Hillery as a partner. This collaboration lasted for two years, during which time Hillery participated in over fifty dirigible flights and piloted his brother's airship on over fourteen long distance trips. In 1908 Hillery terminated his partnership with Lincoln and headed for Howard Gill's Baltimore.

A close friendship developed between the two men based on their infatuation with free ballooning. Beachey became a regular in Howard's inner circle, and even

6   **AERO**   *December 31, 1910.*

HOW TO BUILD A NEW CURTISS-TYPE BIPLANE

By Howard W. Gill

[Editor's Note.—In this detailed explanation Mr. Gill endeavors to instruct the constructor in the making of every part of the machine. It is perhaps needless to say that not every one who is clever with the saw and hammer can do all of the work successfully. The construction of aeroplanes is work that requires craftsmanship of a special order, and even the best woodworker may not always be successful the first time in aeroplane work. Unless one has had experience in aeronautic construction it is recommended that he order the wood parts from some concern that has built successful aeroplanes and has had thorough practice in aeronautic construction. The first cost may be a little more, but this should prove economy in the end.]

Throughout the country the Curtiss type of plane seems to have met with the most popularity among the amateur builders, more of this type having been built than any other. One reason for this is undoubtedly the fact that these machines can be easily taken apart for transportation, and can be packed in a much smaller space than any of the other standard types of machines.

It has been flown successfully with a great many different motors, ranging from 20 horsepower up to the big Christie 110 horsepower used by Chas. K. Hamilton. Besides the machines turned out by the Curtiss factory, which are all equipped with Curtiss engines, the largest number of these planes have been equipped and flown with the Elbridge Featherweight engines.

During the past season there have been more than 20 of this type of machine assembled at Mineola alone, and among these the latest and the one containing the most up-to-date ideas is that of Talmage. This machine has incorporated in it all of the latest Curtiss ideas and is built with a strength that shows a due appreciation of the strains which an aeroplane should endure.

The design and size of this machine is one that has been found best for an engine of 20 to 35 horsepower; the Talmage machine being equipped with a Boulevard engine of 30 horsepower provided with a Carter carbureter. This engine is one especially built for aeroplane use, but a plane of the same general dimensions and construction has been built and flown by the writer, equipped with a regular automobile motor of the American and British Manufacturing Company make with four cylinders, 4 by 4 inches, developing 26 horsepower. This machine has made several circular flights in the hands of different aviators. From this it will be seen that this size machine lends itself readily to the adoption of quite a variety of motors.

In general design the Talmage machine has been improved along the lines of the latest advance in plane design. The biplane box type of front elevator has been replaced by a single plane of larger surface. This plane is double covered and is braced by a central mast with wires to the four corners of the plane. The ailerons, which in the past have been located between the main surfaces, have been replaced by wing tips located on the rear edge of each wing. These are arranged to work both up and down, so that when one side is pulled down the opposite side is pulled up, offering an equal resistance to both sides. By operating the wing tips in this manner, the tendency to turn is neutralized and it is claimed there is no necessity to use the rear rudder in connection with the wing tips in maintaining lateral stability.

Often, in the building of a plane, it is desired to incorporate original ideas in the construction of the details, and this can often be done to an advantage, but it is well to remember that those details given here are the ones that experience has proven most suitable, and when substitution is made, it should be done only after careful thought and it should be seen

to that the substituted parts are of equal strength in both design and construction. Often the breaking of a wire or joint that was a little too light is the cause of a great deal of added and unnecessary breakage and expense.

In making, or having made, the woodwork for a plane it is generally policy to have all the woodwork made at one time and to finish all the parts before work is started on assembling. In the past this has been an impossibility. "Complete plans" sold have been found lacking in a number of important measurements, and those given have often been of such a general nature that it has been necessary to build a machine and assemble it one piece at a time. This means a delay not only costly in itself, but doubly so as parts made one at a time are always much more expensive.

The number of missing measurements is impossible of realization except to those who have undertaken the construction of a plane from a set of the so-called "complete drawings," generally occupying one or two pages. Without all the dimensions of a machine it will be necessary time and time again to stop work on different parts till the assembling has progressed further. The delay caused by this method of building requires weeks for what should be accomplished in a few days.

Where the dimensions have been most lacking of all is in the detail—especially as to the gauge of tubing, size of wires and thickness of metal. And it has been lack of information on just these points that has proved the Waterloo of so many novices.

In building an aeroplane it is impossible to put in a large factor of safety as in other branches of engineering. To do so would mean too much weight, and as a result they are built with a small factor of extra strength, and tubing one gauge too light in a running gear will cause considerable damage to the machine in landing.

In the making of parts where tubing is employed it should be remembered that to obtain the proper gauge is as important as the correct size. In the past, in making Curtiss-type planes, it has been customary to use tubing of too light a gauge in the landing chassis, and as a result it was almost impossible for even an experienced operator to land without damage, much less the novice. The sizes of the tubing to be given here are, however, amply strong.

The main beams are very blunt oval in shape (Fig. 2) made from Oregon spruce, a wood most generally employed in aeroplane construction on account of its strength combined with lightness. Some of this wood is decidedly stringy and it is this grade that is toughest and best for use in building a plane. Hard for the mill hand to work, on account of this stringiness, it is often cast aside for a less fibrous and easier shaped board. It is well to remember that the harder the wood is to work the more it is to be desired.

These main beams, of which there are two to each plane, run the full width of the machine, but are divided into sections at the stanchion joints.

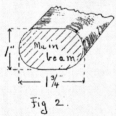

Fig 2.

They are of the same sectional shape throughout, but differ in lengths. The middle and ends are 6 feet and the central sections 5 feet long. This makes 24 of the 6-foot and 16 of the 5-foot sections to each machine, as shown by sketch, Fig. 4.

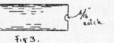

Fig 3.

With the exception of eight of the 6-foot lengths, which are only notched on one end, all of these beams are notched as in

Fig 4

Fig. 2 to fit around the $\frac{5}{16}$-inch stanchion bolts. This can be done with a round wood file, although all wood-working establishments are fitted with machinery for this special purpose.

Howard Gill was Aero's most dedicated contributor (Aero).

secured financial backing from him to inaugurate yet another captive balloon passenger-carrying venture. Lincoln joined Hillery and Howard in the capacity of adviser to the project; but despite the threesome's best efforts, the enterprise collapsed for want of public interest. Undeterred in their love of the sport, on July 29 Hillery and Lincoln took Howard's cousin, Ernest Gill, aloft with Hagerstown, Maryland, as their destination. An unfortunate native of that city, while watching the approaching Gill balloon from the roof of his house, slipped and fell to his death. The balloonists were held blameless.

Howard's growing interest in heavier-than-air flight led him to invite Beachey to collaborate with him in the construction of an airplane. Hillery readily consented, especially since Howard agreed to bankroll the undertaking, and the pair brought engine designer Harry S. Dosh on board. The

Howard W. Gill (*Aero*).

men next obtained permission from Glenn Curtiss to take measurements of his biplane then on display in a New York City department store, after which they proceeded to construct a modified version of the craft in Dosh's Baltimore garage. This hybrid plane boasted a reworked and lightened U.S.-British 26 hp automobile power plant of Dosh's design. With the biplane finished, Beachy and Gill learned that an aviation meet was to be held at Los Angeles, California, in January 1910. The prospect of large cash pots persuaded the Gill-Beachey-Dosh team to enter their creation.

The Los Angeles International Aviation Meet, which took place at Dominguez Field outside the city, was the brainchild of two well-known barnstormers, Charles Willard and Roy Knabenshue, and was funded by area businessmen who knew nothing about aviation. The ten day contest, beginning January 10, featured ten aircraft, seven balloons, and three dirigibles. Los Angeles promoters guaranteed famous French aviator Louis Paulhan a generous remuneration to merely compete, which he did, thereby qualifying the happening as an international event. Clifford Harmon, Charles K. Hamilton, Glenn Curtiss and Willard were recruited to give the aviator roster star quality. Well over 200,000 spectators witnessed the aerial extravaganza. Gill and Beachey eyed the several contests planned for amateur aviators with dreams of substantial prize money and national exposure.

Although the official program listed Howard as the aviator of the Gill-Dosh machine, and despite the fact that neither Gill nor Beachey had ever flown an airplane, it was somehow decided that Hillery would take the controls. He made several short straightaway hops prior to the meet, but suffered bad luck on opening day when his motor backfired during warm-up and ignited the lower wing. Attention to this damage kept everyone busy until the fourth day, when the Gill-Dosh creation was again wheeled out onto the field. This time Hillery took off, flew down the designated course, and rounded the first pylon before the motor overheated, causing him to lose altitude and pancake in and demolishing the craft's undercarriage in the process. He tried again the next day with similar results. On January 19 Beachey flew much better and, after flying nearly two miles, just when a win seemed within his grasp, he was compelled to suddenly dive to avoid colliding with Paulhan, who appeared directly before him. Again, he suffered a bad crash but escaped injury. Many in attendance were amazed that Hillery performed as well as he did, considering that he was innocent of any flying experience whatsoever; despite this lack of training he reportedly became the sixth person in the United States to make a complete circle in an airplane.

Following the Dominguez Meet, Howard and company remained in Los Angeles to rebuild the Gill-Dosh machine, which included additional modifications and refinements. Hillery spent even more hours improving his airmanship, and by early spring he was flying a few exhibition dates at nearby California towns.

Then, on February 12, an unwelcome intrusion from Howard's private life threatened to hamper the team's progress. Gill was named defendant in a suit for breach of promise filed by Miss Minnie King Broumel of Baltimore, who claimed $100,000 in damages. A tearful Minnie told reporters that Howard and she became engaged in December 1908, and that subsequently he went to Saranac Lake for his health, returning in August 1909, when, she claimed, the date for the wedding was set for September, but was afterwards postponed until January 5, 1910. The plaintiff admitted that Howard and the Gill family had given her valuable wedding gifts. The mother of the intended bride filed examples of the wedding invitations and letters of regret as exhibits in the case.

From L.A.'s Hotel Bachelor, Howard gave the press his side of the story:

> It is true we were engaged.... Miss Broumel and I were engaged to be married on January 5, but some time before I left Baltimore to come here to the aviation meet she broke the engagement, not I ... so the suit is a great surprise to me.... I am obliged to stay here now to continue aviation experiments with Mr. Dosh, but I shall go to Baltimore when the suit is tried.

Howard failed in his attempts to shake this unsavory story and by late August he was "on the fly" back in Baltimore, avoiding the sheriff's many attempts to serve him a writ in the Broumel case. The suit brought by Howard's chief rooter during his many balloon ascensions went nowhere, and over a year later her lawyer's papers continued to collect dust in the clerk's office of the court of common pleas.

In April the Gill-Dosh Aeroplane Company was established in Los Angeles to build planes and schedule exhibitions. The incorporators, Gill, Dosh, and Beachey, set a price of $3,500 for their new flyer with an updated Dosh-built American-British motor. Aiming to construct a novel product, they eliminated the front elevator and thereby, according to Flying Pioneers' historian Harold Morehouse, fashioned the first so-called headless biplane in the United States — a feature soon adopted by other aircraft builders, including the Wrights and Curtiss. What free time Howard managed to find was devoted to teaching himself to fly.

The Gill-Dosh team competed in the first national aviation meet for novices held at Washington Park, St. Louis, Missouri, beginning July 11 and pitting Howard and Hillery against eight competitors. Collective wisdom dictated that the partners enter both planes, and on July 12 Gill suffered a crash while practicing in the old biplane, falling from a height of fifty feet to the ground. Rushed to a nearby hospital by car, Howard was diagnosed with a broken nose, a fractured rib, and multiple bruises and contusions. Gill himself, later attributing the accident to inexperience, recounted that he had flown over an orchard and was crossing a road when a team of horses pulling a hay wagon took flight and ran away. This action startled Howard and he changed his course, ascending fifty feet, when his machine suddenly plummeted to earth. The crestfallen airman spent three days in bed.

Meanwhile, Beachey performed well with the new headless machine. When the contest ended on July 16, Gill's group repaired the old machine he had wrecked and eventually sold it to St. Louis's Tom Benoist, and, looking forward, sending Howard's premiere creation on an odyssey of unusual twists and turns.

Together with E. Percy Noel, a newspaperman, Benoist began the first aeronautical supply house in the U.S. His St. Louis company was called the Aeronautical Supply Company, later shortened to Aeronsco. In October 1910, Noel started publishing America's first flying weekly, titled *Aero*, after which he sold his interest in Aeronsco to Benoist, who by 1910 was manufacturing full-sized kits of several contemporary aircraft. On September 18, 1910, with no previous experience, Benoist flew his recently purchased Gill-Dosh biplane at St. Louis's Kinloch Field. The following January he opened a flying school at Kinloch, employing revamped versions of Howard's old modified Curtiss.

In late May 1911, Michiganders Lionel DeRemer and George McBride, owners of a small Bay City movie house, witnessed Gill fly as a Wright exhibition pilot at nearby Saginaw. Convinced that they wanted to learn to fly, DeRemer and McBride bought Howard's old engineless Curtiss from Benoist's supply company. Following its arrival, the would-be aviators installed a locally built two-cycle Pierce-Budd motor in hopes of becoming accomplished pilots. Unfortunately, the usually cautious DeRemer began taxiing practice in too much wind and demolished the biplane. Dejected but unscathed, DeRemer awarded McBride his interest in the movie theater as payment for his loss in the airplane venture.

By late 1910 the Gill-Dosh-Beachey association was nearly moribund largely due to Howard's expanded interests. He closed the year exhibiting his headless machine first at the Philadelphia Aero Show in early November, and then at the St. Louis National Aero Show, held in the city's coliseum between November 17 and 24, the latter event marking the termination of the partnership with his friends.

Gill's growing notoriety in aviation circles caught the attention of Orville Wright, and in the early spring of 1911 "Orv" invited Howard to Dayton for a visit. The young man's reserved demeanor and past record of aerial achievements impressed his host, so before leaving, Howard was invited to join the Wright family as first an employee, and even a possible pilot. Gill accepted gladly, arriving in Dayton for instruction as the spring flying school classes began in April. The twenty-eight-year-old student received his first spin in a Flyer B with Cliff Turpin on April 10, his actual lessons slated for a week later. Gill, however, surprised his instructors, Turpin and Al Welsh, by soloing after only three hours and eighteen minutes in the air during the interim, thereby technically finishing his instruction on April 15. Despite his display of aerial proficiency, available evidence suggests that Gill submitted to the full course of instruction and even went beyond for additional practice on his own.

Howard finally arrived on May 1, when he joined the Wright exhibition team. A month later he made his debut at Saginaw, Michigan, on Decoration Day, billed as "the new Wright flier." The Dailey brothers managed the demonstration, having leased a nearby summer park called Riverside, with flights originating from an adjoining field rented for the purpose. A canvas wall was erected around the field, but in spite of this visual obstruction the countryside was full of deadbeat sightseers who had arrived on clogged dirt roads. Gill performed three flights which included straight and fancy work. His gallery delighted most in the roller-coaster phase in which Howard gave the machine an up and down motion similar to the action of a scenic railway car — a technique known as "scooping." Somewhere in Gill's audience, enthusiasts DeRemer and McBride clapped wildly, imagining themselves at his controls.

Gill's next date occurred at Quincy, Illinois, where his customary three flights "brought round after round of applause." On his first flight he circled a nearby racetrack and then proceeded to cut figure eights. After this show, Howard soared off across country at a height of 300 feet to the town's country club just beyond the field, where he flew about over the golf links, then returned to the airstrip. His second demonstration was more daring as he executed dips and spiral glides galore. On the final flight, Gill reached an altitude in excess of 7,000 feet and circled about far beyond the perimeters of the field. Taking along a camera, he snapped pictures of objects on the ground to be peddled to interested spectators. At one point, Howard was seen overflying the town of Quincy, as pedestrians pointed up at him and waved. Having been in the air for one hour and twenty-seven minutes, Gill's day bordered on perfection as he brought his Flyer B in for a landing. He descended to within 18 feet of the infield of the racetrack where the flying grounds were when he killed his engine, thinking to glide safely into the enclosure. The wind, however, suddenly died and he lit in the track instead, smashing the biplane against the fence. Shaken but unhurt, Howard climbed out of the mass of splintered struts and tattered linen.

Now hailed as the "new star-duster of the Wright team," Howard's next engagement brought him to Meridian, Mississippi, on July 4 and 5, where an overflow crowd paid a hefty admission price to witness an airplane fly. In repayment, the locals savored the full repertoire of stunts known to exhibition birdmen, including the

Dutch roll, which Gill accomplished with an alarming disregard for his machine slipping sideways.

On his last flight of July 4, Howard clawed for altitude, and had reached nearly 3,000 feet when his manager, A. Roosevelt, glimpsed a huge black cloud rapidly approaching from the south. Binding two handkerchiefs together, he tried in vain from the center of the field to wave Gill down, but the star attraction, not having seen the cloud, rose even higher in wide circles. The public, ignorant of the threatening storm, kept their eyes on the Flyer while its pilot sailed ahead, unmindful of the gale overtaking him from the rear. As the storm reached the flying field, snapping the spectators' tent poles and shredding its canvas, Roosevelt became hysterical in his attempts to attract his boss's attention, while women screamed for him to descend before it was too late.

When Gill swung around over the stand for another pass, he faced directly into the churning cloud which by then had reached him. His Flyer rose briefly, and then, with a downward motion, it rocketed for the ground, gyrating uncontrollably as repeated gusts struck its wings. As the machine, with its tail high in the air, disappeared behind a large stand of trees off in the distance, there came a hush over the crowd, which stood transfixed in the rain throughout the dive. The next moment, ruining their clothes on a barbed wire fence surrounding the field, the gallery raced for the trees behind which the craft had disappeared. Howard's chief mechanician was the first to reach him, finding him unhurt and nonchalantly inspecting his plane for damage.

That night, when Gill was interviewed at the Meridian Hotel, he said:

> It was my worst experience yet. The wind wasn't so strong, but the gusts were terrific, and with my feet braced as hard as I could, on three occasions I was thrown completely out of my seat and only regained it through my hold upon the levers. A machine of less structural strength than the Wright would have been torn to pieces in the air.

As Howard talked, he was reclining in his bed, and across his chest reporters noticed one long, thin, blue mark, while two purple and red marks, comparable to those that would be inflicted by a whiplash, were across his legs, showing where he had been catapulted against the wires of his aircraft.

From Meridian Howard traveled to New York, where he was scheduled to fly for his F.A.I. license on July 12 at Nassau Boulevard, Long Island. Prior to his test, Gill rose into the air to become accustomed to the allotted machine on hand and gave an extraordinary exhibition of fancy flying. The official meeting of the New York Aero Club was postponed, as well as all other work in the vicinity, while the crowd watched Gill go through his bag of aerial stunts. His official flights were made without a hitch, and in every case he did more than was required. Most impressive were his landings, which were made within 67 and 72 feet of a predetermined point after the motor had been switched off while the craft was still in the air. Howard's exams were witnessed and sanctioned by Aero Club of America officials W. Redmond Cross and J. Campbell Wood.

Curtiss barnstormer John Alexander Douglas McCurdy undertook the world's first long-distance oceanic flight on January 30, 1911, flying from Key West, Florida, to Havana, Cuba, a distance of 95 miles over shark-infested waters. Within sight of Cuban beaches and a mile short of his destination, an oil leak forced him to land in the water. He was immediately rescued by a U.S. vessel, but not before a circle of sharks surrounded his bobbing machine as McCurdy perched on its upper wing. Although he came short of completing his flight, Cuban authorities agreed that the daring aviator would get the contracted $10,000 prize. Later that evening at a banquet in his honor, McCurdy was presented with a small package — presumably his prize money. It was not until later, however, that he would discover only scraps from a Havana newspaper in the envelope awarded him by the president of Cuba.

Less than seven months later, Miami's mayor, E. G. Sewell, besought the Wrights to come down and offer his citizens a perspective on flight. Orville sent Howard on July 20, who performed some flying over the future site of Hialeah for a $7500 fee. Mayor Sewell then tried to persuade the brothers to base a pilot training school within his precincts, but they were disinterested. Gill received notice in the local press as being the first pilot ever to fly an airplane into greater Miami. Unsatisfied with this lesser accolade, Howard eyed a much greater record — the successful completion of McCurdy's failed Key West to Havana attempt. Even before he fulfilled his Miami engagement, Gill wired Orville on July 18:

> Miami to Cuba would be a history making flight similar to the crossing of the English Channel. No where else in the world could such an easy flight be made that would make as much of a reputation. Its accomplishment would call attention to the Curtiss failure and this failure would add to the prestige of having made it and add to the publicity secured. The exhibition department would find contracts easier to secure if fair managers occasionally heard of some of the newspapers reported flights as having been made by a Wright aviator. Had engine cover off at Meridian and both it and machine in perfect condition. If you will loan me [a] machine [I] will equip it with flowers and pay all expenses of flight.
>
> Gill

Orville squelched the proposal and Howard's ambitious nature began to fester.

Gill next appeared at the highly touted Chicago Meet held at Grant Park between August 12 and 20. This contest proved to be a particularly bloody affair, with St. Croix Johnstone and William Badger being killed, and Arthur Stone, Cal Rodgers, Oscar Brindley, and Al Welsh involved in near-fatal accidents. Howard specialized in endurance and altitude flying, his highest flight in the latter event reaching 8,786 feet. He was aloft every day except Sunday, when Wright pilots did not fly. While there Gill did some flying in a clipped wing special Wright speed plane dubbed the "Baby."

On August 16 Howard had just completed what appeared a flawless landing when his craft suddenly checked as it skimmed across the ground at forty miles an hour and toppled over with terrific force. He was pinioned for a second between the tangled wires and taut fabric of the Baby Wright. The first spectator at the crash site grabbed Howard's extended hand. "We thought you were killed," he shouted. "Naw, I'm not even hurt," replied Gill, wiping dirt from his eyes, "but look at this machine. It's a wreck."

Howard owed his life to the new feature of construction used in the Baby Wright biplane. The engine, instead of being located in the rear of the aviator's seat, was positioned to one side. Closer inspection revealed that Gill's Model R flipped over when its wheels hit a rut, thereby snapping the skid supports and ensuring the crash.

Howard enjoyed better luck at the Harvard-Boston Meet held from August 26 to September 6, where he took first place in both the landing accuracy and bomb-dropping contests. Tragedy struck at the conclusion of the Squantum aviation exhibition, however, when Gill's brother, Royal Warfield Gill, who had attended the contest in support of his brother, was riding back to Baltimore in a rented chauffeur-driven limousine when the vehicle struck and killed the young son of ex-Representative Fred W. Whitcomb of Holbrook, Massachusetts. After spending a short time in Quincy's jail, Royal was eventually exonerated by a coroner's jury. Two weeks later, while still under a manslaughter charge, Howard's brother was also sued for breach of promise by a fetching Baltimore damsel.

Undoubtedly, the adverse notoriety associated with these untoward events, coupled with his own pending legal problems with Miss Broumel, affected his concentration somewhat on-field; worse still, however, was the nagging idea that the Wrights were holding him back in the flying profession. Writing from the Blackstone Hotel in Chicago on September 5, he alluded to his frustrations in a none-too-carefully worded letter to Orville:

Dear Mr. Wright:

I have been thinking over my contract with the Company, and while I have no reason or desire to quit the Company's employ at the present time, I feel that the agreement to refrain from flying for a year after leaving the Company may prove very disadvantageous to me in the future — especially, the longer it is put off. It is natural that I should desire to become as well known as possible, and while flying is still a source of newspaper comment and cross-country flights a means of becoming known, I would like to be in a position to take advantage of such opportunities should they come my way....

It would seem that you have placed a definite money value on the training of an operator by teaching anyone for $500, and this being the case, it should be fair to both for the Company to agree that after the first of the year, I could have my release upon the payment of $500 for my training and the giving of a thirty days' notice. I appreciate the kindness with which you have treated me and I have no fault to find with the Company's treatment or my salary ... but I feel that circumstances may arise which would make it unsatisfactory or disagreeable for me to continue with the Company. It is hard to believe that under these conditions you would desire to retain the services of an unwilling employee.

For your information, it should be interesting [for you] to know that the existence of the contract under which you now hold your aviators is a continual source of argument among them, and is a publicly known fact as well, which makes it constantly referred to by outsiders in a manner that makes one doubt if they have not shown poor judgment in entering the employ of the Wright Company.

Howard's itinerary directed him to Minneapolis, where he flew with Frank Coffyn at the Minnesota State Fair. A 50-mile-an-hour gale slammed Coffyn's fragile biplane to earth during preliminaries on September 5, leaving a debris field from which he casually walked away. Gill followed Frank's act, rising to 300 feet, but remaining aloft a mere thirteen minutes. The following day was a complete wash, but on September 7 both Howard and Frank made flights, thrilling the fairgoers with swoops and circles. Gill performed an ocean roll while Coffyn flew around the field below him. Then Howard headed toward St. Paul and, after a few minutes of further aerobatics, returned, landing in front of the grandstand. On September 8 he made the first passenger flight ever performed from a Minnesota field, carrying a local newspaper representative up for half-an-hour. After this feature, Howard climbed to 5,500 feet, much to the merriment of the galleries.

From his three-day Wahpeton, North Dakota, date beginning on September 29, Howard wrote Orville, reaffirming their earlier conversation in which both men agreed that Gill would leave Wright employment after the first of the year. The young man promised to help keep expenses down and "the good will of the company up" for the duration of his time with them, concluding:

> My connections with the company have been most pleasant and my one and only reason for leaving is the fact that I will have better opportunities to do flying, that doesn't require any special ability, but that on account of the record or the way it is done, will help to make me better known.

In the wake of an October 6 Salem, Ohio, stopover, Howard proceeded to St. Louis where, on October 19, he established a new American endurance record of 4 hours, 16 minutes, and 35 seconds, besting the late St. Croix Johnstone's time. Reaching an altitude of 7,000 feet, Gill maintained a triangular course of more than thirty miles — nearly freezing before he came down. He celebrated his feat by indulging in an orgy of passenger-flying.

In early November the Wrights abandoned the exhibition business and released their "road pilots," including Howard, who had already planned his exodus. Howard returned to Baltimore for a time both to look after his motorcar dealership and to negotiate for another flying position, which he thought possible with the [W. Starling] Burgess Company & [Greely S.] Curtis of Marblehead, Massachusetts. Fearing the long arm of Wright attorneys, many sensible prospective employers of a former company flyer faced several prudent considerations: First, did he leave Dayton on good terms and with a commendable performance record?; second, did he fulfill his contractual obligations?; and third, did he satisfy all royalty and rental payments to the coinventors of flight for the use of their machines? Few licensed constructors of Wright aircraft dared incur the brothers' displeasure by hiring a pilot who had previously run afoul of them. On November 13 Gill wrote Orville:

> Since leaving Dayton I have been traveling throughout the East and have just returned from Marblehead, Mass. While there I had a talk with Mr. [Greely S.] Curtiss [sic] ... find that they are considering sending a representative to the Pacific Coast this winter. However, Mr. Curtis stated very emphatically that he would not consider any of the Wright Co's former aviators without first having conclusive proof that the aviator had secured complete release from your Company, and knowing that the acceptance of a position with them was thoroughly agreeable to you.

From my conversation with you when in Dayton (at which time we talked over these very points) I felt that there would be no trouble in securing your approval of my accepting a position with the Burgess Company & Curtis, so wired you from Marble-head, but up to the present time have not received your reply. I am very anxious to know how you feel about this and would appreciate hearing from you at once.

Although your Company has no exhibition work for me, I intend to continue in the aeroplane business. I can easily connect with an unlicensed firm, but it would undoubt-edly place me in an embarrassing position in the present Patent Litigation, and I also personally feel very much safer in a Wright type machine.

In going to the Coast with an aeroplane I feel sure that I will get my share of the exhi-bition dates, and it would seem to me best for your Company that I go as a representa-tive of the Burgess Co. & Curtis with an aeroplane of their manufacture, in which case it will mean that your Company will secure your daily exhibition royalty.

Trusting that the delay in answering my telegram was caused by oversight and that I will hear from you upon receipt of this, I am

Orville immediately granted Howard his unconditional release, thereby clear-ing the way for his association with the Marblehead group. Gill was assigned as one of its instructors to be stationed in Los Angeles to begin a Burgess flying school, and as he had received instruction in piloting water craft back in Massachusetts, both land planes and aeroboats were shipped there for his use.

Howard started flying a Burgess-Wright Flyer B with a peppier 60 hp Hall-Scott motor, as he desired more power and a machine that would climb faster with a passenger. His students arrived on January 6, 1912, including Harry and Silas Christofferson, who flew with Gill three days later. From this time on Howard was constantly involved with his pupils and doing considerable flying.

The annual Los Angeles meet held at Dominguez Field between January 19 and 28 offered Howard a diversion from his daily instructional chores. It was to be a large affair with sixteen contestants and a colorful flying circus. He gave Orville his impres-sions of the forthcoming event on January 2:

The meet out here seems to be sort of getting on the bum, and it looks as if it might wind up in being an exhibition of the Curtiss team, assisted by the local aviators, their taking the gate receipts as their pay....

Both [Cliff] Turpin and [Phil] Parmalee are out here, and have formed a partnership with Roy [Knabenshue], who has been trying to secure exhibition dates for them, upstate. From the way they talk it hasn't been very profitable, and I believe Turpin is get-ting quite disgusted with their prospects.

Dick Ferris, who is managing the meet here, has secured the services of Bill Pickens, who was formerly press agent for Barney Oldfield.... Pickens is certainly getting the papers to boost the meet, but it is mostly very sensational, such as women aviators, loop-ing the loop and etc. It will be interesting to see if he can get the people to come out.

During preliminary flight trials on January 12, the local constabulary wheeled up to Dominguez Field and summarily deputized Gill, along with meet participants Glenn Martin, Parmelee, and Turpin. Their mission was to locate two fugitives, from the air, who had wounded a deputy sheriff and had fled into the dense woods bor-dering the San Fernando Valley. Using field glasses, Howard and the others thought they had spotted the desperadoes, but after diving to treetop level the airmen discovered that the life forms were dogs. Returning to the meet site, the flyers had to admit failure; however, all four believed that they had been among the first to support law enforcement through aerial surveillance.

The opening attraction of the Dominguez meet left 75,000 spectators breathless as Lincoln Beachey and Parmelee performed variations of their "Dives of Death." Following this show Howard flew in the first race against four competitors: W.B. Atwater, Farnum Fish, W.B. Cook, and Turpin. While each man ripped off mile after mile in their frenzy to best the others, a big gas bag was seen filling in the center of the field before the grandstand. Suddenly the sphere shot up in the air. Dangling from its bottom was a young woman, who waved at the crowd. The balloon rose to about 800 feet and then the damsel cut herself loose, and, equipped with a parachute, dropped about another fifty feet before the chute opened and scotched her fall. She floated earthward and again was seen to cut herself loose, bringing the crowd to its feet with a yell. It represented a new stunt: a second parachute attached to the first one. The diminutive woman settled easily to the ground. Gill, having finished his race and passing by in his biplane, landed long enough to pick her up and fly his pretty passenger back to the center of activities.

There were other carnival-like antics. In Howard's next appearance, he and Parmelee started on their search for a gentleman who was playing the part of a fugitive from justice. The human decoy ran from the center of the field and attempted to hide from the aviators. For a half hour the two flyers zoomed back and forth across the adjoining fields and the quarry was never once sighted. Dejected, Gill and Parmelee returned to the front of the grandstand and reported the escape of the malefactor. Then there was the pigeon-shooting event, which caught nearly everyone's attention. The birds were freed from a biplane flown by Parmelee, while Howard carried Warren Wood, commodore of the South Coast Yacht Club, who was armed with a shotgun. Three of the pigeons were bagged by Wood, and the excitement of the hunt drew the airmen miles away from the course.

In attempting to glide his powerless plane to earth in darkness from an altitude of 400 feet, Howard crashed on a barbed-wire fence a mile southwest of the grandstand on January 25, his machine ground-looping in the process. Falling from his seat, he was pinned under his radiator, which rested on the left side of his back. The engine was destroyed. Two mechanicians ran toward Gill and removed him in an unconscious state from the demolished craft.

Turpin sped to the scene in his car, which had been hurriedly equipped with blankets and cushions. A physician summoned from the crowd found Gill to have three broken ribs, a facial laceration, and possible spinal injuries. Taken to a Los Angeles hospital, doctors there predicted that Howard would be laid up for six weeks. While coming out of the anesthetic, he kept murmuring: "Corkscrew, corkscrew, warping lever, motor worked all right, rudder jammed, spinned around."

Poor Howard had been plagued with a series of minor accidents and delays ever since the meet opened. For two days he waited for a new power plant, and then was forced to await the arrival of a new fly wheel from San Francisco for his recently acquired motor. During the delay, Gill took up the wife of a local dignitary, employing his old engine. It malfunctioned, and he had to volplane down 200 feet into a plowed field. Ironically, his new motor served him no better the next day and with even far worse results. To the end, however, Gill never admitted that his near-fatal accident was the fault of his machine, blaming instead the onset of darkness, and going so far as to have Parmelee and Turpin attest to the airworthiness of his Burgess-Wright craft. Howard's crash finished the Los Angeles Burgess School. While Howard was hospitalized, Knabenshue presented him a silver trophy from the Aero Club of St. Louis commemorating his endurance record flight made the previous October.

After leaving the hospital in early March, Gill returned to Marblehead, where he did some additional test and instructional flying for Burgess during the spring months. On May 5 he attended Walter Brookins' called meeting at the Hotel Manhattan to form the Safe and Sane Club, an association of the country's leading aviators now pledged to ending aerial tomfoolery on the exhibition circuits and elsewhere. The former Wright trick flyer confessed that he was moved to take this action following the death of flying great Calbraith P. Rodgers, who died attempting to execute one of Brookins' stunts. From the audience, Howard recalled out loud the steep-banked flying of Brookins that drove the Boston crowds wild at the city's first air meet, and nettled his host further by reminding Brookins of Wilbur Wrights' frequent admonishments:

> You know that Wright always used to tell you after you swung around at so steep an angle that if the spectators could see the sky between your planes [wings] that you were straining the machine far beyond safe limits. And you would always reply: "Well, I get away with it, Wilbur, and the crowds fall for it great."

Although Brookins spent the rest of the conclave repairing the damage inflicted by Gill's recollection, his good-natured heckler willingly joined the group. Eight weeks later, at a New Haven, Connecticut, date, Howard drove his biplane into Yale's baseball field after banking too sharply in a turn.

Early in 1912 Howard made plans to compete for a long-standing *Scientific American* prize of $15,000, which Edwin Gould, the son of railroad magnate Jay Gould and patron of aviation science, had offered to the successful inventor of a practical aircraft with two or more separate engines and propellers. Gould's aim was aerial safety, believing that a multi-motor machine would allow the pilot, should one power plant become disabled, to stay aloft by starting his second engine. The rules stipulated that the motors run in unison and separately, and that the aircraft must remain airborne for at least one hour over a prescribed course. Hempstead Plains Aviation Field on Long Island, New York, was selected as the trials' site and July 4 the contest date.

Gill personally financed and designed his machine, which consisted of standard Burgess-Wright biplane wings, a fuselage with a Hall-Scott 60 hp V-8 cylinder engine in the nose (prototype of the 1913 Burgess-Wright Model F), driving two tractor Wright-type propellers, and a standard 4 cylinder Wright engine halfway between the wings driving two standard Wright pusher propellers. All were driven by the usual Wright chain drive, so either motor alone, or both, could be operated at will. Howard successfully conducted the first flight tests of this novel craft on floats in early May at the United States' first hydroplane meet at New York. A minor setback occurred the following month when a gust of wind overturned Gill's biplane while he was skimming across a bay off Peaches Point near Marblehead, Massachusetts, requiring him to cling to his creation until rescued.

Meanwhile, one after another of the competing Gould entries dropped out until Howard was the only one left. It was then announced that there must be at least two machines contesting, so the $15,000 prize was withdrawn. After having funded the project himself, and considering the extent of his work, he tried to get the *Scientific American* committee to award him something, but to no avail, which was a disillusioning experience for him. Orville wrote Gill later in the month: "I have read with indignation of the treatment you received in the Gould competition. The rules were most ridiculous and very unfair."

Howard limited his flying during the summer of 1912, dividing his time between his Baltimore business interests, his work for the Burgess Company, his support of Percy Noel's newly titled aviation magazine, *Aero and Hydro*, now based in the "Windy City," and his preparations for the ten-day Chicago meet at Cicero Flying Field beginning September 12.

In mid–July Gill inquired of Orville whether or not he could secure two of his machines on either a daily rental basis or a percentage of his winnings:

> I should like to have one of your EX or new Military Scouts equipped with a six cylinder engine for altitude and speed work, and a standard "B" without engine, as I have a Hall-Scott eight cylinder 60 hp motor weighing 265 lbs. And it has been giving splendid satisfaction. This motor has turned one of your standard sets of propellers over 500 revolutions and I am confident could be made to turn them up to 530. It seems to me that this should be a good combination for quick starts, accuracy in landing, and weight carrying.
>
> I am leaving today for a month's rest and camping trip in the Adirondacks, so should be in ideal condition at the opening of the Chicago meet.

Four days later, Orville, ever the businessman, responded that he could make no promises about the availability of Wright machines for the Chicago event, and pointed out:

> Some time ago I had a six cylinder motor put on the No. 1 EX machine, and had no difficulty whatever in climbing more than 600 feet a minute; the light scout, however, is a still faster climber and also a much speedier machine. The light scout will have a speed of about 65 miles an hour; the EX approximately 58 or 59 miles with the six cylinder motor.
>
> It is quite probable that we will have a "B" machine or two on hand that we could rent, but, of course, we do not wish to bind ourselves in such a way that we cannot sell these if the opportunity is presented.

Angst-ridden about which Wright speed model would serve his purposes best, Howard wired "Orv" on the morning of August 15 that he would be arriving in Dayton before nightfall to talk over the problem. In the end, both mentor and protégé agreed that the EX offered the most potential for success.

Months prior to the Chicago date, Howard began to experience a sense of growing foreboding concerning his aerial career, based largely on his continuing and, it seemed to him, ill-fated string of unavoidable accidents. In late August he wrote his brother, Royal Gill, of his intention to leave aviation, concluding, "It's but a question of time.... I'm going to quit before it gets me." Then, on September 12, at the close of a day of extraordinary flying, Howard was forced to make a quick descent by reason of high winds and engine trouble. As he touched down, his machine suddenly began skidding over the field at twenty miles an hour, struck a hummock, and abruptly swerved toward a wire fence. Gill jumped from his seat into the front rigging of the craft and then onto the field as attending mechanicians grabbed the EX and guided it from its ruinous course. Turning to his rescuers, Howard quipped, "I'm

Howard Gill prepares for his race at Cicero Field, Chicago (Official U.S. Navy Photo, courtesy of the Glenn H. Curtiss Museum, Hammondsport, New York.)

beginning to be afraid. If I live through this meet, I am going to cut out aviation forever."

Just before climbing into his cockpit on the late afternoon of September 14, he called to a friend to throw him a heavy oil coat which the fellow was wearing. "I'm likely to bring back some blood on this," said Gill, with a chuckle, as he slipped it on. The friend jokingly retorted, "Gill is as safe in these machines as if in a bus on the ground." To this, Howard replied, "When you go up you never can tell what shape you will be in when you come down."

The next to the last event on that day's program was the biplane scratch race of 20 kilometers. Entered in this contest were Gill in his EX, Anthony Jannus in his Benoist tractor machine, Horace Kearny in his Curtiss, Martin in his Martin biplane, and Fish in his Wright. All but Gill and Jannus had completed their twelve laps around the field and the sun had set when these two contestants started on their course. There was still one more event on the card — the monoplane scratch race for the same distance, and Belgian George Mestach was the sole entrant.

Gill and Jannus raced their biplanes around a course marked by pylons. That contest had been completed but Howard had not yet landed when the officials told Mestach to take off. The Belgian believed he was to be the only one aloft, racing against the clock, not other airplanes, and failed to see Gill's EX ahead of and below him. The undercarriage of Mestach's Morane-Borel monoplane struck and splintered the tail assembly of Howard's biplane. Mestach managed to survive his crash with multiple lacerations, but Howard perished after his spinning EX fell fifty feet to the ground. A crowd of 50,000 spectators stampeded toward the mangled aircraft seeking crash relics. The police and meet officials, led by D.D. Griffith of the contest committee, attacked the mob with clubs while automobiles formed a protective circle around the stricken flyers. Griffith ordered the cops to club newspapermen who had rushed to get the facts. Alderman John Toman of the Thirty-fourth Ward interfered at this juncture. He directed the constabulary standing near him to leave the journalists alone. A policeman replied that he had his orders from the meet officials. "I don't care from whom you get your orders," stormed Toman. "The newspapermen have a right to get

One Aviator Killed, Another Injured, in Mid-Air Collision.

George Mestach.

Howard Gill.

Tragedy at Cicero Field: Howard Gill (left) and George Mestach (*Chicago Daily Tribune*).

the facts here," he insisted. "Clear the other people out ... but leave the newspapermen alone."

Gill was removed from the wreckage with a broken back and a crushed chest, the result of his body having taken the full impact of the Hall-Scott engine located behind his seat. He died on the way to St. Anthony de Padua Hospital. Brother Royal, who witnessed the tragedy, accompanied Howard's body back to Baltimore by train, but not before wiring editor Percy Noel, his mother, Alice, vacationing in Atlantic City, and Orville. Wright told the Dayton press that he classified Gill as a most proficient aviator, considering that he had only two years' experience. Mindful of the chagrin and disappointment the *Scientific American* had brought to Howard in life as sponsor of the Gould Prize, it is ironic that the journal's obituary of him concluded, "To his lasting credit be it said that he was one of the few aviators in this country who took an interest in a prize which was offered solely for the purpose of making flying safer." Gill was laid to rest in Baltimore's Greenmont Cemetery. His prize money of $882.00 was later remitted to the family.

Back at Cicero Flying Field a crisis had developed. Complaints abounded among the flyers that the fatal race should not have been held so late in the day, when the sun was almost gone and with near zero visibility. Before Gill and Jannus started their laps, the participants testified at a coroner's inquest, Howard told Aero Club of Illinois officials, many of whom were not aviators, that it was too dark to race and that an accident would happen if more than one aircraft went up. Statements were made that the contest committee had forced the aviators to fly in the twilight, for fear of disappointing the crowd. Mestach testified that he had also protested flying in the darkness and had been assured that his monoplane would be the only machine flying. The outraged flyers adopted their own set of rules and conditions under which they would continue to perform in the meet, one of which was that no contests were to be held under unfavorable weather or lighting conditions. Howard's comrades placed the blame for his death squarely with the presiding officials for permitting crowd satisfaction to trump flyer safety. Not one member of this group blamed Mestach for Gill's fatal plunge.

There were several considerations which influenced Gill's decision to quit flying: his family's repeated urging after the Dominguez Field crash; his belief that he was jinxed; his distress over the growing disinterest in pilots' safety as exhibited by both the public and meet promoters; and, most of all, his concern for the loss of so many of his flying associates. Howard had long ignored the fact that the one activity which made him feel so alive could also — for whatever reason — kill him. And yet, for the year 1912, a total of 151 members of his aerial fraternity worldwide joined him in death. As Brookins concluded in his prophetic "Safe and Sane" address, "We learn to love our friends who fly, and to esteem them after they have won great honors.... It is a great burden on the heart to carry a memory of so many who had very brilliant careers that were unnecessarily short."

Three

ARCH FREEMAN

Pioneer Flying's Man Friday

Archibald (Archie, Arch) A. Freeman's early years are largely shrouded in mystery. The birth records for the town of Flushing, Long Island, New York — housed in the Queens County Municipal Archives — where he was born do not show his name, leading one to suppose that his parents, the E.G. Freemans, did not think to report this happy occasion to the civil office. Moreover, the two marriage licenses associated with Arch's crowded life did not reveal his date of birth. What's worse, in 1918 Dayton, Ohio, Freeman's second wife and by then grieving widow, while recollecting for the coroner her deceased spouse's age as twenty-eight, could not call to mind his birthday. Then, there was the respected pioneer aviation historian who indicated that Arch had appeared in vaudeville as a youth, a fact seemingly beyond documentary proof or disproof. Conceding that Freeman was the recipient of a superior secondary school education in Flushing's public schools, nevertheless, the *Boston Daily Globe*'s report that he graduated from Syracuse University was erroneous. With so much biographical ignorance and misinformation connected with Arch's beginnings, where does one pick up the thread of his career as a budding turn-of-the-century aviator?

As assistant and beginning student of one of Orville Wright's principal flying instructors, Arthur L. Welsh, he attended with his mentor a private aerial exhibition orchestrated by Robert J. Collier, head of P.F. Collier & Son Publishers, editor of *Collier's Weekly*, and influential aviation enthusiast. Although Arch barely made the *Who's Who in America* guest list, what he witnessed at Collier's country estate, Rest Hill near Wickatunk, New Jersey, from October 14 to 16, 1911, must have fired his imagination — the perfect confluence of wealth and flying.

Collier's social extravaganza on October 14 included a foxhunt, a polo game, and plenty of airplane flights prepared by the publisher to cap a protracted housewarming party. On the first day there was to be a ten-mile hunt from East Freehold to the polo grounds on the Collier estate, with two machines circling overhead. Tom Sopwith, the celebrated British aviator, received instructions to pilot his Wright B (Sopwith also brought along his Blériot XI) and carry James H. Hare, Collier's personal photographer, who was to snap shots of the chase. Al Welsh, aided by Arch as his ubiquitous grounds crewman and all-around man Friday, flew Collier's Wright B, named *Laredo*, taking his host from Rest Hill to East Freehold. Arriving there, Collier dismounted his biplane and mounted one of his eighteen polo ponies before leading the hunt. Over three thousand local farmers, enticed by a complimentary breakfast served on Rest Hill's sprawling lawn, cheered on their benefactor. Later on there were passenger-carrying flights — of which Freeman eagerly partook with Welsh and Oliver G. Simmons at the controls — and a polo match between the Rumson and Wickatunk clubs.

Perhaps O.G. Simmons, more than anyone else at Collier's posh event, inspired Arch Freeman to pursue flying. The aspiring novice identified with O.G., which was not the case with Collier's retinue of social swells. Arch learned that the thirty-three-year-old flyer had been the Army Signal Corp's first civilian aircraft mechanician, servicing the army's premiere Wright machine at College Park, Maryland, and later at Fort Sam Houston in San Antonio, Texas, where Lieutenant Benjamin D. Foulois put Uncle Sam's No.1 Flyer through its paces. Simmons remained with the one-man, one-aircraft U.S. Air Service into the spring of 1911. At that point the Signal Corps accepted the loan of a new Wright model from Collier — the very biplane flown by Welsh at Wickatunk — which Lt. Foulois then flew, along with Wright pilot Phil O. Parmelee, over the Rio Grand from Laredo to Eagle Pass, Texas, the following spring. Collier had dispatched his photographer to the border for pictures and to oversee the use of his plane, and when the Signal Corps returned *Laredo*, he instructed Hare to offer Simmons a job as his pilot and mechanician. O.G. left the military on July 14 to work at Collier's private Wickatunk airfield.

About noon on the final day of Collier's fete, Arch wheeled out *Laredo* from its hangar and gave it a customary preflight check. Shortly thereafter, its owner and O.G. climbed aboard and off they went. Flying over Lakewood, Collier headed toward open country, followed by several dozen automobiles. Circling above John D. Rockefeller's estate, Collier decided to put down, making a pinpoint landing near one of Rockefeller's grazing horses. The sudden descent of the machine frightened the animal, which reared up and fell back, breaking a blood vessel and dying a few minutes later.

Shaking off this untoward incident, Collier inquired of several bystanders the way to Allaire, his destination. After checking his Wright craft for damage, Collier and O.G. were aloft again. *Laredo* flew well for about two miles before its motor gave signs of distress, necessitating an emergency landing in an unwelcoming cornfield. Pilot and passenger were scratched and bruised, but not otherwise injured, an imperfect ending to full days of nonstop flawless entertainment. Collier's lavish, three-ring circus affair impressed Freeman every bit as much as it did a *Washington Post* reporter:

> Across the private polo grounds of the Collier estate, the aeroplanes have been flown successfully on a 10-mile fox hunt.... Mr. Collier sat with Mr. Welsh ... in one machine. Accompanying Mr. Tom Sopwith ... was Mr. Jimmy Hare, who took photographs. Mr. Richard Harding Davis lent the dignity of his presence. Five thousand guests ... followed

in automobiles. And—oh, yes, Mr. Collier also wore a pink coat, thus making the whole affair not only wholly triumphant, but exceedingly recherché as well.

From this watershed event in his life, Arch returned to Welsh's Nassau Boulevard classes held at the Wright flying school extension on Long Island, New York. He subsequently obtained pilot's license no. 84, dated January 10, 1912, at Dayton, Ohio, along with fellow graduates Farnum Fish of Los Angeles, California, Frank Champion of Sherman, Texas, and Earl Dougherty of Des Moines, Iowa.

By late May 1912 Freeman had scarcely set foot in Boston, Massachusetts, and already his aerial exploits as assistant flying instructor at the nearby General Aviation Company flying school at Atwood Park, situated in Saugus, were the talk of the city. The field's location, with the broad Lynn Marsh in front and the ocean only a mile away, made for an ideal aviation field. It was here that Freeman instructed, and he frequently made flights over Revere, which created a huge public stir among the thousands who patronized the beach. A *Boston Daily Globe* reporter sized up Freeman's flying ability in the following passage:

> Freeman is a daring aviator, but he is always "safe and sane," so much so that the pupils at the school, both men and women [4], have the greatest confidence in him—a very necessary thing for an aviation instructor to possess. His control of the machine is perfect at all times and he banks and turns with the greatest ease. He has good "air instinct," and he doesn't seem to get "air foolish" at any time.

Although Arch reported to his boss and head instructor, Harry Nelson Atwood, he did most of the flying with the school's forty-three pupils in a Burgess-Wright Model B biplane. The reasons for Arch's work overload were Atwood's aversion to teaching and his recently acquired desire to fly the Atlantic Ocean. In retrospect, Freeman's decision to sign on with Atwood may have been the worst mistake of his life.

As with many of the civilian alumni of the Wright flying school, Atwood had gone into exhibition work at numerous county dates, competing for the lucrative long-distance prizes offered by national newspapers. Harry left Dayton set on winning the $50,000 Hearst Prize for the first coast-to-coast flight. The Hearst competition stipulated that the flight would have to be completed by October 1, 1911. Unable to raise the money for such a venture in the time required, Atwood settled on a shorter but still headline-grabbing flight from St. Louis to New York via Chicago. The publicity, he expected, would secure financial backing for the longer flight. Flying out of St. Louis in his Model B on August 16, he landed nine days later at Governors Island. His endeavor garnered national attention, but no sponsors. Meanwhile, a colleague, Calbraith Perry Rodgers, met the challenge by flying from Sheepshead Bay, Long Island, New York, to Long Beach, California, setting down in the surf on December 10, eighty-four days of pure hell after leaving Sheepshead Bay. Arriving well beyond the Hearst deadline, Rodgers settled only for the record.

Frustrated by his perceived bad luck, Atwood meant to eclipse Rodger's feat by pursuing his original dream of flying the Atlantic Ocean. Wary of raising money through the dicey medium of publicity, he settled on opening a flying school. "I

Arch Freeman (left) and mentor Al Welsh ("Jack" Stearns Gray, "UP": A True Story of Aviation).

should be at the head of the school, but would only give what personal instruction was necessary," he resolved. "I do not like to teach myself, and while the school was in session I should probably take long cross-country flights." The school became a blue-sky springboard for his projected transatlantic venture and, best of all, Harry corralled some backers with Arch and Ripley Bowman, a fellow instructor, to do the grunt work.

Atwood's General Aviation Company incorporated in February 1912 as "New England's latest and greatest aviation enterprise." After transforming an old racetrack into Atwood Park aerodrome and establishing a dock for hydroplanes at a nearby shore, Harry took over a defunct aircraft manufacturing company in Boston, where his students would supposedly learn aeronautical engineering and mechanics. The new CEO signed aboard for three years, claiming $250,000 in capital for his company, offered in preferred and common stock. The outfit's newspaper and prospectus, *Aviation News*, presented an unbelievable menu of pie-in-the-sky organizational objectives.

Once the school opened, with Freeman on the payroll, Atwood's students sat and fretted, waiting to fly. Student Melvin W. Hodgdon complained that about half the pupils waited around for Wright training, given by either Arch or Harry on the one Wright machine available, the craft Atwood had flown from St. Louis to New York. "With only one plane for two instructors, bad weather, strong winds, mechanical problems, and failure of the instructors to show up, it was thus a fortunate pupil who received more than two lessons a week," fumed Hodgdon. Since four hundred minutes were stipulated as the required flying time to complete course requirements, it took three or four months to graduate. Henry Roy Waite managed to take two lessons with Atwood. On each of the five minute flights, Harry did not utter one word in the air or on the ground. Waite would eventually learn to fly on his own.

Conditions were even more abysmal for the Curtiss novices, who were left to run up and down the field in a "ground hog," an aircraft that never left the ground. With Arch perched on the wing to prevent a student from hopping the device into the air, "the plane roared down the field at thirty-odd miles an hour," recalled Hodgdon. "The run lasted about fifteen seconds but it took usually ten or fifteen minutes to position the plane for the return 'flight.' Lessons were only given when there was no wind or the Wright plane was not using the runway. Few students got more than three or four runs a week." Atwood also advertised instruction in a nonexistent Blériot XI, his exasperated monoplane enthusiasts being told that a certain Sr. Guisseppe Colucci had been dispatched to Europe to purchase one for their use.

To be fair, conditions were not always wanting and grim at Atwood Park. On May 16, Atwood, disgusted with a month-long overcast over Saugus, consulted his personal meteorologist, who assured him that he would reach sunshine above the cloud bank. Taking his employee's word as gospel, Harry soon packed a Panama hat as Freeman and fellow instructor Ripley Bowman pushed his biplane out to the field. Once aloft, Harry kept climbing to an altitude of 1,200 feet; but he only found more fog, more rain, and the beginnings of frostbite. Spiraling down 1,000 feet Harry glimpsed the dim outline of rooftops, so he went up a bit and descended more cautiously — more housetops. Flying level, he dropped even more, until he spotted a clearing and landed in the Lynn marsh, being nearly blinded by the driving rain. His Panama hat sat next to him still in its box. Late that afternoon Freeman and Bowman were seen hauling the Burgess-Wright from the marsh on a jerry-rigged cart over to the Saugus hangars — no doubt cursing their employer's weather guru under their breath.

Then, on May 20, Freeman and his mechanician/pupil, Henry Roy Waite, bombed fortifications and battleships at Boston Harbor. Taking off from Atwood Park at 4:25 A.M. they flew across the Lynn marsh, passed over Revere, and finally reached Winthrop, where the action commenced. Circling 700 feet in the air above Fort Heath, the two birdmen dropped three sixteen ounce flour bombs in paper bags; so skillfully were the missiles aimed that one hit a range-finder, a second struck a gun pit, and the third landed on the fort's embankment. Fort Banks — headquarters of the Boston Artillery District — was then attacked with similar results, its sentries

milling about and pointing skyward in panicky consternation, especially when they
saw the white balls strike and then erupt into geysers of flour dust.

The flyers next hovered above the battleships *New Jersey*, and *Rhode Island*
anchored in Boston Harbor, showering the vessels with "bombs." Freeman claimed
three strikes on each ship: stern, midship, and bow. Buzzing over the Charlestown
Navy Yard, his Burgess-Wright made a beeline for Saugus. Arch's entire flight took
forty-five minutes round-trip, during which time twenty-eight miles were covered,
the biplane's speed ranging from forty-five to sixty miles-an-hour.

The demonstration came about as the result of a hotly contested debate between
Saugus aviation students and officers of the affected forts as to whether the gar-
risons might be assailed by men in "heavier-than-air" machines, and whether destruc-
tion could be wrought before the raid was realized. Freeman and Waite made their
point.

On the occasion of H. Roy Waite's 90th birthday, Early Birds celebrants hon-
ored the event with a cake and a memorable ode which read in part:

> Roy wanted to fly but [Harry] Atwood said, "No! If you touch those levers, then out you
> go!" Roy paid for more rides. Flying was his dish, with Atwood, Arch Freeman, and Far-
> num Fish. But Roy, instead of just thinkin' and guessin', decided he'd teach our Armed
> Forces a lesson. So in 1912, on the 20th of May, Roy and Arch Freeman, before the dawn
> of day, loaded an airplane with deadly power —12 bombs, made of bags filled with one
> pound of flour. They flew to Fort Heath and there they dropped one. It landed kerplop
> on a ten-inch gun.
>
> Another one hit on a range-finding station. Then on they flew to their next destina-
> tion. Fort Banks was their target. Soon it lay below. Our Roy took aim and made a good

**Roy Waite (left) and Arch Freeman after the flour-bombing of Boston Harbor (http://his-
toricaircraftpictures.com/WAITE).**

throw. Three times he cast. He threw them just right. The Fort was clobbered with splotches of white.

Next to the Navy Yard. There they could see the warships *Rhode Island* and *New Jersey*. Six bombs were heaved out and downward they sped. Within each bag was a note which read: "What if this bomb, instead of flour, contained nitroglycerin's deadly power?"

Roy and Arch Freeman then homeward flew. Roy wondered what the Army and Navy would do. But those officers said with a disdainful grunt, "That's only a dern fooly Early Birds stunt."

Nine years later came Billy Mitchell's shocker when battleships went down to Davy Jones's locker.

In hindsight, Arch's prescient demonstration went far beyond skylarking, as trumpeted by the military and political establishment of the time. The *New Jersey* would be decommissioned at the Boston Naval Shipyard on August 6, 1920, and sunk by friendly fire, together with her sister ship, *Virginia*, a little over three years later. Freeman's secondary target, the USS *Rhode Island*, was sold for scrap the same year as the *New Jersey* sinking.

In one of the first exhibitions of air prowess over naval power, Brigadier General William "Billy" Mitchell led Martin MB-2 and deHavilland DH-4 biplanes carrying 600 and 2,000 pound bombs against the *New Jersey*. Despite these and other significant aerial demolitions of capital ships, the General Board of the Navy continued to tout the battlewagon as "the element of ultimate force in the fleet and all other elements." For his nuisance role in continuing to advocate the primacy of air power, General Mitchell was eventually court-martialed.

Scarcely had the local and national public digested Arch's landmark assault on Boston Harbor's fortifications and U.S. Navy dreadnoughts riding at anchor — marking a not altogether welcome change in the course of American military history — than the pride of Saugus was airborne again. Taking off on the morning of May 25 from Atwood Park at Cliftondale with passenger George C. Parker in tow, Freeman flew to West Lynn at 200 feet and circled the General Electric River Works while 7,000 employees applauded his aerial capers from the plant's windows and grounds. Eyeing an inbound Boston and Maine express train chugging across the West Lynn marsh, Arch headed his biplane down the track, caught the train, held it neck to neck for three-quarters of a mile, then passed it and returned while the express's passengers spilled out onto the rear platform or leaned from the coach's windows to cheer. Flying back over Lynn, Arch dropped a small United States flag, a sponge, and two letters on Fairchild Street.

His adrenaline level still high, he took to the air again late in the afternoon and headed for Revere Beach, again skimming the ground. With him was the manager of one of the "shows" on the beach who expressed his delight in seeing his adult arcade from a different perspective. Performing figure-eights over the beach around the State Bathhouse, Arch volplaned just above the breakers and flew low up and down the beach a few times where those on the boulevard and shore could plainly see his passenger. Then, he rose, circled once and sped away over the marsh to Saugus. A perfect day was had by all.

On June 1, the finale of a three-day meet at Atwood Park, the exuberance of crowds running into the thousands belied the underlying woes of Harry's organization. During the event, aerial great Lincoln Beachey led off pitting his Curtiss biplane against a host of motorcycles, after which he rose a mile in the sky and plummeted to earth, pulling out at the last moment. By mid-day, aviators Philip W. Page, Frank J. Terrill, and Atwood were performing some fancy exhibition work, followed by C.C. Bouette's parachute drop from a balloon high over the spectators.

Following these spectacles, Arch jumped into Atwood's craft and climbed to 3,000 feet before executing a beautifully symmetrical volplane to earth without "jarring a single guy wire." This segment was followed by a bombing contest during which junior officers from the *New Jersey* and the *Rhode Island*, Arch's former imaginary enemies, went aloft with Freeman to try their skill at dropping flour-laden missiles on the outline of a battleship drawn on the aviation field.

Finally, the U.S. Postmaster General's office had granted permission for the establishment of an air postal route between Lynn and Saugus during the three days of the aviation meet, with drops occurring each day. On Arch's first run representing Atwood's "Skyline Mail Service," the mailbag fell in the ocean and was later retrieved. On his next attempt, Freeman successfully deposited his cargo of 2,000 letters and postcards in the middle of Lynn Common.

By late spring of 1912 both Freeman and Atwood were flying distant exhibition dates when not performing at Atwood Park, sometimes together and sometimes individually. Towing the tired Burgess-Wright from one engagement to the next, they motored from the White Mountains to Sherbrooke, Quebec, to the lakes in New Hampshire and to Bangor and Portland, Maine. Atwood grew tired and disillusioned in his attempts to raise money for his ocean flight.

From the incorporation of his enterprise back in January 1912, Harry had claimed that his people were secretly building a machine for his projected transatlantic crossing — a revolutionary design which would accommodate three-quarters of a ton of fuel. At the same time, the secretary of the navy was importuned to assign six cruisers, stretched across the ocean, to serve as refueling stations for his anticipated flight from Newfoundland to Ireland. As for the construction particulars of his mystery aircraft, Harry was maddeningly vague. He tried to interest Orville Wright in his scheme, but without success. His former boss, Starling Burgess, listened to his ideas for a monster biplane equipped with pontoons; but, again, who would pay him for constructing such a craft? Even President William Howard Taft vetoed naval involvement in Harry's undertaking at a White House meeting; perhaps he had knowledge of his guest's many aerial "near-misses."

Despite his employer's improbable machinations and untimely absences from Atwood Park, Arch faithfully served Harry as flying instructor, chief mechanician, and deputy administrator under the worst possible conditions. On June 10, 1912, with its students in a quandary about the future of the flying school, the promoters of the General Aviation Company announced that Atwood had resigned and would be taking the airfield's only machine with him. The backers gave as Harry's excuse his newly discovered preference for exhibition over instructional flying, which, he claimed, stemmed from his disenchantment with employee Freeman as a result of his Boston Harbor raid. There were vague promises that another aircraft would be purchased in the near future, but nothing more. Despite the alleged bad blood between Harry and Arch, the two flew away together in the company's battered old Burgess-Wright. "Many local people lost money on this, having taken stock," a Lynn newspaper lamented. Not one student had completed their training. Atwood would live another fifty-four years, a life filled with many adventures and misadventures; but he would never fly the Atlantic on his own.

While none of Arch's students had completed their formal training, a few nevertheless believed that they had accrued sufficient instruction to allow them to solo. Jack McGee, Harry Jones, and the legendary Ruth Law bought planes and took their first solo flights at Saugus during the summer of 1912. Roy Waite acquired Atwood's famed Burgess-Wright and followed his classmates' example. McGee, Jones, and Law remained at Saugus an extra few weeks to refine their airmanship before leaving. Waite, however, established yet another school at the now defunct Atwood Park, and remained there until the winter of 1912-1913.

After leaving Atwood Park, Arch again took brief positions as assistant flying instructor with several concerns, most notably the Thomas Company of Bath, New York. At the Thomas school of aviation, he trained in both the 65 hp Kirkham 1-6 pusher — aka Thomas Headless Biplane — and the 65 hp Kirkham tractor version, which was later dropped in favor of a return to the pusher line. His free time was devoted to exhibition work at various New England points.

In 1912, William A.P. Willard, who had helped manage the 1910 and 1911 Harvard-Boston meets, organized an air meet at Squantum. Appearing in this contest, Freeman vied for honors with the likes of Blanche Stuart Scott, Harriet Quimby, Lincoln Beachey, Charles K. Hamilton, Glenn L. Martin, Charles T. Niles, Philip W. Page, and George A. Gray. Willard offered a wide array of events: speed, bomb dropping, aero baseball, racing, and quick-starting.

On July 1, Quimby took Willard up as a passenger in an attempt to break Englishman Claude Grahame-White's speed record time around Boston Light. With a huge throng watching, first Willard, then Quimby were somehow thrown from the plane, and they plummeted a thousand feet to their deaths. The tragedy cast a universal pall which virtually ended the contest.

Arch had his 80 hp Burgess-Wright out on the "getaway" testing its souped-up power plant well before the competition began. Despite adverse weather conditions, he went up and remained aloft for several minutes, during which time he flew two laps around the prescribed circuit before descending. Just as Freeman was about to land, a powerful air current caught his machine and nearly caused him to ground-loop, forcing him to rise again before he finally landed.

California's Farnum T. Fish, the "Boy Aviator" and Arch's old classmate at Simms Station, defeated Freeman in a five-lap passenger-carrying event, with Arch and his old pal Roy Waite settling for second place. In the bomb-dropping sequence Freeman placed behind leader Paul Peck in an event history dictated he should have won. Following the Quimby-Willard disaster, Freeman lightened the general mood with several exceptional exhibitions, to the delight of his fans. On the final day of the meet, Arch took to the skies with Martin, Hamilton, Page, and Fish in a five-man flying show. The airmen flew in a forty-mile-an-hour wind during their finale. Arch and the others jettisoned toy bombs which marksmen on the field tried to hit with rifles and shotguns. Boston Red Sox star Johnny Murphy then attempted to catch a few of their baseballs dropped from 600 feet in the air.

On July 7 the *Boston Daily Globe* paid the aircraft piloted by Freeman and his fellow Burgess-Wright flyers a back-handed compliment:

> The Burgess-Wright machines flown by Page, Freeman, and Gray are so far ahead of the machines Wilbur Wright brought to the 1910 meet that there is no comparison. These are also wonderfully stable machines and yesterday it was demonstrated that they can stand the roughest weather. The only handicap in these machines is the motor. The Wright motors are not as powerful as the motors used in the Curtiss biplanes. Speed adds greatly to stability in a flying machine if the aviator is skillful.

Apparently unbeknownst to Arch was the fact that he had participated in a meet unsanctioned by the Aero Club of America. The club's ban stemmed from the late Willard's refusal to deposit before the Squantum event with "some responsible bank" an amount equal to the sum of prizes to be awarded. Because Freeman had flown in an unsanctioned or outlawed meet, both he and seven other licensed aerial performers were suspended for six months. Poor Arch had been awarded his pilot's license no. 83 on January 10 in Dayton, and already he was in hot water; still, it was comforting for him to learn that the brief excommunication did not apply to private exhibition flying.

In the fall of 1912 Freeman widened his geographical horizons, flying dates at Newark, Ohio, on October 2, both performing stunts and carrying passengers; appearing on October 11 at Suffolk, Virginia, with a similar program; and later that month offering an expanded show and carrying passengers at Riverview Park, Louisville, Kentucky. Arch worked for New York aviation promoter John S. Berger, who, the previous March, had been charged by Waycross, Georgia, authorities with the misappropriation of sponsors' funds and misuse of the mails. While a member of Berger's stable of aviators in 1913, Freeman formed a bond of friendship with Howard Rinehart, a fellow Wright graduate.

The colorful Berger telegraphed Arch's application for a place in the *New York Times* Aerial Derby, to take place at Oakwood Heights, Staten Island, New York, on October 13. Held to commemorate the forthcoming tenth anniversary of the first successful flight of Wilbur Wright, the race was scheduled to be flown around Manhattan Island. Freeman's manager used his flyer's role in the 1912 Boston Harbor bombing incident as an effective promotional gimmick. At the last minute, however, Arch failed to obtain a Wright machine and his bid for top honors evaporated.

As with his flying career, Arch's domestic life had its ups and downs. In late December 1912 he had married Helen Stevens of Brookline, Massachusetts. Because his bride expressed her distaste for aviation, Freeman publicly announced in the press that he would give up the sport. He went back on his word, and the marriage fell apart.

The following year, Freeman settled down to regular employment as an instructor with the Wright Company at Mineola, Long Island, New York, continuing in that capacity through the spring of 1915, even after Orville sold his interests to an eastern group. Then, in 1916, Arch became involved with his friend from the John S. Berger troupe, Howard Rinehart, in a private aviation venture backed by Edward A. Deeds, vice president of Dayton's National Cash Register Company; two Dayton bankers, the Harold E. Talbotts, senior and junior, and inventor Charles F. Kettering — with Orville as a consultant. The Dayton-Wright Airplane Company was capitalized on paper at $500,000 with Deeds as president and Kettering as vice president and technical adviser.

Meantime, Rinehart persuaded management to establish a flying school and construct a new much needed trainer in the bargain. The Wright Field Company was formed, land secured, and North Field laid out on the site which later became McCook Field.

Harold Talbott, Sr., decided that his company's "first shot" machine should be called the FS, so the trainer Rinehart had asked for became the FS-1. It took South Field constructors only eight weeks to complete the craft. It was a standard wood and fabric craft with two bays (the upper overhand braced by twin struts), ailerons on the upper wing, a balanced rudder without a fixed fin, a two-wheeled landing gear with tail skid, tandem cockpits, and the engine cowling and top surface of the fuselage, around the crewmen, of metal. A Hall-Scott 4-cylinder engine of about 100 hp was installed. Freeman tested the new model at South Field and declared it to be a docile trainer. The FS-1 was then flown to North Field where Rinehart and Freeman were instructing for the Wright Field Company. Two weeks later a second such trainer, the FS-2 was made available. Employing these ships, Howard and Arch taught a number of civilian and U.S. military students to fly, including forty-one wartime Canadians sent there under contract with the American government. The visiting Canadians trained for the coveted pilot's certificate which was a prerequisite for admission into the Royal Flying Corps and the Royal Naval Air Service. Through Arch's tutelage these men would go on to distinguish themselves in the Great War, winning nineteen combat decorations between them.

By late 1917 North Field had been taken over by the army and renamed McCook Field, ending the work of the Wright Field Company. The two FS trainers were sent to South Field, now the experimental field for Dayton-Wright. Management ordered that one FS be installed with a radio, and Arch made a number of flights in the trainer, talking from a point over the Soldier's Home at Dayton to Army Signal Corps staff using Kettering's radio set in his home at Ridgeleigh Terrace. Although the FS passed muster as a trainer, its adaptability at South Field was limited, and it was eventually replaced by the Wright modified Standard J-1 trainer.

Rinehart had been named head experimental test pilot back in April 1917, when

Dayton-Wright became a reality, and had been given a flight staff, which included Arch. Following the Army's lease of North Field as a central engineering post and experimental flying depot, Howard, Arch, and Bernard L. Whelan relocated to the Experimental Station at South Field near the Dayton-Wright plant. At this location the threesome conducted the first flight tests of the Standard J-1 trainers, and in early November Rinehart flew the first Dayton-Wright–built DH-4.

As World War I began to take its toll on Allied aircraft, Dayton-Wright's officials had anticipated that 3,500 warplanes could be produced before the end of 1917, sparked by a congressional appropriation of $640 million dollars. A technical delegation, working in concert with Allied aviation experts, selected the British deHavilland DH-4 as the design most suited to U.S. manufacture.

The DH-4 was a two-bay biplane of 42 feet, 6 inch span; the fuselage, somewhat tapered in appearance, was about thirty feet long. With a gross weight of nearly 4300 pounds, the deHavilland was armed with two Lewis guns mounted on a Scarff ring in the rear cockpit and one or two forward-firing machine guns. It could carry 322 pounds of bombs over a range of 100 miles and could be fitted, on reconnaissance missions, with cameras and wireless telegraphy.

Dayton-Wright had won the deHavilland bid; Washington ordered 400 J-1s to be filled by year's end, and an unspecified number of DH-4s were due the spring of 1918. Rinehart and Freeman did considerable test flying in that first DH-4 during fall trials, laying the foundation for several thousand U.S. versions of the British combat plane.

Reports of the initial flight of the original U.S. deHavilland were so hair-raising that they defy belief. According to bystanders, Rinehart took the plane up and proceeded to stunt it with rolls, loops, and other aerobatics. Arch went along in the gunner's bay. During inverted flight, the wood screws holding his seat stripped and Howard nearly lost his passenger. Poor Freeman's screams were lost in the DH-4's slipstream. "When he (Rinehart) came in for a landing," an observer recalled, "we could see Arch standing up waving something over his head. This turned out to be the gunner's piano-stool type of seat. The only comment he had to make was as to how funny he would have looked when we picked him up with the seat still strapped onto his sitter."

Aside from the many headaches involved in the complete revamping of the British deHavilland to U.S. standards, Arch was involved with Howard in other experiments, such as the deployment of the aerial radio telephone and the search for an effective synthetic fuel for the DH-4's Liberty engine. After full-time production on the deHavilland began in early 1918, Freeman became a member of the staff of acceptance pilots performing shakedown flights as they rolled off Dayton-Wright's assembly line. Then tragedies befell two of Arch's fellow flyers in DH-4s at Dayton.

Since leaving Dayton in December 1913, Rinehart's former instructor, Oscar Brindley, had been detached by the Wright Company as a civilian flight instructor to the army. He received a commission following the declaration of war, and his experience qualified him to evaluate the fitness of new experimental aircraft. On May

2, 1918, Major Brindley and an accompanying colonel, Henry J. Damm, arrived at South Field to test a DH-4. After a friendly round of greetings with former pupils Rinehart, Freeman, and Whelan, the major climbed into a deHavilland and took off on a series of projected tests. On his second flight the plane's engine seized, and Brindley and Damm plunged to their deaths in full view of scores of onlookers. Ironically, on the exact same day, one of Arch's old instructor colleagues at Saugus, Ripley Bowman, while with the naval air service fell 4,200 feet while making an aerial survey at Hampton Roads, Virginia, and received injuries which kept him in ill health for the remainder of his life.

On May 10, Lieutenant Frank Jefferson Patterson, son of one of the founders of Dayton's National Cash Register Company, was assigned to the 137th Aero Squadron at nearby Wilbur Wright Field. His instructions were to conduct tests on the DH-4 and Bristol fighter aircraft. Little more than a month later, Patterson and an observer went aloft in a deHavilland to test newly installed machine guns synchronized by Nelson interrupter gear equipment. Their instructions were to fire a number of rounds into the field from ascending heights. On the third trial Patterson's wings collapsed and completely separated from the fuselage, leaving it to race across the field at full power after it crashed. The machine was totally destroyed and its crew crushed beyond recognition.

The funereal atmosphere encompassing Dayton-Wright and the surrounding area due to these accidents was somewhat alleviated by the summer meeting of the Society of Automotive Engineers held at Triangle Park on June 17 and 18 to honor the achievements of Orville Wright. Sponsored by SAE president Charles Kettering, the two-day occasion fairly exuded a martial theme, with displays of Liberty engines, Allied and German aircraft, simulated bombing attacks on fixed positions and "Hun" infantry, and a spectacular aerial sequence led by Howard and Arch. The *Dayton Daily News* reported:

> The afternoon program was the signal for the most sensational flying ever seen in this city. As accustomed as Dayton people have become to airplanes, thousands were gazing skyward Monday afternoon [June 17] as scores of machines soared over Triangle Park or came over the city. Some of the most daring stunts imaginable were pulled. Five big battle planes [DH-4s] vied with each other in the maneuvers while 15 smaller planes were constantly on exhibition with air tricks of all kinds. Particularly clever and daring flights were made by aviators Rinehart and Lewis, Freeman and Doolittle, of McCook aviation field. Flying at a speed of 125 miles per hour, the machines came so low at times that they narrowly missed brushing the treetops in the park. Three of the battle planes had never been flown before and on one the wings had been attached only a few hours before.

Clearly Freeman was no stranger to danger as an acceptance pilot, but to stunt an untested aircraft over thousands of spectators added an unacceptable level of risk to the show — or so thought the local reporter whose last sentence may have been more of a critique than a comment.

On June 27 Arch Freeman, with Rinehart and Benny Whelan looking on, forfeited his life under the same circumstances as did Oscar Brindley. Whelan recollected:

Archie was testing one of the production models. It had that disease, whatever it was, which caused the engine to lose power suddenly—just like Brindley's test ship. It would stop when about fifty feet high, but skillful Archie would do a one hundred and eighty degree turn and land back at the field. The mechanics would go over the fuel system, especially the carburetor, and then try another takeoff. The third time it quit again; the wind had come up and Archie tried to make a full 360 turn but couldn't do it. The ship pivoted on one wing in a turn and struck the ground with great force, his head hitting the instrument panel and Liberty ignition switches temporarily burying themselves in his forehead. They were in the closed position. I guess it was Archie's last-second gesture, but a futile one.

Running over, three of us piled into [a] car and headed for the nearest [Miami Valley] hospital. I held Archie in my arms but [I could] see he was dying. The new doctor in emergency held a stethoscope near his heart region. Mike Eversole [Dayton-Wright aviator attached to the Signal Corps] spoke out brusquely to the doctor—"For Christ Sake! Do something; don't stand there like a wooden Jesus!" The doctor looked at him and said, "This man is dead."

I called Monty Williams, [Dayton-Wright's] General Manager, and he said, "you better tell Helen [Gray Freeman], Archie's [second] wife, so I had to do so. She met me so cheerfully, it was hard to do. She headed for the hospital. Helen danced to the orchestra at the Miami Hotel and she and Archie had recently been married. After Archie's death Howard and I remained the only test pilots on the wartime Dayton-Wright payroll.

While Archie lived he was a most able pilot. The type of accident that led to his death, being like Brindley's, [was] almost certain to be fatal. In life from day to day he carried a jovial spirit and was missed all the more for it. Frequently at the end of the day Archie, Howard and I would stop at the Miami Hotel for a drink, with Archie having more than was good for him, and providing the fun for the others. He always bought a newspaper, but I never saw him read one. One night he chose a girl's coat to wear home, but it would be back the next morning. He is not easily forgotten.

Arch Freeman. From the Freeman Scrapbook (courtesy Dr. Mary Anne Whelan).

Helen Gray Freeman accompanied her husband's body by train back to Flushing for burial. The couple had been married less than a month. Flying Pioneers biographer Harold E. Morehouse concurred in Whelan's poignant recollection of Freeman, observing that he was "A small, slightly built fellow, with a quiet soft-spoken, pleasing personality and an ever-cheerful disposition, he was loved and respected by all who had the good fortune to know him. An active, skillful pilot who loved to fly, he gave his life to the cause of World War I."

Four

GROVER BERGDOLL

Early Aviation's Loose Cannon

Less than seven years following the Wright brothers' first heavier-than-air flight at Kitty Hawk, North Carolina, men of wealth in America were abandoning polo fields, yacht basins, and race tracks in pursuit of a new leisure-time diversion — amateur aviation. Foremost among this privileged class appeared a Philadelphian named Grover Cleveland Bergdoll. Known alternately in the local press as Playboy of the Eastern Seaboard and Million-Dollar Flyer, this handsome, charming, and always willful scion of one of Philadelphia's richest families — the grandson of the founder of the Bergdoll Brewing Company (1849), with real estate holdings in the millions — was destined to play a significant role in promoting the cause of early sport flying in the United States.

Grover Cleveland Bergdoll was the youngest of five children (after Louis, Charles, Erwin, Elizabeth) born to Louis Sr. and Emma Bergdoll. Following a difficult birth, he entered the world on October 17, 1893, with a broken arm and a severely bruised head. The toddler lost his father at age three, and his $5,000 a year allowance scarcely compensated for the seizures he endured well into his teens. Grover's mother managed her home, her real estate interests, and the family brewery by day, and pored over her accounting books by night. Despite her demanding schedule, Emma always found time for Grover, perhaps because of his physical afflictions. He became her favorite. Growing up in this environment Grover did what he pleased, especially if the activity garnered him attention.

As a teenager Grover relished his close association with brother Louis, who was one of the country's foremost exponents of professional racing and, later, aviation. The owner of Philadelphia's Bergdoll Motor Car Company, he spent his considerable free time with Grover on the eastern auto racing circuit, competing in road, hill, and beach events driving vehicles primarily of the Bergdoll design. In early 1910 Louis purchased a Blériot XI from department store magnate Rodman Wanamaker; and although he never took to the air himself, he allowed his general manager, William E. (Willie) Haupt, to fly the machine. There is evidence that Grover also taught himself to fly the monoplane during the hectic summer of 1910, abetted by Haupt's

Louis (left) and Grover Bergdoll aboard the Flyer (*Philadelphia Record*).

with several of his passengers who attempted to wave to people below or otherwise shifted their weight unexpectedly, thereby causing his craft to veer alarmingly off course. He flew local photographer Charles M. Clark over many of Philadelphia's landmarks on one occasion, and the shutterbug's bulky camera made for hazardous flying. With regard to crowd recognition, Bergdoll compromised by asking his riders to wiggle their feet as a friendly gesture to the multitude on the ground.

His grand event came on August 16, when he performed the first flight ever between Philadelphia and Atlantic City, New Jersey. Bergdoll's course led from Eagle Field to 69th and Market streets, then down Market Street to the city hall. He circled William Penn's statue, and then flew down Market Street to the Delaware River, across to Camden, New Jersey, and followed the Reading Railroad tracks to the shore. Grover planned to land on the boulevard as near to Atlantic City as possible. His aim was to set down on the beach, but the authorities refused to prepare a landing site there. The flight of seventy miles was made in an hour and twenty minutes at the rate of seven-eighths of a mile a minute.

Grover having left his destination late in the day on his return flight, the onset of dusk forced him to look for a landing spot outside Berlin, New Jersey. Meanwhile,

CHARLES
KRAUSE AND
GROVER C.
BERGDOLL IN
MACHINE READY
TO FLY

1912

PHOTOGRAPHS BY A STAFF PHOTOGRAPHER OF "THE PRESS."

Charles Krause (left) and Grover C. Bergdoll were in the news (Bergdoll Family Papers, Bergdoll Scrapbook, 1912–1920, undated clipping).

the proprietor of a dahlia farm, L.K. Peacock, was distracted by an approaching noise in the sky. Looking up, he saw a frightened goose being pursued by a dark speck which he took to be a hawk. The farmer grabbed his rifle and prepared to fire at the supposed predatory bird when he made out two men seated in a strange contraption — Bergdoll and his mechanician. Grover quickly landed and Peacock, dropping his weapon, raced to the plane, hardly noticing that his unannounced guests had destroyed many specimens of rare dahlias. "Safe!" yelled Grover as he alighted from his Flyer. "It would have been risky to go further," he opined, turning to his mechanician. It was then that the winded Peacock blurted out just how close the two men came to being shot.

The next morning Grover and his associate tried repeatedly to take off, but the soggy earth held the machine fast. Realizing that he would not be able to free his plane for several days, Bergdoll simply tossed a piece of canvas over his motor and left for Philadelphia. As soon as the men were out of sight, Peacock's gathering neighbors approached the unguarded aircraft and proceeded to test its wires, pull its levers, and inspect its mud-encrusted engine.

Grover aced the tests for his pilot's license at Eagle Field on September 16, 1912, and received FAI license no. 169 nine days later. In celebration, he flew over the Bryn

Louis Bergdoll at the helm of his Blériot (*Fly*).

Mawr horse show on September 28, distracting the spectators' attention away from the victory ride of the contest's first-place winner. Bergdoll circled the field and stands, dipped, veered, and cut figure eights for about fifteen minutes. Within two minutes of the first sound of his engine the seats were emptied. A society reporter covering the event wrote:

> Dignity and clothes were forgotten in the wild rush to gain the open ground, where no canopy blocked the view skyward. Meanwhile the various events in the ring went merrily onward, unwatched except by judges.
>
> It might be well, after this experience, for the next Horse Show Committee to invite this aviator to come and sit in a box by himself, where he can be seen by all without interrupting the show.

In October Grover began ballooning lessons with Charles G. Clark, an acquaintance connected with the United States Signal Corps. That same month he performed with Clark at Llanerch, flying about Clark's balloon while a third person parachuted from its gondola before a throng of 4,000 onlookers.

The year 1913 brought Grover legal complications and aeronautical vexations. On December 21 of the previous year, he had been involved in a nightmare wreck in which six passengers were injured. Arrested and released pending a hearing on $1,000 bail, Bergdoll was immediately rearrested for two other misdemeanors dating back to November 1911. He plunked down another $1,000 and stormed out of the magistrate's office. All three violations carried charges of assault and battery, aggravated assault and battery for running into a mounted policeman's horse, reckless driving without lights, driving without licenses, discharging firearms in a reckless way, resisting arrest, and shooting at a police officer with intent to kill. With twenty-five outstanding warrants on him, Bergdoll joked to a reporter that if convicted on every charge against him he would be jailed for fifteen years.

In early January 1913, Grover received notice that he would not receive a Pennsylvania automobile license that year. This action was taken at the behest of Delaware County chief of police James Donaghy, who filed a personal complaint against Bergdoll with the state highway department. The irate twenty-year-old called a press conference as a demonstration of his defiance:

> The refusal of my 1913 license does not stop me from registering my car. I may be wrong, but I am under the impression that when an owner registers his car he can drive the car without a driver's license, provided he has an owner's license. I am also under the impression that drivers' licenses are only required of taxicab drivers and paid chauffeurs.

Going further, Grover swore out warrants against Chief Donaghy and the Bryn Mawr businessman with whom he collided on December 21, 1912. A Montgomery County editorial declared that Bergdoll was in desperate need of either "a straight jacket or a whipping post."

On March 1, Grover sped through the town of Ardmore, Pennsylvania, scattering little printed cards with the neat inscription of "Good-bye, fare-well — the Ardmore cops can go to hell!" He also displayed on his racer a huge banner declaring, "I have my license." Following his visit with a friend there, Grover was arrested and jailed for thirteen hours in the town calaboose. At his hearing the presiding magistrate was informed of the string of warrants out for Bergdoll, so he attended to the defendant's latest offense, collected $1,000 in bail and remanded Grover to the Media, Pennsylvania, authorities on a charge of contempt of court. Before leaving, Grover paid the bail of a drunk who had shared his cell.

Once outside the courthouse, Bergdoll was required to drive the attending constable in his racer to Media; they were closely followed by boisterous partisans. At his hearing, Grover entered bail "on the bench warrant which had been issued on his failure to renew his bail following a delay in his trial" for the December 21, 1912, smashup. The judge kept him handcuffed before, during, and following his hearing; "a thing not at all to the liking of the aesthetic young son of a wealthy brewer," quipped the press.

Grover was tried and convicted of reckless driving and assault by a Norristown jury in early March 1913; Judge Aaron S. Swartz sentenced him to three months imprisonment. There would be no retrial or other legal finagling in the wake of his unsuccessful appeal to the superior court in Pittsburgh. Bergdoll's jailers pronounced him a model prisoner who read voraciously, tutored other inmates in the basic skills of reading and mathematics, answered roll call, ate prison food without complaint, and even prepared for his forthcoming reentrance exams for the University of Pennsylvania Law School.

Bored and lonesome, Bergdoll spelled out his woes in an undated letter to his old mentor in Dayton:

My dear Orville:

It is just about a year ago today that I left Dayton, after being trained by [Al] Welsh out at Simms Sta. I told you then about my trouble with the police, well they have been after me ever since and now,—they have succeeded in putting me in jail for three months. My Model B will be idle for a time now. Does it not seem to you that aviators are very *unfortunate* persons? Bad luck seems to be their only lot. If they are not killed, they go to jail, if not to jail, they go bankrupt and so on down the line; it is pretty tough, though I still am a bird even if I am in a jail (jailbird).

How is the new tractor type selling?

Really, to tell the truth, I do not think very much of a tractor biplane. I am stuck on the "Baby" type which you refused to sell. Now if you will decide to part with those two "babies" which are in the building opposite the shop, can't you make me a price? (I hope the flood has not damaged them.) I have made over two hundred flights with my Model B and the only thing broken was a wheel base, caused by the wheels getting hot and freezing tight to the axle, and thereby twisting it off. I like the Baby type, because it is much easier to handle.

How is Mr. [Arthur] Gaible? I hope he escaped the flood. I guess he did as it is not likely that aeronautical people would drown in *water*??

It is very unpleasant to be here, but "rather here than where poor Welsh [killed in a flying accident] is."

Please write at once [and] also enclose particulars about the tractor type.

> Yours respectfully,
> Grover C.A. Bergdoll
> Montgomery Co. Jail
> Norristown, PA.

The reply came:

My dear Mr. Bergdoll: April 19, 1913

I am sorry to see such a fine bird caged, but sometimes such is necessary.

As to the "Baby" machines to which you refer, I do not think that it would be advisable for you to purchase these, as they will not compare at all with our newer model, which we have been selling to the Government. If you contemplate getting a fast machine, I would only recommend this new model "D."

We are not building a tractor machine. Our single propeller machine — Model E — has a single propeller, but the propeller is in the rear instead of in front. This machine is intended especially for exhibition purposes, and is made to be knocked down and assembled rather quickly.

We are getting out some new hydroplanes this season, which I think would probably interest you. When you are free, we would be glad to have you come on to Dayton to see them and the new models.

> Very truly yours,
> The Wright Company
> President

There was also unsettling family news from beyond Bergdoll's cell: confirmation that his brother, to whom he owed his love of flying and his first aircraft, had lost his automobile company to bankruptcy. In time, creditor claims against Louis arising from the business's insolvency would climb on appeal to the United States Supreme Court (1926) and continue to be litigated in Pennsylvania's lower courts for years thereafter.

Grover left the Norristown lockup on July 7 with the best wishes of its warden. He went directly to his mother's residence, but left after telling her that he would be at the Eagle Field hangar. Once there, Bergdoll tuned the long dormant Flyer's engine and examined the machine with the exception of its guide wires. Then, for several days, inclement weather postponed much-anticipated flights he had planned. During this interim, Grover happened to notice that someone had apparently filed into each of the biplane's steel guide wires during his incarceration. Had he not caught this alleged act of deliberate sabotage, his craft would have collapsed after he had reached a height of several hundred feet. Bergdoll told reporters that he considered the vandalism a deliberate attempt on his life.

With great determination Grover wheeled his Flyer out of its hangar onto the Pennsylvania Aero Club field at Broomall. It was the afternoon of July 13 and his first time aloft since prison. His original intention was to fly over the police station in Ardmore and then to circle the Norristown jail for the benefit of the warden and turnkeys, but the weather prevented these sorties. About 7:00 P.M. the wind abated and he went up, barely clearing treetops at the end of the runway.

Grover executed some fancy turns, after which he tipped his craft toward startled fans from about 150 feet. The crowd stampeded, and he flew over them, looking back and grinning. A young woman standing in an automobile became so caught up in the show that she clasped her hands and shrilled, "Ooooooh, Grover! That was fine, fine." Everyone gathered around to shake his hand when he landed. Again, he went up, and again he dipped his airplane (scooping) toward the milling people, sailing low, men, women, and children running and throwing themselves on the ground. The star attraction thoroughly enjoyed the performance.

A reporter subsequently interviewed Bergdoll about his trial, incarceration, and plans to study law. Bergdoll was unrepentant about his charges of police harassment and their objective to frame him yet again. With respect to his legal studies, he said, "The reason I started on this plan to become a lawyer is that I wanted to find out how it was the law could keep pestering me all the time." Asked whether he planned to take his plane with him to law school, Grover answered in the affirmative, and added that he would also include several racing cars and a few motorcycles as well. Toward the end of his interview, an elderly woman, who had been gazing first at Bergdoll and then at his Flyer for some time, asked him the purpose of the plane's large gasoline tank. "Oh, that," he stammered, "why — uh — that is for coffee. You see, we put the coffee in the tank. The engine heats it. Then, while we are making a flight, we just put a cup under this small spigot, here — see? and get a drink. It's a good arrangement."

Clearly Grover's plans for law school were more extracurricular than academic in nature. In the end he returned to the University of Pennsylvania, not necessarily because of its reputation, but rather its closeness to his base of operations. Since his waking hours revolved around the world of flight, Bergdoll elected to share his passion with fellow classmates.

Grover lamented the fact that aeronautics had become "a back number" at the university since George A. Richardson and A.T. Atherholt took the intercollegiate balloon race in June 1911. It was small consolation to him that Richardson also captured the "aeronaut" prize, flying the winning glider in a match race between Swarthmore, Harvard, and his own alma mater. He felt himself ordained to further this modest legacy.

Bergdoll's first priority was to get himself elected vice president of the freshman class, which he accomplished by promising a "fair deal," a student newspaper, and a "real aeronautic club." Usually collegiate campaign promises fade quickly, but Grover made every effort to keep his word. The twenty-year-old offered the university's nascent flying group the use of his machine and Eagle Field. On weekends he served as both pilot and instructor to many of his campus chums.

Regrettably, Grover's self-financed student newsletter met with less success. Initial issues contained racy articles on the fairer sex, unflattering profiles of Dean William Draper Lewis and selected instructors, a vitriolic attack on Philadelphia's new municipal court, and a promised exposé titled "A Ninety-Day Visit to a Two by Four County Jail"—Bergdoll's diary penned at the Norristown cooler. When Dean Lewis called the offending editor to account, Grover threatened to transfer to Columbia University, citing that institution's devotion to "absolute freedom of the press" and its geographical proximity to Broadway. The dean responded to his freshman editor's ultimatum with a deafening silence, so Bergdoll packed his bags.

On August 3, 1913, Grover's flying antics forced a gallery of 1,000 gapers to duck as he buzzed them from above. Between sunrise and sunset that day he made seven flights with and without passengers. Performing near Haverford College, Bergdoll winged his way only twenty-five feet from the ground, and later he raced motorists on the Eagle Road. Flying back to Eagle Field alone, he cut several figure eights not more than forty feet above the crowd. A disapproving Clarence P. Wynne, president of the Aero Club of Pennsylvania, complained to an attending reporter that Grover was taking too many risks. He also grudgingly conceded that his friend could qualify as "one of the most expert aviators, and by far the most daring aviator in this part of the country."

In less than two weeks Grover flew again, without incident or a stopover, from Llanerch to Atlantic City. At one point during his second flight there he reached an altitude of 6,000 feet. Desirous of maximum exposure, Bergdoll circled repeatedly over Atlantic City's beach area near the Steel Pier before landing fifty feet from the surf. The young adventurer had flown right across the state of New Jersey. "As easy as running an automobile," yelled Grover, as he alighted from his plane, "and not half so risky in some ways," he added, perhaps reflecting on his many clashes with the Pennsylvania highway police. He carried no passenger, deciding earlier that the air was too laden with moisture to warrant any extra weight to his machine.

Once again, President Wynne tempered Bergdoll's post-flight euphoria with a letter of warning that if he wished to fly over Philadelphia—or any other city—he must do so at an altitude of 5,000 feet or higher; otherwise, the Aero Club would pull his pilot's license. According to Wynne, all the air under 5,000 feet belonged to "the common people." Bergdoll, the president pointed out, had maintained a constant altitude of 400 feet over metropolitan areas during his trans-New Jersey flight, a fact based on the stack of complaints he had received.

Immediately following this notable feat, Grover left for Europe in quest of a high-speed racer with which to compete in the September International Coupe d'Aviation Race at Reims, France. He set his sights on Armand Deperdussin's swift machine. The 1912 French flyer was a braced high-wing monoplane, two-king posts on the forward monocoque fuselage carrying a skein of wires to support its slender wings. The aircraft's lateral control was achieved by wing warping and it boasted a fixed undercarriage and tailskid. Power came from two Gnôme rotary engines mounted on a common crankshaft. From Grover's perspective, its oversized spinner seemed to transform the sleek craft into a winged bullet.

Deperdussin's creation was the first to shatter the 200 kph (124 mph) barrier, as well as to capture both the Schneider Trophy and the Gordon-Bennett Aviation Cup in 1912. An avid reader of aviation periodicals, Bergdoll was well aware of the racer's pedigree. What he did not know, however, was that the Deperdussin Company teetered on the verge of bankruptcy, and that its founder would be arrested for embezzlement.

The Bergdoll family opposed Grover's plans for competing abroad. His mother even offered him a substantial sum of money if he would abandon aviation altogether. Rather, his kinsmen urged him to renew his study of law. But there was a more pressing reason for him to remain in the States. He was scheduled to appear in court on multiple driving violations and an assault charge. Ignoring this legal commitment, Bergdoll simply told everyone that his impending trial had been postponed with the approval of the district attorney until the December term, when he expected to return.

Philadelphia's "rich young speed fiend" had made prior arrangement with the

Grover Bergdoll's wayward aircraft, the Bechereau Deperdussin 1913 Racer (courtesy the author).

Deperdussin Company to deliver a 160 hp racer to him on his arrival in Paris. When he appeared, however, he discovered that Deperdussin had given his plane to Maurice Prévost, the French aviator. Adding insult to injury, this was the machine Prévost piloted to victory in the Gordon-Bennett competition.

Grover was told that the company could not build him another racer in time for the September 29 meet. Still hopeful, he next went to the Morane-Saulnier group and experienced the same frustrating results. Even the Gnôme Motor Company refused to sell him a 200 hp engine for an as yet unprocured aircraft. He gave up and came home, complaining all the way that Prévost was "connected" with Deperdussin and that there were no Aero Club of America representatives in France to further his cause.

The Aero Club of Pennsylvania condemned the "dilatory tactics" employed by French aviation manufacturers to prevent the United States from competing in the 1913 Gordon-Bennett contest. The immediate reason for Bergdoll's undoing, declared its president, was the fact that the owner, Deperdussin, had been jailed and his company put in the hands of a receiver, thereby upsetting the firm's workforce. President Wynne concluded:

> As the result of Bergdoll's unfortunate experience, the Aero Club will begin a campaign to have American aviators' machines built entirely by American workmen with American material, so that no such fiasco can occur again. By next year we hope to have a first class aero manufacturing plant established here so that Bergdoll or some other aviator can take his machine with him when he goes abroad to take part in the next Gordon-Bennett contest.

Due to his sojourn in France, Grover had forfeited his mother's bail bond of $1,000 as a result of missing a 1913 court date which stemmed from a former charge of speeding, reckless driving, and assaulting a local policeman. In June 1912 Grover was tried on these counts at Norristown and assessed a $75.00 fine. Chief Donaghy of the aggrieved officer's township dismissed Bergdoll's sentence as insufficient and ordered that a new warrant on the same offenses be issued. Disagreement among an intermediate jury over Bergdoll's guilt had forced the presiding court to carry his case over to the fall 1913 term, which he missed.

Did Grover care about being a fugitive from justice? Not at all. His response to the press was "Ich ge Bibble," loosely translated as "I should worry." He staunchly maintained that it was impossible for him to be present at the trial, blaming the constabulary who continued to harass him and who refused to bind his case over for another term. Bergdoll obviously believed that the authorities would allow this involved legal matter to drop. Subsequent events proved otherwise.

On October 13, 1913, Emma Bergdoll appeared before the Media, Pennsylvania, court, asking that Grover's bail bond be returned to her. The presiding judge ruled that the money would be returned if her son's case were disposed of by the December term. The defendant was then called to the bar, but he could not be found. Two deputy sheriffs went looking for him.

Outside the courthouse the lawmen spotted Grover and called to him. Instead of responding, Bergdoll started his powerful Erwin Special racer and sped off in the opposite direction. He kept driving in and out of the adjacent streets, followed by the deputies and his mother on foot. Periodically, the playboy fugitive stopped the vehicle and waved to his exasperated pursuers and then drove on.

When Grover eventually came to trial the jury deadlocked as to his guilt. Bergdoll testified that he had taken the plaintiff, policeman Ignatius Mullen, for a dangerous mugger instead of an arresting officer. The fact that the cop had been out of uniform back in November 1911 saved Grover from a conviction.

Ever since the 1913 Gordon-Bennett race, Grover had sought to update and expand his options in aircraft. Perhaps more important, he wanted to see his old flying guru again and savor the ambience of Simms Station. On Christmas Day he wired Orville: "Would like to try out your Flying Boat [Model G] and also Model C. Will this be OK if I came to Dayton. Wire at once." The following day Wright telegraphed back: "Weather too cold for water flying at present. Have asked our Mr. [Grover] Loening (designer of Wright's 'Aeroboat') who is now in New York to call upon you." Apparently Orville missed Bergdoll's holiday wish to simply be invited to Dayton, and the two never met again.

For nearly eight months Bergdoll puttered quietly about Eagle Field, continued to fly recreationally, and participated in an occasional automobile race. With time on his hands as he was no longer in law school, he turned to science as a distraction. On June 8, 1914, a fifteen-year-old Philadelphia boy, Joseph F. Shevlin, was playing near a garage on North 29th Street in which Grover had his X-ray apparatus installed. Bergdoll invited the youth to be the subject of an experiment. Shevlin placed his hand where Grover directed and in a few minutes the rays had inflicted third degree burns at a point two inches above the wrist. Bergdoll's human guinea pig ran home and a physician was summoned. The doctor treated Shevlin over the course of fifty appointments in a successful effort to save the hand from amputation. A common pleas court subsequently awarded the teenager's father $500 in damages.

In late August of 1914 Grover offered his services and his plane to the German government's early war effort at the kaiser's consulate in Philadelphia. The unlikely volunteer told Dr. Arthur Mudra, the consul, that he had applied for acceptance through a desire to follow the flag of his forefathers. Bergdoll was taken aback when informed by the consul that he could neither enlist nor send his Flyer abroad. Dr. Mudra explained that as an American citizen of a neutral power, the only course for him to follow was to reach Germany and enlist there. As for the airplane, it could only be regarded as war contraband and therefore must be left behind. After considerable soul-searching, Grover went nowhere. The idea of leaving his Flyer behind struck him as peculiar, perhaps signaling the prospect of his induction into the infantry rather than the Imperial Air Service. In a final defiant gesture to the Allies, he sent a letter to one of the Philadelphia newspapers, predicting a German victory in the global conflict, and signed it "Llodgreb C. Revorg," his name spelled backwards.

During the fall of 1914 Bergdoll returned to his second passion: auto racing. And why not? He had raced against many professionals, winning over such men as Barney

Oldfield, Ralph de Palma, and Bob Burman. Grover ran well at the Brighton Beach
Race Track on Labor Day and pressed de Palma at the Interstate Fair raceway in Tren-
ton, before blowing a tire on the backstretch. Then, as usual, bad luck and youthful exuberance placed him at odds with the law. On October 25 Bergdoll's Erwin
Special racer slammed into an oncoming vehicle, sideswiped a tree, and plunged
through a hedge before overturning. It caught fire, temporarily pinning Grover and
his mechanician underneath. Unfortunately for the pair, their old nemesis, Chief
Donaghy, covered the accident. Both men were held under a $500 bail bond. Fam-
ily attempts to have Grover forfeit his driver's license rather than face yet another
trial collapsed. Nevertheless, Bergdoll's defense attorney bought the youthful offender
delay after delay by pleading his client's poor health.

Grover left Philadelphia for San Francisco on February 1, 1915, accompanied by
two assistants and a new Erwin Special rebuilt especially for the Vanderbilt Cup Race.
On February 27 he crashed into a retaining wall during trial laps. Thrown free of the
racer, he fell headlong into a barbed wire barricade and suffered a concussion and
severe facial lacerations. False reports circulated that he had been fatally injured. Four
days later, Grover's trial was postponed again due to his California accident. Over
the next eight months there occurred ever more driving violations, bail bond post-
ings, and "no shows" for Bergdoll in the Norristown courtroom.

The frustrated authorities ultimately submitted their warrants on Grover to the
Bryant Detective Agency, whose operatives cornered the fugitive in a Philadelphia
garage on October 6. Desperately fighting back, Bergdoll was secured only after four
of the detectives held him pinned against the seat of his "Big Red" racing car, while
the other three placed handcuffs on him. The bruised and battered bounty hunters
relieved Grover of a loaded revolver on his front seat and served him with multiple
summonses, not only for speeding violations. One summons commanded him to
appear at a special hearing on October 18 to show cause why his brother, Charles,
should be prevented from seeking the appointment of a lunacy commission to inquire
into Grover's sanity.

At that trial, Emma, as always, leaped to her son's defense, announcing to
Philadelphia's fourth estate, "This is the last straw, and I wish you would make it
emphatic that ... I will spend my last cent to prevent them trying to make my boy
out as insane. I wish you would say that I make the assertion that Grover has more
sense and is better equipped mentally than either of his older brothers, Louis or
Charles. They are the ones who are behind this latest move."

The trial began in the court of common pleas on the appointed day in December with Joseph Gilfillan representing Charles Bergdoll and N.H. Larzelere appearing for Grover. Larzelere demonstrated that his client owned an impressive library
and a well-equipped workroom in his home; that he possessed an above average
knowledge of the law; that he had mechanical patents pending; that he had undertaken over 500 flights; and that he did not read dime novels, imbibe to excess, nor
consort with improper women. Alienists, race drivers against whom he competed,
aviators with whom he flew, the warden of the county jail where he spent three

MRS. BERGDOLL SEEKS FLEEING SON: 'A MAN WITHOUT A COUNTRY'

GROVER CLEVELAND BERGDOLL

Grover Bergdoll on the lam (Bergdoll Family Papers, Bergdoll Scrapbook, 1912–1920, undated clipping).

months, his mechanicians and girlfriends, all testified that Grover was a sober-minded, God-fearing youth.

Just prior to Grover's case going to the jury, Gilfillan shouted in his summation, "Where is the mother of this man? They do not dare produce her." There was an instant of agonizing silence as everyone but the speaker turned to look at Emma, who had been muttering remarks and crying during the course of the trial. Before the attorney could resume, however, Emma leaped to her feet and exclaimed, "Here is his mother! He is a liar!" Court officers tried in vain to quiet her. Emma was warned that she would be removed from the proceedings unless she controlled herself. "I know," she cried, "but he lies; he lies." That the interruption had its effect on the jurors was evident in the way they leaned forward suddenly in their chairs as she spoke. After this outburst, Gilfillan confined himself to the legal points of the case.

In his summation, Larzelere drew the picture of the two brothers, Charles and Grover, sitting with their attorneys at opposite tables and the old mother watching from her chair in the center of the room. Tears filled the eyes of many present that afternoon: "Think of these two men," he began, "the same blood coursing through their veins — brothers fighting against each other." With this statement, Emma broke down, and her sobs drowned out the voice of Grover's attorney as he spoke:

If you render a verdict against Grover Bergdoll you reduce him to a miserable cipher. You indict him forever as a legal imbecile. He cannot marry, his estate will be gone, then where will he go? Charles Bergdoll was trying not only to take his brother's money, but to ruin him forever. The only designing person to whom Grover Bergdoll fell a victim was his own guardian and brother.

It took the jury fifteen minutes to find Grover Bergdoll "mentally sound."

The bitterly contested trial proved significant, aside from Grover's clear access to his million dollars, in that it brought about a family schism. Louis and Charles shunned Emma and their younger brothers, Grover and Erwin, for years to come. The pair went so far as to change their surnames. Louis became Louis Bergson and Charles, Charles Braun. Grover, beset by a sense of persecution arising from his innumerable scrapes with the law, his local unpopularity, and particularly Charles's lunacy petition, tried to drown his anxieties in a flood of activity. Racing faster in more speedways than ever before, Bergdoll counted on youth, good looks, and wealth to overcome his tumultuous past.

In late 1914 Grover packed away his Flyer in the Bergdoll Machine Shop several miles from Eagle Field, where it stayed until 1933. What possessed him to take this action? Had Grover reached all of his goals in aviation, or did he once again crave the close-quartered competition of the racetrack? There is no way to know. On December 3, 1933, his machine was removed to the Camden County Vocational School in Merchantville, New Jersey, where Arthur Arrowsmith and his students painstakingly restored it. Orville offered ceremonial assistance when he visited Philadelphia for the 30th anniversary of his first flight. Less than a year later, Bergdoll's Flyer, number 39, which had logged 748 flights without mishap, made a commemorative flight for the 31st anniversary of the Wrights' first successful effort. In January 1935 the craft was placed in Aviation Hall at the Franklin Institute. Sixty-six years later, Grover's pride and joy was removed from Aviation Hall to be restored again. It was returned to the institute and reassembled during the summer of 2003.

At the outset of America's entry into World War I, friends and family maintained that Bergdoll was conflicted about fighting against his ancestral homeland. He reportedly applied for a commission in the Army Air Service and was refused. Soon thereafter Grover was drafted into the infantry, which he resented, and went into hiding for two years. When apprehended by the authorities he was tried and sentenced to five years imprisonment. Eluding his captors, however, Grover fled to Germany, where he was to remain off and on for the next 19 years, avoiding various schemes to kidnap him hatched by ex-doughboys who sought to return him to the United States.

While on an automobile excursion in May 1927 with his new wife, Berta, Grover learned that Colonel Charles A. Lindbergh had flown his single-engine monoplane across the Atlantic Ocean in an unprecedented solo flight. Bergdoll, who had not flown in over a decade, sensed a powerful urge to fly. His life since the time at Eagle Field had been interspersed with desperation and sorrow, but his early flying days had been the productive apex of an otherwise misspent life. A month later, while on a similar jaunt across the Fatherland, Grover stopped his car in a little hamlet called Hoexter and walked into the Berlin Bureau of the Associated Press to send a telegram:

> Will the constructor of the *Spirit of St. Louis* or the *Columbia* deliver a plane with the Wright motor in short order? I am anxious to fly from Europe to the American interior until the gasoline gives out, as soon as an airplane can be obtained. No German plane capable of this flight is obtainable at present.

There came no answer from the Lindbergh camp. Charles Levine, who accompanied Clarence Chamberlain on his Atlantic flight, informed Bergdoll that the *Columbia* was not for sale. To a proposal that Grover be allowed to accompany Chamberlain on a return flight to the United States, Levine replied that he and Chamberlain were going back to New York City together.

Because his numerous appeals for clemency to President Franklin Roosevelt fell on deaf ears, Bergdoll lost heart and returned to the United States in 1939 to stand trial. His conviction for draft violation and desertion a foregone conclusion, Grover received his original five-year term and an additional three years for escaping federal custody. He served four years and ten months at Leavenworth and was paroled on February 3, 1944.

In June of 1942 Grover wrote the Justice Department from Leavenworth with an outlandish proposal: that he, at forty-nine years of age, be allowed to enlist in the Army Air Corps. He reminded the attorney general of his dated aerial accomplishments, his pro-American spirit, and his desire to "send Hitler to his doom." Grover's lawyer even predicted that his client's enlistment might provoke a popular uprising among Bergdoll's following in the Third Reich. Then, there were the plaintive letters from the prisoner's wife to Grover's old friend in Dayton.

Orville had watched and listened to the Bergdoll saga for a quarter century, and by the summer of 1942 he had seen and heard enough. On June 28 he gave a stunning interview to a local reporter in which he recalled Grover as "one of his most brilliant flying pupils," who for years had been maligned by a national press at the instigation of the United States Army. His anger mounting, the seventy-year-old inventor disclosed that at the time of

Bergdoll in Germany during the early twenties (*Philadelphia Bulletin*).

the 1939 dedication of Wright Brothers Hill, the picturesque memorial park outside Dayton, attempts were made to keep Bergdoll's name off the list of early Wright flying students who trained under him at nearby Simms Station. The committee members in charge, Orville complained, were acting at the behest of army officers. When Grover's mentor refused to budge on the issue, these same gentlemen suggested that just his initials be used as a way to conceal his identity. Orville told them that if they omitted Bergdoll's name from the plaque, he would not allow his own to be included as well. Orville said, "A man is entitled to his place in history, with his good deeds recorded along with his transgressions. The plaque was a historical record and I contended that every student was entitled to recognition."

Orville insisted that Grover had offered to go into the army's air service at the outset of World War I, but was rejected, he believed, because of his German parentage:

> That was nonsense about him having been so pro-German. He had some feeling for Germany, as did many other Americans of German descent, but he loved this country, and, if it came to a choice between the two, he would certainly have chosen America. Before the draft issue came up Bergdoll was widely recognized as a flyer. One early flying magazine said that no flyer in the country had contributed more to the popularization of flying with large numbers of people.

WRIGHT BACKS BERGDOLL

Inventor Says Former Air Pupil Has Been Punished Enough

DAYTON, Ohio, June 28 (*P*)— Orville Wright, co-inventor of the airplane, asserted today that it was "time to stop making a national scapegoat" out of Grover Cleveland Bergdoll, now serving a prison sentence for evading the draft in the last war.

Bergdoll, a flying pupil of Mr. Wright's thirty years ago, recently requested permission to serve in the Army Air Forces.

Mr. Wright said in an interview that he was not defending "slackers," but that he believed Bergdoll had been punished more severely than any other draft evader of 1917-18.

The 70-year-old inventor said that admission to the aviation section of the Army Signal Corps had been refused Bergdoll and that resentment probably prompted his resolve not to serve as an infantryman and his ultimate flight from this country.

Orville Wright speaks out! (*New York Times*).

The personal view of the coinventor of flight was that Grover made the army look "silly" by eluding its guards and escaping to Germany, and for this act he became its "scapegoat." Asked if he meant to lodge a formal clemency appeal to the government on behalf of his friend, Wright responded that he had not decided, but he concluded that his former pupil had been treated unjustly.

At this juncture, Fred C. Kelly entered the scene. A writer involved with an authorized biography of the Wright brothers, Kelly fretted about Orville ever approving his manuscript. Eager to please the inventor and to disengage him from Bergdoll's adverse press notoriety, either he proposed to Orville or Wright mildly suggested to him that he investigate Grover's true intentions with respect to the Great War. Four months later Kelly wrote Orville his findings:

November 5, 1942

Dear Mr. Wright:

While in Washington last week I decided to make cocksure of the Bergdoll matter and went in to see your friend, General [Henry "Hap"] Arnold. I like him immensely. He was frank and unassuming and said he "never heard the story about Bergdoll having tried to get into the air corps before becoming a draft evader, but that it might be true." He added: "If the Army blundered in his case, maybe I was the one who did it." You know, of course, that he and Bergdoll came from the same town. He called in Colonel [H.W.] Shelmire, who also came from the same town and knew Bergdoll all his life, and asked him to run down the facts. Shelmire also impressed me as very high grade. He showed no prejudice at all; just said he didn't know anything about it one way or another but would get the facts for me. Yesterday I got the enclosed letter. Of course it is still possible that the story we heard is true, but evidently it would be prudent to lay off of it and not appear to be whitewashing Bergdoll. But there could be no harm in saying, that, nevertheless, regardless of what he did or may have done about the draft, he did much for aviation ... and so on.

P.S. The fact that Bergdoll's wife never replied to my letter now seems a bit significant.

Colonel Shelmire's enclosed letter completely persuaded Kelly of Grover's guilt, despite Orville's earlier misgivings:

November 3, 1942

Dear Mr. Kelly:

Following our conversation the other day, I have had a very complete investigation made of the case concerning Grover Cleveland Bergdoll.

The records of the Department of Justice and the Adjutant General's Office have been very carefully checked and there is nothing on file to support the contention that Bergdoll requested appointment to the Air Corps (Aviation Section, Signal Corps) during the past war.

We find, however, references to a letter Bergdoll wrote to the *Philadelphia Public Ledger* in July, 1918, offering to surrender to the authorities provided he would not be punished and that he would be admitted as an instructor of aviation instead of being drafted.

It further appears that in the trial of [Carl] Neuf and [Frank] Zimmer, the two Americans who attempted to apprehend Bergdoll in Mosbach, Baden, Germany, Bergdoll testified under oath that he had written such a letter to the *Ledger* but that "it was considered as a ruse."

This seems to me to take care of Bergdoll's contention that he had applied for admission to the Air Corps as a pilot, because the records definitely show that he did no such thing, and he became a fugitive from justice before he attempted to bargain his way out of punishment and even that was later admitted to be a ruse.

Doubtless upset by Kelly's letter, Orville nevertheless gave no further interviews on the Bergdoll matter.

Grover Bergdoll in later life (*Philadelphia Bulletin*).

Grover sold his estate near West Chester, Pennsylvania, in 1946 and relocated to Virginia, near Richmond, where he resided until his death on January 27, 1966, at the Westbrook Psychiatric Hospital at age seventy-two. He was survived by his ex-wife and eight children.

Perhaps one finds it tempting to categorize Grover Bergdoll's career as one of extreme recklessness, pampered indulgence, and complete self-absorption. His youthful contempt for authority and the rule of law; his seeming disregard for human life on Pennsylvania's highways; his family squabbles; his disruptive behavior at the University of Pennsylvania; and his numerous bizarre experiments might be regarded as manifestations of an imaginative yet troubled mind and, even more, the tragic prologue to his role as America's most celebrated draft dodger.

If one redeeming attribute shines bright in Bergdoll's otherwise clouded life, however, it was his capacity as an aviator. In two years time he logged an amazing 748 flights with a total of 312 hours and 34 minutes in the air, all without a single accident. Flying Pioneers' biographer Harold Morehouse said it best:

> Flying pioneer Grover C. Bergdoll was a wealthy sportsman pilot who took up flying purely for pleasure, and did an unusually thorough job of it. He established a splendid flying field and facilities, putting his plane to daily use, taking up hundreds of passengers, demonstrating the airplane as a sport vehicle, and established an enviable record in the care and skill he exercised in its operation. It is recorded that he never had an accident during his flying career. While he later became nationally known as a "Notorious Draft Dodger" his name must be well recorded in American aviation history.

Five

GEORGE GRAY

Flying the Resort Circuit

George Alphonso Gray's prismatic personality reflected the conservatism of a small-town banker, the daring of a trapeze artist, and the entrepreneurial spirit of a Wall Street stockbroker, at once conflicting and complimenting characteristics which made him one of pioneer aviation's more interesting yet enigmatic flyers. Self-effacing and taciturn to a fault, Gray, nevertheless, had a firm understanding of his legacy to early flight in later years. When the compilers of *Who's Who in Aviation* notified him of his inclusion in the 1942 publication, Gray responded with his customary caution tinged with a seldom displayed hint of pride: "What is the obligation to be included in this? Let me know, please before you go ahead. I would like to be in it because of my children."

Gray was born to James Madison and Annah Clough Gray on September 23, 1882, at Blue Hill, Maine. A descendant of one of the state's first families, George traced his line back to Queen Anne of Holland. His father was in the lumber business. With five brothers and a sister to command his attention, young Gray's childhood effectively prepared him for the give and take of life. Following his graduation from the local high school, he went on to Blue Hill's prestigious academy, but did not receive his diploma. When he was 19, Gray moved to Boston, Massachusetts, and took his first job with the Warren Steamship Company. He worked for a number of companies after that, involved with night work, until his health broke under the strain. Finally, George obtained daytime employment as an engineer for the New England Telephone Company, after which he spent a year with the Bay State Auto Company.

George's interest in flying dated from his attendance at the Harvard-Boston Aviation Meet held at Squantum, Massachusetts, from September 2 to 13, 1910. There he witnessed the civilian and military applications of aviation as performed by some of America's and Europe's leading pilots, including Walter Brookins, Ralph Johnstone, Glenn Curtiss and Charles Willard, as well as two prominent British aviators, Claude Grahame-White and A.V. Roe. With monoplanes, biplanes, and even a triplane showcased, Lieutenant C.A. Blakely, USN, reported as an assigned observer to his superiors at the Navy Department: "I consider the maneuvers at the Harvard-Boston Meet as most remarkable, as every machine readily responded to the will of the aviator and all who came to the grounds as skeptics went away marveling."

Spurred on by what he, too, witnessed, Gray committed himself then and there to the challenge of flight. George tried to interview some of the flyers and look over their planes, but failed in both attempts: "I left the grounds very enthusiastic, however, and said to myself, 'If those fellows can fly, why can't I?'" He inquired of several of the gentlemen connected with the meet where he could obtain books on flying, but they were unable to help him. Gray was informed that there were two flying schools in existence: one being operated by the Wright brothers in Dayton, Ohio and the other by the Curtiss Company in Hammondsport, New York.

The manager of the Wright School told Gray that he would receive a course of instruction in aviation for $750, the lessons to include short flights at different intervals by their instructors, the entire time of which would not exceed 240 minutes — a period considered sufficient to learn to fly. Gray forked over his fee and received his contract, and was ordered to report to the factory on the following morning. There he met the superintendent, who escorted him through the plant where Wright Model Bs were being constructed. After several days in the assembly building, Gray was led to the flying field, which was six miles from Dayton. Once on site, the first things he saw were two aircraft housed in a large wooden hangar. George was introduced to instructor Al Welsh, who pridefully informed him that he was one of the early pupils personally taught by Orville Wright, as well as one of the premiere pilots selected for the Wright exhibition team. Although Gray would come to view Welsh as a superb flight instructor, he considered him less than a first-rate exhibition pilot.

Several introductory trips to the field sufficed to prepare Gray for his initial lesson, which was short. Since he had never flown before, naturally the twenty-eight-year-old New Englander was nervous. Nevertheless, he took courage and received a five-minute flight:

> After I landed I felt very strange and came to the conclusion that I would never make an aviator, as it was not at all what I had expected. I told Mr. Wright that I thought it would be no use for me to continue, but he said they [students] all felt that way on the first flight, and that I would feel much better after I had made several.

George and his fellow pupils were asked to report at the field between 6 and 7 o'clock in the morning to make flights before the wind rose. Afternoon flights were also slated for 5 o'clock when the wind had subsided. His instruction lasted six months. Sixteen weeks into Gray's course the weather turned cold, so Orville considered it best to send him to the Wright School at Nassau Boulevard, Long Island, New York, where he was to finish his instruction. Once embedded there, Gray discovered that he was running alarmingly short of funds, so he was given the privilege of sleeping on a cot in the hangar. Al Welsh completed George's lessons, although he did not take his test at that time.

Gray returned to Dayton and petitioned Orville for a job, but failed in this effort, being consoled by Wright, who explained that the company had discontinued making contracts for exhibition work, that his sole objective now was to instruct fledgling aviators, and that fairness dictated that his displaced exhibition flyers should fill the new instructional slots. Gray then explained to Orville that he desired to obtain his pilot's license. Wright responded that if George wished to do this, he must secure $1,000 as collateral and pay $50.00 for the use of a plane. George confessed that he was broke. Orville cryptically responded that he would see what could be done. A few days later Wright told Gray that there was a plane at the field which he and Wilbur owned jointly, whereas the other machines in inventory were the property of the company, and that if he desired he could use that plane. Within the week George reported to Simms Station and prepared the designated aircraft with the help of Welsh, after which he successfully flew a planned course around the field. Gray was subsequently told to show up several days later for a second flight, this time before a representative of the Aero Club of America. The candidate reached an altitude of 150 feet in a steep climbing angle when the motor died, and his not pushing forward on the elevator quickly enough to put the machine in a gliding angle caused the craft to fall backwards, then turn over and plow into the ground. Orville's ship was totally demolished. This catastrophe ended Gray's flying that year, being the fall of 1911.

Dejected, and with neither money nor a job, Gray returned to Boston seeking employment. Once there, he gained a position with a canning company, selling its products to retail grocers. In the spring of 1912 Gray met William A.P. Willard, who confided to him that he [Willard] was endeavoring to promote an aviation meet in July. Willard introduced George to a prospective backer for this event. Gray's sights, however, were on his future flying career, not just a forthcoming event. He proposed to this gentleman that they collaborate on a partnership basis and become involved in exhibition work. The senior partner, according to George, would furnish $5,000 for a Wright machine and he would fly the craft; and they would split the profits equally. His would-be benefactor declined the offer. Soon thereafter, Gray learned during a visit to the Burgess Company that he could rent a plane for $500 a month, payable in advance, providing he post $1,000 to cover any possible damage. Returning to his reluctant partner, George advised him of Burgess' conditions, whereupon the gentleman agreed to a union of money and talent, and made arrangements for a plane.

Although Gray had once indulged himself on borrowed wings, the *Rockland (MN) Courier Gazette* noted that Gray was lately known for preferring "sudden and unlooked-for stunts," such as his recent flight over Boston harbor when he sailed above and circled repeatedly the mammoth Cunard liner *Franconia*. During a June 1 meet at Atwood Park near Cliftondale, Massachusetts, George displayed his flying acumen before thousands of onlookers. As Gray and his passenger, Clifford L. Webster, sailed past a cheering grandstand, the latter stood upright on the plane's foot guard, free and clear of the aircraft, doffed his cap, and waved both hands and sat down again. Webster weighed 174 pounds, and when he rose he brought this weight nearly three feet forward of the plane's center of gravity. This trick required Gray to lift the tail elevator as Webster stood and lower it as he sat down. Many spectators agreed that this display of solid airmanship rivaled Lincoln Beachey's best efforts on that particular day.

Gray's first contract was with a company that agreed to pay him $500 for two flights each of fifteen minutes duration. He performed the flights, but had difficulty obtaining his fee, finally resorting to paying $100 to an attorney in the collection of his money. Between his exhibition dates, George courted William Willard, who had made advances in arranging an aviation event at Squantum July 1–8, 1912. According to Willard, the promoters would pay Gray $1,000 to fly, and that he could possibly realize prize money in the bargain.

Gray procured his pilot's license, no. 142, dated June 23, performing before an Aero Club of America representative at Atwood Park in Boston. With his license in hand, he again met with Willard and agreed to fly at his Squantum show, providing that he would be participating in an Aero Club sponsored contest. George knew that the ACA would not sanction a meet unless the money had been put up to cover his contract. He inquired of the Aero Club and learned that the forthcoming program had not been approved. Instead, he won an agreement from the board of trade in Somerville, Massachusetts, to provide two twenty-minute flights on July 4, for which he received $1,000.

Gray's budding aviation career was nearly ended on the evening of July 8, when he and a passenger went down in Nahant Bay off the coast of Winthrop, Massachusetts. From all accounts, the cause was attributed to control problems. Gloomily perched on George's converted Burgess-Wright equipped with pontoons, the pair languished for over two hours before being rescued by launches from the Lynn Yacht Club. The local authorities opined that both men would have drowned but for a calm sea and the newly attached floats which kept the wreck from sinking. A passing trawler affixed a line to Gray's damaged bird and towed it to port.

With several flying dates behind him and $750 in contract money in his pocket, the future looked promising for George. And despite his qualms about the Squantum meet, Gray could not resist the lure of competition. A.J. Philpott, aviation reporter for the *Boston Daily Globe*, noted his dramatic arrival on June 30, 1912:

> A rather unexpected feature of the afternoon's flying was the appearance of a flying machine on the northern horizon, coming toward the field across Boston Harbor and Dorchester Bay. This proved to be George Gray, who started out from Saugus about 4 o'clock in his Burgess-Wright biplane on a "joy ride" with Miss Ethel Davis of Bar Harbor.

After cruising over the Lynn marshes and Revere for some time, Gray and his passenger had headed south for the contest held at Atlantic, flying over Chelsea and East Boston, across the harbor and bay, and then remaining airborne around Atlantic for a half-hour before landing. While Gray and Miss Davis hovered over the Atlantic aerodrome, there were also aircraft being flown by Lincoln Beachey, Charles K. Hamilton, Glenn L. Martin, and Philip W. Page. The spectators were riveted by the whirling melee of machines, with Page over a mile above their heads, Beachey, Hamilton, and

Martin hotly engaged in a speeding contest at a lower altitude, and Gray arriving somewhere in between. After everyone else had landed, Beachey unveiled a new aerial trick from his repertoire of stunts: dipping sideways across the aerodrome, recovering himself, and then dipping back toward the opposite side, all at a speed of 60 mph. With Squantum's preliminaries behind him, Gray bade Miss Davis adieu and flew his colleague Farnum T. Fish back to Saugus, both men readying themselves for the main event. For a tragically compelling reason, George made little more than a cameo appearance at the Squantum event, although reporter Philpott praised his brief but "splendid" aerial contributions.

Unfortunately for Gray, not only did he receive negligible profit from Squantum, but the unexpected flying deaths of internationally acclaimed aviatrix Harriet Quimby and her passenger, promoter Willard, so depressed George and his backer that the latter abruptly terminated their partnership. He had shaken Harriet's hand and wished her luck right before she got into her monoplane, fully expecting to follow her flight. The flying disaster essentially ended the meet and his chance to close on a more auspicious note. By mid–July Gray was bereft of an airplane, and in possession of only $750 with which to further his flying career.

Still, George realized that there would be considerable work for him as an exhibition pilot at various northeastern county fairs. Gray approached several "men of means" about forming another partnership with a fifty-fifty split in receipts if they would supply him with a plane. He was told that aviation constituted a passing fad, that he was insane for wanting to fly, and that he should get into some stable line of business. Undeterred, George decided to pitch various companies about endorsing their products on the wings of his as yet nonexistent plane. Of course, the prospective firm would have to purchase him a machine.

While strolling down Battery March Street in Boston one afternoon, Gray spied a candy factory festooned with advertising material. He accosted the manager with his usual offer, producing his license and a folder of newspaper clippings. The manager inquired as to what an airplane would cost, and when presented with the figure of $5,000, he declined. George countered that he would advertise his product if the manager would pay $500 for the rental of a plane for a month's time and post $1,000 to cover damage to the craft. The boss decided that he would "think over" this offer. As Gray was leaving the factory, he was stopped by the manager's son, who had overheard the earlier conversation. The young man told Gray that he was interested in aviation and he would lobby his father to accept Gray's proposition. A few days later George learned that his offer had been accepted, providing he would secure enough contracts to cover his first month's expenses, which included reimbursing the manager for the rental plane, and the transportation of himself and a mechanician to the place where he had secured his initial contract.

Scarcely out of the manager's office, George encountered a friend who owned a cottage at Rockland, on the coast of Maine, and who revealed that his neighborhood had scheduled a centennial celebration there in late August. At his pal's insistence, Gray visited Rockland's board of trade and persuaded its director to include his exhibition flights in the overall festivities. The board agreed to pay $750 for two flights, and allow George 35 percent of the gate receipts. After throwing in the use of the local fairgrounds to make his flights, its director also consented to pay the transportation of Gray's plane from Boston to Rockland. With one date in the bag, George set his sights on Old Orchard Beach, where a Labor Day fete had already been planned. In no time, he concluded a contract with the Business Men's Association to perform two twenty-minute sorties for $1,200; however, this was not a guaranteed payment: no flights, no fee. Gray also made a side agreement with a local entrepreneur for $200, giving the hustler the privilege of tenting his rental machine and charging admission to see the plane.

George returned to Boston and presented his hard-won contracts to an impressed candy maker who, in turn, wasted no time in arranging with Burgess-Wright for an aircraft with his advertisements on its wings. The Model B was ready in several days and Gray took it to Rockland. The New Englander's premiere flight there went without a hitch, but during his second time aloft Gray's motor stalled, and he was compelled to set down atop some spruce trees. With the help of several bystanders, he succeeded in getting his ship down and back to the field. The *Rockland (MN) Courier-*

A rear view of "UP." George Gray and mechanician Chauncey Redding discuss the flying conditions of the day at Old Orchard, Maine ("Jack" Stearns Gray, *"UP": A True History of Aviation*).

Gazette reported that the stalwart pilot got out of his wingseat and calmly climbed down to the ground. Unfortunately, there was no alternative but to chop down the cradling trees in order to retrieve George's aircraft.

Warming to the life of an exhibition pilot, George moved on to Old Orchard Beach, where he flew flawlessly, collected his money without incident, and even padded his earnings by carrying passengers. Favorable publicity came his way during this Labor Day event, especially when he defied good judgment by flying over Portland with a passenger on September 7 during a violent thunderstorm. Lightning flashed all around them, with rain and wind battering their machine. The credit for a safe landing went to Gray's mechanician and passenger, Chauncey Redding, who held his cap over the magneto to keep it dry, thereby preventing the motor from quitting.

While at Old Orchard, Gray learned of a county fair to be held at South Paris, Maine, the following week. Anticipating a flying date during the town's annual extravaganza, he offered to provide three spectacular flights for $1,000. Local officials countered that someone could buy a farm thereabouts for that kind of money. Instead, George received an offer of $750 for five flights, one on the first day of the fair at 4:00 P.M., and two on the remaining days, scheduled for 10:00 A.M. and 2:00 P.M. As always, he was to be paid only for flights made. Gray acceded to these terms, providing he be permitted to tent his plane in the north end of the racetrack and levy an admission charge of ten cents a person to view the Model B. Five flights later George pulled out of town with over a thousand dollars in his pocket and a damaged machine to show for his trouble.

During his South Paris show, Gray was approached by a Canadian promoter who guaranteed him $600 and 50 percent of the gate receipts to fly from a Montreal racetrack, which was located in the French section. He discovered on his arrival that the city's press had stirred up tremendous enthusiasm among the citizenry which, in turn, brought out huge crowds. Unfortunately for George, his motor went on strike, and he was compelled to announce to the multitude that he would be unable to fly. Inasmuch as local advertising had literally vouchsafed his performance, and poor Gray being the only feature on the program, the mood of the crowd turned ugly, and its spokesmen began to cry "Fake," rushing in and beginning to tear his machine to pieces. Gray ran toward several rather indifferent policemen and displayed his license from the Aero Club of America, which demanded (in French) the protection of both pilot and aircraft from mob depredations. His actions saved the already damaged biplane from total destruction. With the assistance of his mechanician, George succeeded in having the ship towed away to a temporary place of safety. From there, the machine was again removed to a wooded area on the outskirts of Montreal. Remaining in the city overnight, Gray awoke the next morning to find himself attacked in the papers. That day he noticed an advertisement in *Billboard* magazine of a fair in Malone, New York. Contacting the manager of the association by telephone, George negotiated a contract for $600 for two flights, after which he rented a car and proceeded to tow his plane to Malone. The roads were impassable, however, necessitating a stop in an intermediate hamlet where he procured a forty-foot railroad car, loaded the plane, and shipped it on ahead.

At the U.S.-Canadian border, Gray was requested to furnish entrance or cus-tomhouse papers for the admission of his plane, documents he had neglected to obtain before leaving Montreal. He argued that there were no aircraft manufactured in Canada and that his machine was a product of the United States. The border agents were unmoved, and after debating with them at length about admitting his craft, George stalked out of the customhouse. Just outside, he met an old comrade who was also an agent. After explaining his dilemma, Gray's friend wired Montreal for the necessary paperwork, while releasing pilot and plane into American territory.

Because of this border-related red tape, George had barely two days to prepare for his Malone date. Much to his pleasant surprise, the mayor of the town invited Gray into his home and facilitated the flyer's preparations in every possible way. The day after the close of the Malone fair, George met a local character, A.F. Cooper, also known as Caribou Bill, who resided at Saranac Lake, New York, and who had been taking moving pictures of his flights. Eager to have Gray perform back home, this homespun personality invited George to perform at Saranac Lake. Gray told his new acquaintance what amount he would demand for a day's work of flying, plus expenses for himself and his mechanician, not counting transportation costs. Bill refrained from guaranteeing a definite purse, but believed that George would make more than his specified figure. For his part, the Saranac Lake native promised to secure the use of the resort's racetrack and also guaranteed hotel expenses for the Gray team, asking only that George allow him exclusive filming rights while there. With the county fair season over late that October, Gray decided to fill the Saranac date.

As usual, George was operating against the calendar with less than a week to make his New York commitment. Panic set in when he learned from the Malone rail-way agent that the freight car in which he had shipped his aircraft from Montreal to Malone was no longer available. Faced with no apparent option, Gray decided to make the trip by air, dismissing the agent's dire warnings against his attempting to fly over the Adirondack Mountains.

George returned to Malone's Howard Hotel and poured over a map of the state of New York, discovering that it was approximately 85 miles as the crow flies from Malone to Saranac Lake; worse still, of that distance about 72 percent of the way would be over the Adirondacks. It occurred to him that along much of his penciled route it would be freezing at the altitude necessary for him to clear the mountain range that time of year, exposed as he would be to the biting winds in his open Model B. He had made up his mind, and not even the protestations of his mechanician could persuade him otherwise. A brief parting visit to the mayor's home to thank the fam-ily for their hospitality and to confide what he planned to do, and George was off. In a final gesture the mayor called to George that he had $50 left from a slush fund, and that he would give it to him if he agreed to fly over Malone on his way to Saranac. Gray accepted. The news of George's flight swept over Malone like wildfire, and crowds gathered on rooftops across town, particularly that of the Howard Hotel where his mechanician was to remain until he received his boss's telephone message to come to Saranac.

Gray left Malone on October 1, 1912, at 4:00 P.M., climbing to reach an appropriate altitude before leaving the town's precincts so that he could negotiate the distant mountaintops. His flight went smoothly for the first hour and he covered nearly half of his projected time in the air. He then noticed that his fuel connection from the tank to the engine was leaking, which had already cost him 25 percent of his fuel supply. Gray pulled out his pocket handkerchief and deftly tied it around the connection to staunch the flow. Flying on, he became exceedingly cold, as he had not dressed for the occasion. A quick check of his watch showed it to be 5:50 P.M., and, looking down, he could not see anything. George flew for another twenty minutes before dropping down in order to locate a landing spot. Continuing to glide, Gray finally spotted a small dwelling, a large barn, and a level field nearby. He set down, climbed out of his wing seat, switched off the gas, and came face-to-face with the owner and his brood of youngsters.

The farmer wanted to know if Gray's conveyance was an airship. George replied in the affirmative. He apologized for frightening the cow and the man's children, and for the loss of spilt milk, the unintended result of his abrupt arrival. Shifting his gaze between pilot and plane, the awestruck native introduced himself as Mr. Martin and assured Gray that he was most welcome. Martin invited Gray over to his house, where the latter finally succeeded in getting warm. He asked his host as to his whereabouts, and was disappointed to learn that he had landed in Bloomingdale, New York. When Gray asked Martin the way to Saranac Lake, the farmer took him to the front door and pointed out lights in the distance which marked his destination — eight miles away. George then inquired as to the location of the nearest telephone, so that he could ring his mechanician in Malone, and was told there was one a quarter of a mile away at a place called Fletchers Farm.

Martin immediately took his guest to that location in his horse and buggy. When the men reached their destination, Gray noticed that the farm was a tuberculosis resort. The women residents were so excited about hosting an aviator that they nearly overfed Gray, plying him with six bowls of soup. After dinner everyone at the sanitarium was loaded into vehicles and returned to Martin's place to see the aviator's flying machine. Having spent the night with his host, the next morning George learned that he had landed at the base of White Face Mountain — the highest summit in the Adirondacks. To his dismay, he was apprised that he had nearly set down on top of this peak by mistake, and most assuredly would have frozen to death as a result.

Gray could not take off from his landing spot, so Martin tore down an obstructing fence and loaned him a horse with which to tow his plane to a more spacious field. Flying to Saranac, he descended into the town's racetrack and ensconced his machine in a tent previously erected by the fair officials. Because George's flight from Malone to Saranac had created so much publicity, he was able to charge the public an outrageous sum of one dollar to inspect his ship. The following day Gray received a telephone call from a lady inquiring as to his price to fly over her cottage on Saranac Lake. George replied that he would take the commission for $150. She accepted and sent her limousine for him the next morning so that he could pinpoint her residence from the air. It turned out that the lady's tubercular husband had been homebound for many years, and she wanted to afford him the thrill of seeing his first flying machine. Poor Gray subsequently learned that his client was a millionairess who would have been willing to pay him many times his asking price for the flight.

On October 4 Gray fulfilled a staggering schedule, with a general exhibition, two aerial displays over nearby sanitariums, a flight over Saranac, and passenger-carrying hops, all of which netted him a thousand dollars. The star attraction was George's 20 lap race with one F. Paul Stevens in his 60 hp automobile around the resort's racetrack. Saranac's favorite son prevailed against Gray only because the latter had too many short turns to negotiate in the air. Approximately two thousand spectators were on hand, and 40 percent of the gate receipts went toward the support of Fletchers Farm sanitarium.

Two days later he carried a special passenger, twenty-one-year-old Edith "Jack" Stearns, who would later become his wife. "Jack" Stearns met Gray for the first time

Gray and company at Saranac Lake. George is leaning against the plane's blinker with a cigar in his hand. Standing at center (in the checkered shirt) is Caribou Bill ("Jack" Stearns Gray, "*UP*": *A True History of Aviation*).

on the morning of October 5, at Saranac Lake where she was vacationing. They met over the telephone through a mutual friend. He had stopped at a small Saranac hotel near the racetrack/flying field so that he could be near his plane. Gray's concern had to do with souvenir hunters, who were known to strip a machine in a matter of minutes. Stearns recalled her direct approach with this cocky young birdman:

"JACK": "I am Miss Stearns from [Culpeper] Virginia. I would like to take a flight with you. I have wanted to fly for years."
GEORGE: "Well, young lady, I am sorry, but you will have to keep on wanting. This is no place to fly women, and besides I am here only for exhibitions. Pardon me — goodbye."

Gray's brusque manner made her more determined than ever to fly with him. The following morning "Jack" rode her horse, Punch, to the makeshift airstrip. There she met a barker who demanded a dollar from her to see Gray's machine. Just then, George walked up; Stearns recalled: "I knew he was the aviator because I had seen his picture spread all over several newspapers. He had puttees on, a dark red sweater rolled up around his neck and his cap was turned backwards! That was the unfailing sign." Gray inquired what the trouble was, squinted his eye at the gateman, and told him to admit Stearns.

The next day "Jack" was back at the racetrack pursuing her objective with grim resolve:

Aviator Gray and I went thru that gate together, and I "registered." He had nice eyes! He was about twenty-eight years old. There were many people looking over the plane, who had been separated from their dollars. I took inventory of my progress towards a flight, and thought so far so good! I noticed the wings of the airplane were scribbled all over with autographs — some of celebrities. I humbly added mine!

Circling about the main attraction, Gray's following asked him the same old tiresome questions:

GALLERY: "Do you fly this thing?" GRAY: "Sure."
GALLERY: "Who invented it?" GRAY: "The Wright Brothers."
GALLERY: "Does your head swim up there?" GRAY: "Never."
GALLERY: "Don't you fall sometimes?" GRAY: "I'll never fall but once."
GALLERY: "Man, you are crazy." GRAY: "Sure. You'll be some day."

In the wake of these interrogations George performed a flight, and on landing his fans rushed to the plane yelling, "You ain't so crazy after all!"

"Jack" introduced herself to Gray as the previous day's caller, and again pestered him to take her on a flight. Finally surrendering to Stearn's cheeky persistence, George agreed to take her up that very afternoon. Before he fulfilled his promise, however, he had to put on his customary derring-do show, executing the devil dip, the ocean roll, the sharp banks, the spiral, and the vol pique. His dips over the crowds created a near-panic. At 5:00 P.M. head mechanician J. Chauncey Redding had three-strapped Stearns into her wing seat before Gray even arrived. Somewhat amused, George leaped into his seat and took off. Redding yelled after her, "Hold on tight, aw! But what's the use; if you fall you fall." Gray flew "Jack" over the town's racetrack, Saranac Lake itself, and both Whiteface and Saddleback mountains. In the process of landing, he had to dip at the milling spectators to frighten them away from the field. With Stearns still strapped into her seat, the mechanicians immediately towed Gray's Model B into a large tent where a barker began shouting through a megaphone to the multitude: "One dollar to see the [first] lady who flew over the Adirondacks." An irate Gray bounced out of his seat and started to berate the fair manager, telling him that "Jack" was a private flight passenger and that his actions were unacceptable. Forty dollars had exchanged hands before George stopped the sideshow. As the couple walked back to "Jack's" hotel, a band in the distance struck up "Dixie" in her honor. In the lobby, Stearns wrote Gray a check for $50.00, while the flyer's newly acquired entourage clamored for autographs. George never cashed the check.

Edith "Jack" Stearns was quite a personality in her own right. A native of Richmond, Virginia, the name "Jack" was given her at birth. A tomboy during her childhood, she sported bobbed hair and wore Buster Brown suits. Later "Jack" attended Mary Baldwin Seminary in Staunton, Miss Jennie Ellett's School for Girls in Richmond, and Stuart's School in Washington, D.C., where she served as captain of the baseball team, graduating in 1907. As a teenager "Jack" hunted the 2,500 acres of Farley Plantation, her father's [Franklin Stearns II] country home near Culpeper, Virginia. Young Stearns was later invited to a weekend visit at the White House in the spring of 1908. This signal honor constituted a return gesture for her family's hosting

"Jack" Stearns' Certificate of Flight ("Jack" Stearns Gray, "UP": A True History of Aviation).

of a hunting party at Farley the preceding autumn which included Ethel, President Theodore Roosevelt's youngest daughter. "Jack" took the wrong train to Washington and arrived early and therefore unmet. Following a brief conversation with an incredulous cop after telling him her destination, a hansom cab was summoned and she was transported to the White House. That evening "Jack" sat to the right of President Roosevelt at dinner, and later accompanied T.R. and family to the District's Columbia Theater.

Unlike the dashing young aviator who had just entered her life, Stearns was the beneficiary of privilege and social position in her native state. Family money provided her the wherewithal and

Edith "Jack" Stearns Gray ("Jack" Stearns Gray, *"UP": A True History of Aviation*).

leisure with which to pursue many agreeable pastimes, but none more agreeable to her than horseback riding. As an accomplished equestrian, "Jack" understood the importance of a proper habit, so, following her first skyride with Gray, she decided to treat herself with an altogether different outfit for what she hoped would be a lifetime of flying. Briefly returning to Washington, Stearns commissioned Julius Garfinkel & Company to make an aerial costume of her design. The flamboyant togs included a Norfolk jacket coat with hood attached, a broad belt, riding breeches, and a white cap with a big "VA" on it in red, standing for Virginia. Thanks to George, she had recently captured the title of first woman to fly from the Old Dominion, and she wanted everyone to know it. The standout material Stearns selected for this suit was white polar cloth. A pair of gun metal boots and matching gauntlets rounded out her garish ensemble. Sartorially resplendent and eager to join Gray on the exhibition circuit, "Jack" now elected to abandon her enviable station in life for George's company, the thrill of flying, and the lure of the open road.

From Saranac Lake Gray and "Jack" flew to Plattsburg, New York, after which George flew across Lake Champlain to Burlington, Vermont, on October 19, where University of Vermont students were treated to his peerless stunt flying. With the end of the exhibition season in late October 1912, Gray and Stearns returned to Boston, where he purchased a new Burgess-Wright machine ("UP") and prepared to leave for Florida.

Before leaving town, in celebration of his first anniversary in aviation, Gray announced on November 10 that he and his mechanician were planning an endurance flight from Boston to Seattle, Washington, covering the route from Bean Town to Chicago in a sizzling twenty-four hours without alighting once. Such a feat, if accomplished, would win for him both endurance and speed records, and the implied eclipse of Calbraith Rodger's transcontinental effort the previous year. Exuding confidence, the brash young birdman captured the imagination of his Boston audience in somewhat overblown rhetoric:

> As they used to say on the plains, I shall ride light; that is, there will be nothing on the machine but what is absolutely necessary to sustain flight. Of course, on the first leg — the longest of all ... we plan to carry along some sandwiches.... For the trip I shall have two Burgess-Wright biplanes, one to be used regularly, the other in case of emergency.... We shall be able to carry forty gallons of gasoline, and this should sustain us for the first-planned leg of the trip. The start will be made in April [1913].

The cynic might rightly surmise that George's imagined project was little more than a publicity stunt, as there was no mention of financial backers or definite logistical details. Regrettably, his hoped-for undertaking never left the ground. As he subsequently passed through Virginia, Gray awed crowds with his fancy flying during a long visit at his lady friend's home before collecting "Jack" and moving on to the Sunshine State.

While Gray and Stearns dallied at Farley Plantation, George's attractive hostess persuaded him to give an aerial benefit for a tubercular friend convalescing back at Saranac Lake. The town's fairgrounds were not conductive to takeoffs and landings, so the couple compromised on short hops, promising longer and higher efforts if the local folks were not happy with the early offerings. Three hundred feet in the air, Gray's engine quit. The pair could not make it back to their point of origination in a gliding machine, and with no suitable place to set down, Gray spotted a train chugging along just below them. Devoid of options, they dropped like a stone, taking out a high fence — posts and all — which bordered the railroad tracks. Neither "Jack" nor George were hurt, and with only slight damage to the plane. Stearns offered to return the gate receipts intended for her girlfriend's sanitarium expenses, but the hometown crowd refused the money. Moved by her neighbors' generosity, she cajoled Gray into circling the entire county of Culpeper on December 14, one week after their accident near the Southern Railway tracks. On that day "Jack" was presented a loving cup by the citizens of Culpeper.

Gray arrived in Jacksonville on January 1, 1913, and prepared "UP" for extended flights down Florida's eastern coast. Newspaper coverage followed in his wake and, as a result, he began receiving requests to fly packages and letters as a special delivery messenger. Railroad tycoon and hotel magnate Henry Morrison Flagler was one of George's main customers, who then resided at his Hotel Ponce de Leon in St. Augustine. Gray and the multimillionaire discussed the future of aviation in the U.S. Post Office Department during an audience called by Flagler, and when the two men parted company George's host provided him with a letter of introduction addressed to the managers of the eighty-four-year-old mogul's Florida East Coast Hotels, direct-

"Jack" and George Gray at Farley Plantation, Virginia ("Jack" Stearns Gray, *"UP": A True History of Aviation*).

ing them to furnish the flyer complimentary accommodations at their facilities. Gray's benefactor had less than six months to live.

Staying in St. Augustine for nearly three weeks, Gray performed several flights, resulting in his being the first man to fly over that city, a feat for which he received a bronze medal. During this interim George severely damaged "UP," but his machine was repaired at Flagler's Florida East Coast Railroad shops without cost to him. From St. Augustine, Gray flew to Daytona, a distance of some 110 miles. He remained there for the winter, subsequently laying over at the Ormond Beach Hotel, where he briefly established a business carrying passengers. Many of his clients were resistant to distance or altitude flights, claiming problems with vertigo and opting rather for low-level flying. Consequently, George adopted hop flights, whereby he would fly down an unobstructed beach at ten feet above the sand and surf, land the plane, and fly back. This approach allowed his customers the sensation of flying without adverse physical side effects. Gray eventually settled on a scale of prices—$10 for a hop of about half a mile, rising only ten feet in the air; $15 for a flight of about 100 feet altitude;

and $25 for a 200 foot high flight. Many apprehensive passengers would take the $10 ride, find they enjoyed the experience, then take the $15 sortie before indulging in the "big ride." One fellow and his wife took the whole package one morning, and blew $100 finding out how it felt to truly fly. Finally, for the hopelessly faint of heart, George and "Jack" allowed these patrons to be photographed in "UP" for a nominal charge.

Top: "Jack" Sterns Gray and George Gray at Farley Plantation. The arrow pointing to their punctured wing is where they took out a fence in preference to a freight train. *Bottom:* Gassing up before a flying date. Geoge Gray is at right ("Jack" Stearns Gray, *"UP": A True History of Aviation*).

Conversely, Gray sometimes earned his money the hard way at Ormond Beach. For example, an elderly lady asked him for a flight. As she climbed aboard the plane, George told his mechanician to not only strap her around the waist, but to also strap her skirts about her ankles. The woman's skirts were huge, of several layers, and made of brown taffeta. As the mechanician was about to execute Gray's directive, his passenger gave him a look of disapproval, informing him she wanted her feet free. George hollered, "Let her go," to his assistant, and away "UP" rose. When the Burgess-Wright had gotten up to around 200 feet the spectators below witnessed what appeared to be a field of brown cloth hiding both Gray and his passenger. In desperation, George nose-dived to earth, suffering a rough but otherwise damage-free landing. While being assisted in having her clothing disentangled from the plane's many parts, Gray's disgruntled passenger vented her rage at him: "You are no kind of an aviator and no gentleman to scare me like that! I won't pay you a cent." "I don't want your money," he snapped, "or any more passengers like you! You nearly killed us both with those skirts." George later revealed that he had scarcely risen twenty feet before his terrified client began hitting him and screaming to let her down.

While at Ormond Beach, Gray and Stearns would frequently pass Ruth Law high in the air; the famous aviatrix was flying from her home base at nearby Sea Breeze. At this time "Jack" harbored aspirations of becoming a pilot, instead of just a "professional" passenger, and Law represented a natural role model. In the end, however, she chose a life with George over her heart's desire, her decision due entirely to his insistence that there should be only one licensed flyer in the family.

In mid–April 1913, George went north to Richmond, Virginia, where he had contracted for an exhibition. He made his required flights, but received no pay, as his freeloading audience enjoyed his performances inside a gateless enclosure and from adjoining hills overlooking the field, without the necessity of paying admission. Adding injury to insult, Gray suffered a bad smashup at another date in the city, largely due to his contractor's misunderstanding of their schedule. He had agreed with a minor league baseball manager to land on the outfield at a local park during a game, as an extra attraction to the fans. George was to set down at precisely 4:00 P.M., and the management promised to clear the field by that time. When Gray came sailing over at the designated time and shut his motor off preliminary to landing, he was shocked to see below him teams still on the field. As his motor had already been killed, the only thing left for Gray to do was to attempt, with the momentum left him, to skim over the bleachers to railroad tracks beyond the stadium while trying to evade a series of wires and a high fence back of the bleachers. While gliding towards this destination, he frantically tried to lift the plane higher, but failed. His craft was heading directly to the center of the stands. "UP" hovered for a second over the heads of the spectators, before careening sideways and crashing just beyond the bleachers, flattening a Coca-Cola booth in its path. A small boy dispensing drinks in the hut was badly shaken up, but he recovered.

Incredibly, Gray scrambled out from under the machine with only scratches. The engine had plowed into the ground about four feet, barely missing Gray. Even before George crashed, Stearns was on the field minus a shoe, trying to get through a police cordon. When she reached him, Gray was fighting mad. Chewing at his ubiquitous cigar he stalked off, looking for the manager. Following the crackup, the couple had "UP" repaired and shipped to George's next engagement. Once again, Gray went unpaid.

But for happenstance and aviation, Stearns would never have wed Gray on June 4, 1913, in Washington, D.C. "Jack's" plan was to fly to the nation's capital, the current home of her parents, with a greeting for President Woodrow Wilson from Virginia's governor, William Hodges Mann. Due to the debacle in Richmond, however, it became necessary to ship "UP" to the site of their post-nuptial engagement and entrain for the District. Stearns was fashionably late for the ceremony and the colorful aviator George W. Beatty, who served as Gray's best man, kept whispering into the groom's ear, "Brace up, old man; this is not a solo." No sooner had the proceedings concluded than the newlyweds were off by rail to Ocean City, New Jersey, Gray's next exhibition date.

George Beatty: Gray's best man and flying companion ("Jack" Stearns Gray, "UP": A True History of Aviation).

Soon the Grays were skimming several miles out into the Atlantic, their machine having been outfitted with pontoons. The contract proved to be a great advertisement for them, and within weeks adjoining resorts were bidding for George's services. As usual, Gray featured his patented "hop" flights between his regular exhibitions. One afternoon "Jack's" share of these comic flights amounted to nearly $100, so she staged a party to celebrate, not anticipating that townspeople and beachcombers alike would join in. As a result, "Jack" had to work overtime the next day rooting for more "hops." If his engine malfunctioned or the weather prevented flying, Gray was forced to redouble his workload the next afternoon. George's shows were scheduled for 2:00 P.M. and 5:00 P.M. daily. The crowds seemed to surge at these hours, and frequently special trains were run from nearby cities to allow inlanders to see his aerial genius.

From Ocean City, the Grays moved on to Wildwood, their succeeding intrastate contract. As Gray climbed into his wing seat in preparation to fly to the resort town, he yelled to his mechanician, Bill Gilbert, "to step on the gas" and beat him there. Gilbert rode top speed at 55 mph, and the Gray's other two machinists were in the back seat clearing the way with pistol shots. "Jack," seated alongside the driver, initially asked Gilbert to let her out of the car, but when he ignored her entreaties she offered him her diamond engagement ring if he would slow down. Orders were orders; so Gilbert continued to barrel down the highway at full throttle. George landed some ten minutes ahead of the automobile, and he was shaking hands with Wildwood's mayor on the beach when Gilbert's party arrived. After "Jack" was introduced to Wildwood's chief executive, the mayor immediately offered Gray's bedraggled wife hotel accommodations.

It was the Grays' custom to fly out over the Atlantic after settling in at a resort. About a mile from the coast "Jack" spotted a shark down below and begged her husband to head for the beach. George climbed to 5,000 feet and relinquished the control levers to his partner while maintaining a level course. Both pilot and passenger knew that with their machine they could glide only one mile to every thousand feet up; hence, they were assured of reaching the beach safely.

While at Wildwood the Grays encountered stiff competition in the person of Pennsylvania aviator Marshall Earle Reid. The Milton native flew a hydroplane; because of the type of plane he commanded, customers seemed to flock to his pavilion. Fighting back, George staged a marvelous demonstration of aerobatics which included the sideslip, the devil's dip, the falling leaf, the ocean roll, the spiral glide, and the steep dive with engine dead. On the final stunt Gray unceremoniously landed in the ocean. Later on that day, Reid had to set down in a shallow marsh. In due course, lifeguards fished "UP" from the water, while tourists pulled Reid from the mire. Those observers who witnessed the two salvage operations thought it odd that a land airship would go down in the sea and a water craft would land in a swamp. The irony of their juxtaposed situations was not lost on either Gray or Reid.

George made his first night flight at this popular tourist mecca. Despite his wife's entreaties not to attempt anything so rash, Gray waved her aside, saying that if a roaring bonfire were to be built for him to land by he would be fine. Besides, he

In the drink at Wildwood, New Jersey, George Gray is being rescued by lifeguards ("Jack" Stearns Gray, "*UP*": *A True History of Aviation*).

argued, the moon would be full on the appointed evening, and should help him, as well as afford a clearer view to the crowd below. When "Jack" stood in front of "UP" in an attempt to block his takeoff, Gray simply flew over her, forcing his wife to dive into the sand. Gray's stunts in the dark sky so excited a spectator near "Jack," who watched him execute spirals while silhouetted against the moon, that the stranger suddenly blurted out, "Three cheers for [Lincoln] Beachey." George's one-woman publicity department immediately grabbed a megaphone, and mounting an old barrel near the huge bonfire built by volunteers, screamed over the din and roar of an agitated gallery, mingled with the whirr of the motor overhead, "That's not Beachey! It's George A. Gray, the daredevil of them all."

For the sake of novelty, at least regarding the Grays' repertoire of aerial antics, the couple staged a harrowing race between their automobile and "UP." The car came in a poor second, having to make countless laps around the track in the dusty wake of George's aircraft overhead. Poor "Jack" had been "selected" to drive the vehicle.

There occurred rip-offs and hoaxes aplenty during the Grays' 1913 tour of the Garden State. At Tumbling Dam Park they barely broke even after the fair manager appropriated the lion's share of the gate receipts. Moving on to Cape May and Avalon, George did secure at the latter resort a one-day exhibition contract to perform for a prospective gubernatorial candidate who was speaking to the converted on the city's progress. Following an ill-advised holiday in Philadelphia, where the couple blew a large portion of their earnings, Gray was duped into a two-flight contract from a fraudulent aviator. The self-proclaimed flyer could produce no license for George, insisting that he had applied for a renewal. Reputedly his plane had not arrived, so he asked Gray to fly for him. Affording this faker the benefit of the doubt and feeling pity for him, the flights were made. "Jack" later recalled George muttering to himself, "He is a new one on me — but they are coming four or five into the field a year now." On this man's word alone, the Grays gave him 20 percent of the proceeds from the two flights. Shortly thereafter, a well-dressed high roller drove up to "UP" during an engagement and asked to be taken on a $50.00 flight. Once back on the ground, the passenger casually left the plane and got into his nickel-plated automobile driven by a uniformed chauffeur, and started off without paying for his sky ride. Gray ordered his mechanician to dash after him, and as George's employee leaped aboard the car's running board, he was advised by the upward-pointing chiseler "to go on up and get it."

Interspersed among the swindlers were equally aggravating flying mishaps which took a toll on the Grays. On one occasion they were sailing over a picturesque country church while Sunday services were in progress. The congregation did not wait for the end of the sermon, but rather stampeded outside in a state of panic. Beckoned to earth by the fuming pastor, George took out a fence in landing. According to "Jack's" recollection of the event, a "material appeal" for forgiveness was offered and duly accepted. In yet another humiliating incident Gray's engine stopped over a New Jersey farmer's tomato patch, and in the course of setting down, "UP's" skids raked up row upon row of the fruit still attached to their vines. Almost simultaneously a full-bearded, tobacco-chewing farmer hobbled up to the biplane piqued by the damage and toting a pitchfork.

Gray instantly produced a ten-dollar bill from his pocket and handed it over to the rustic. In the twinkling of an eye the two men were shaking hands and smiling, and it was the victim who apologized "fer my tomatoes a' gitten in yer way." In leaving, following minor repairs to the machine, the old man cackled, "Ha, Ha, Ha, feathers ain't what they'se cracked up to be — next time it'll serve ye right if ye land in the pig sty." For weeks after the tomato patch incident, "UP" sported a red and gray camouflage pattern.

An unusual setback presented itself when engine trouble forced "UP" down near an alleyway in the suburbs of a tiny New Jersey hamlet. As Gray and his mechanician climbed down from their wing seats, George spotted two goats eyeing his machine. He ordered his man to guard the plane while he went for towing assistance. When Gray returned in an hour's time, he found the Model B's protector asleep under a wing and the goats munching on the wing's rubberized linen fabric.

Barnstorming next took the Grays to Union Lake Park in Millville, New Jersey. A hint of fall was in the air as the couple migrated southward. Their advance man had signed a contract for them to fly at a location on the outskirts of town, and he grossly misjudged the conditions surrounding a proposed landing site. When the Grays reached Millville and checked out the location, they were appalled. For the remainder of the day and all during that night, twenty woodsmen chopped a lane through the obstructing trees for "UP" to take off and land. At 11:00 A.M. the next day, Gray rose from the confined area, flew through the lane hewn hours before, and landed without a hitch. Scarcely had this hurdle been overcome when George's number one mechanician, who had been demoted as a result of sloppy inspection work, drew a pistol on his boss. Luckily disarmed by the number two team member, the offender was sent packing.

Before turning south for the season, Gray committed to three more northern dates: Asbury Park, New Jersey, and Bustleton and Allentown, Pennsylvania. Incredibly, the physical flying conditions at Asbury Park were even worse than Gray's previous contract. Nevertheless, he went for the purse, despite "Jack's" protestations. Up his plane climbed, headed towards overhead wires and trestles, with "Jack" running behind and shouting for him to "shut her off." As she expected, George lacked the distance and speed to clear these obstacles. In a desperate attempt to overfly them, he turned "UP" perpendicularly and stalled it, coming down backwards. His machine fell into Deal Lake, barely avoiding a number of canoes filled with picnickers. The impact catapulted Gray from the plane to the top of a large willow tree nearby. From its pinnacle he tumbled downward before finally hitting the ground. A huge mob gathered at the base of the willow, and "Jack" reached her husband only through the intervention of police. There he lay, unconscious, covered in blood and being attended by two physicians who happened to be present. "Jack" was informed that Gray would live, despite his two cracked ribs, a split shinbone, and multiple cuts and bruises. A car was offered to rush him to the nearby Long Branch Hospital, and two cops and one of the attending doctors went along. Outside the emergency room "Jack" was again reassured that her spouse would pull through, but she was also told that perhaps his flying days were over. On the heels of this mixed report, the ER door opened, and George emerged on crutches. Hobbling over to his wife, Gray's laconic concession statement went, "Jack, why didn't you plug the gasoline tank?" Six weeks after his crash, Gray filled a contract at Bustleton, Pennsylvania, slated to perform ten flights. On the last day the crowd's applause went off the decibel chart when everyone saw George, his crutches at the ready, being helped from "UP" after setting down.

The Grays did not tarry at "Jack's" hometown of Culpeper in the autumn of 1913. Actually, George had already made some twenty-three flights over the area during the past eighteen months; so instead, the pair accepted an engagement at Fincastle, Virginia. Gray flew ahead to the date and "Jack" caught a mountain bus to the village. When she arrived, George was there complaining to the promoters about the field. His initial instinct was to fire his manager, but the gentleman had already absconded with their northern receipts. Despite their unpromising beginning, the Grays more than recouped their losses at Fincastle, and "Jack" bought her first thoroughbred racehorse. Peyton B proved to be a fifth of a mile sprinter, winning most of his races at that mark. Coveting a longer distance runner, she added Ortsen, a steeplechaser, to her stable. Racing these animals on any available track near her husband's flying dates, the horses acquitted themselves admirably. During their months with the Grays, Peyton B and Ortsen, together with "UP," were transported in two separate freight cars. There was no mention as to the accommodations of Henry

Wells, "Jack's" African-American jockey. When the horses could no longer run, they were sold.

From Fincastle, the Grays traveled to Roanoke, Virginia, where they failed to secure sufficient guarantee of their portion of the gate receipts. Managing himself at this point, George followed a simple dictum: there had to be a certified check for a certified flight — no check, no flight. The dates he now filled came from his ads in *Billboard* magazine. Pickup engagements occurred when bids flooded in from towns in the vicinity where he was flying. "Jack" recalled: "I have seen whole mountaineer families arrive in town in wagons with straw for their seats 'dressed up to kill' and ask[ing] the way to the 'flying ship.' One family told me it had traveled twenty-one miles since early dawn, 'to see that man who acted like a bird, get up with his wings.'"

Leaving the hill country of Virginia, Gray shipped "UP" to Columbia, South Carolina, where he had been engaged by New York City aviation promoter John S. "Jack" Berger at Charlotte, North Carolina, to fly with two other pilots at a highly touted "Avi-

Cooley, the Grays' traveling mascot and dedicated protector of their aircraft from all would-be souvenir hunters ("Jack" Stearns Gray, "*UP*": *A True History of Aviation*).

ation Meet," which turned out to be three planes and three aviators. Howard M. Rinehart and Henry Roy Waite were Gray's competitors at this contest, with baseball legend Ty Cobb serving in the capacity of starter.

The Grays reached Columbia in mid–November 1913, and found their mechanicians already assembling "UP" at the fairground. It was George's impression that Waite and Rinehart were Berger regulars; as for his role as a freelancer, he agreed to fly for $600 and expenses. Gray completed his four flights before a disappointingly small crowd, the result of poor advance publicity. Rinehart's showing was mediocre, merely a jump over the racetrack fence due to engine trouble. Waite, however, astonished the Grays by rivaling George's effort in a tailless machine, taking it aloft on twelve separate occasions. On the last day of the meet, Berger reportedly skipped town with the proceeds. Worse still, "UP" was attached for alleged debt left behind by the promoter, of which George had no part in the making. In the end, he lost his contract money, his time, and the short-term use of his plane, while the police sorted everything out. The couple was forced to engage an attorney, and pending contracts in other towns went aglimmering. After three weeks of extreme aggravation, they succeeded in getting their aircraft released.

Exhausted, short of patience, and low on funds, the Grays closed 1913 by landing in Jacksonville a few days before Christmas. They had lost nearly $2,000 in Colum-
bia, and now, as "Jack" later phrased it, "Florida was a bracing demitasse to a bad
dinner." The city's newspapers learned that a Wright aviator was in town and sought
Gray out. Of course, he had done some flying there before; and during his absence,
Curtiss pilot Charlie Hamilton had revived local interest in exhibition shows. At the
outset, George agreed to limited flying over the city and stunting above an ostrich
farm nearby. In less than a week's time, however, he had pocketed a contract for an
entire winter's work seventeen miles from Jacksonville at a resort in Atlantic Beach.

They were given a suite of rooms at an ocean front hotel, a private table in the
dining room, and full access to an impressive menu. In return, Gray agreed to one
flight a day. If the weather turned bad one day, George promised to double up on
performances the next. The remainder of each day was open to him to carry passengers at his own rates. His "hops" again became a popular attraction at $10.00 per
rider. Subsequent to several sensational night flights and hundreds of passenger excursions high above Atlantic Beach, the tourist season petered out, so the Grays seized
a contract when offered it in St. Augustine with a motion picture corporation.

The Grays first project was with Pathé Motion Pictures. They were filming *The
Perils of Pauline*, a popular melodramatic serial in which the heroine, Pauline, is forever imperiled by the scheming villain, Koerner. In one harrowing episode, the fiend
tries to kill Pauline by having her perish in an airplane crash. Under the direction of
Paul Panzer, Gray served as the flying double for the actor who played the unwitting
tool of Koerner, scripted to fly actress Pearl White (Pauline) to her fiery death, but
who himself met a solitary end in a plane sabotaged by Koerner. This part of the film
had to be spliced with the actual death plunge of another flyer in France.

That same winter, the Gray team worked for the Lubin Company of Philadelphia, its management having established a branch in St. Augustine. For six weeks
George served as a flying consultant and participating pilot to help make the film
Cipher Key. Among other exploits, he rescued the heroine from a desert storm and
flew rings around the top of a lighthouse. While flying over St. Augustine, George
was seen making a precipitous dive toward the city. "Jack," meanwhile, was out on
location in a walk-on role. Earle Metcalfe, of the Lubin Company, together with the
leading man, collected "Jack" and rushed her by automobile to the location where
her husband went down. When they arrived, she found that Gray had volplaned
down to a golf course. It seemed that his propeller had fallen off in midair over the
Alcazar Hotel, miraculously with no loss of life.

In late May 1914, the Grays boarded a ship from Savannah, Georgia, bound for
Baltimore, Maryland, after nearly being burned out in the April 2 conflagration that
ravaged St. Augustine. "Jack" had been admitted to a hospital at the time suffering
from influenza and was awakened in the early morning hours by ambulance sirens
and the arrival of casualties. Abandoning her room, she met Gray, who was just arriving to check on her condition. When "Jack" recuperated, the pair was more than
ready to depart the city.

Following a four-day voyage, the couple arrived in Baltimore and went straight-away for "Jack's" country home at Farley Plantation. "UP" had been shipped ahead, with the Grays planning some needed repairs to the machine before an anticipated flying season along the Atlantic coast. They remained at Farley for six weeks, and towards the end of their stay George meant to test the refurbished plane before going north. Unfortunately, on the 2,500 acres comprising the estate, the couple experienced great difficulty locating a level site for an airfield. Finally, after a three-day walk over the grounds, Gray settled on a spot. Word spread overnight among house staff and tenants regarding George's impending test flight, and on the appointed day everyone was in attendance. Gray's flight went beautifully until he started to land. In the second after he shut off the motor and began his glide down to earth, the plantation manager's wife and her two children ran into the path of the oncoming machine. Gray, in desperation, tried to brake the plane's forward momentum with his foot. "UP" scooped up the three and kept on going, plowing through a sturdy farm gate and finally stopping in a muddy cornfield, together with its unscheduled passengers. Amazingly, no one was seriously injured, although "UP" sustained major damage. Six weeks of arduous labor spent repairing the Grays' aircraft had gone up in smoke. As for the northern commitments, George had to forfeit two weeks of the original fee bargained for to hold on to his contract, as he could not arrive on the specified date.

On July 15, the Grays once again migrated back to Wildwood, New Jersey, stationing themselves there, with George performing exhibition flights and carrying passengers between Ocean City, Wildwood, Avalon, and Cape May. As always, "hop" flights were the most attractive to Gray's clientele, but with a new twist: the issuance of certificates of flight by the pilot himself. Following the Wildwood engagement, the twosome worked farther north, to Vermont, New Hampshire, and other New England states, limiting themselves largely to exhibition appearances.

Fulfilling these contracts, Gray decided to leave the exhibition business and turn to different aerial pursuits, basing his decision on economic considerations. Transportation expenses cut deeply into his budget, and the $100 a day royalty payments to the Wrights for the privilege of piloting one of their licensed machines was another financial burden. Finally, the airplane had become a relatively commonplace sight, and with more aviators in the exhibition game, George could command less money for his performances. In light of these fading prospects, he turned to instruction. "Jack" later defended her husband's more mature approach to flight in a rather revealing passage from her memoir:

> His experience warranted this new responsibility. Nor did we wish Orville Wright to count us failures at the crossroads. We wanted to "carry on" and we felt as other pioneers did, that flying at fairs and exhibition work was not the airplane's highest possibility. Flying for the satisfaction of a lot of sensation seekers had always made us recoil.

In a long and somewhat rambling reminiscence of the various eccentricities of early flyers, she noted that Gray, aside from his career-long aversion to wearing goggles, left aviation with a phobia regarding crowds, "and will run a mile to get out of sight of a country fair."

That July George offered his machine and services to the New York National Guard at Camp Whitman, Fishkill Plains, New York. At this encampment, in a civilian capacity, he successfully demonstrated bomb-dropping, carried out observation and reconnaissance flights, and generally presented a very favorable impression of the deployment of aircraft in military operations. The following month, Gray repeated his demonstrations, at the behest of the Aero Club of America, to the Vermont National Guard at Fort Ethan Allen. His efforts won for him an Aero Club gold medal. As a result of Gray's aerial salesmanship an aviation section was added to the state's National Guard.

The need for earning a living persuaded George to open a flying school at Garden City, Long Island, New York, that fall, where he personally instructed for a time. During May of 1916, Gray became involved in some experimental test flying for the Richardson Aeroplane Corporation of Lowell, Massachusetts, piloting its single float tandem wing biplane hydro on the Potomac River at Washington, D.C. As Jack said:

> Often I would sit for hours on the cold bank of that partly frozen river and watch Gray and a mechanician experiment with the plane's lifting powers in those deep waters. He did prove to the inventor that she could fly, but these tests were never very successful. Something was wrong with the mechanism of it. I have never known the outcome of the Richardson ambitions for his tandem seaplane. I hope it proved every bit the success he had dreamed it would be. His ideas were a bit new in 1916 for the generally accepted planes of that day.

Actually, the Richardson tandem hydroplane was considered by the army for service in the 1916 Mexican campaign, but it was never deployed.

In the wake of these trials, the Grays decamped for Canada and opened a flying school, reportedly in Toronto, as a supplementary extension of a large scale training program already in progress for World War I. What followed there is subject to considerable conjecture. Conventional sources maintain that George crashed his machine during training exercises and destroyed it beyond repair. "Jack's" recollection, however, proved to be quite different. According to her memoir, Gray believed that he could "kill two birds with one stone"—help the Canadians train their airmen and make a living in the bargain. He had done similar work at College Park, Maryland, during a part of 1914, and was qualified to train in aerial combat. Given those qualifications, continued "Jack," the Royal Canadian Flying Corps grew to resent George's prolonged resistance to joining its war, despite the fact that he was the citizen of a neutral country. Seemingly this indignation spilled over into the general population, for at some point an unruly crowd, scarcely contained by an indifferent police reserve, totally destroyed Gray's plane. Apparently the attack was stoked by George's intemperate remarks to the mob. Now, without any means to a livelihood, all he could do was to bring home one of "UP's" wing struts as a souvenir to his despondent wife:

He [Gray] forgot to take into consideration the intense feeling for "cannon fodder" of the moment and that they [the Canadian Flying Corps] thought he ought to go after some of that "fodder" for "His Majesty."

I told Gray he would make a sad diplomat. A bit of finessing might have saved "UP" for some museum, and our feelings as well.

In late December of 1916, Gray held a temporary military lectureship in New York City, while "Jack" kept company with her mother in Washington, D.C. The following February she received a telegram from George, who was still "carpet flying" (lecturing) in the Big Apple, directing her to go to the aviation section of the War Department and attempt to win for him a particular job he had learned was available as inspector of aircraft for the government. Admittedly, the job offered modest remuneration, but it held the prospect of promotion. "Jack" stood in line for three hours before finally reaching the office of the chief of the Air Service, Major Henry Souther. She presented him with Gray's flight album and explained that her husband was otherwise occupied. The major asked "Jack" whether or not George attended college and had he "studied about all this," referring to the album. Restraining her outrage at such a question regarding an authentic Wright aviator, she stammered, "Gray can build your old airplanes; he can inspect them, and he can fly them! What more does the Government want?" "Nothing," responded the uncomfortable officer. Asked to come back the next day, "Jack" walked out of Major Souther's office with Gray's job in hand. In this final session she learned from the major that her meticulously kept album of George's career had landed him the appointment.

Gray's first posting was at Plainfield, New Jersey, as inspector of aircraft assembly at the Standard Aero Corporation. In September 1917, he was transferred to the Fisher Body Corporation, Detroit, Michigan, to again inspect planes built there. During both tenures George was promoted twice, having the rank of captain in the United States Army Air Service. His inspection responsibilities were limited to army machines and did not apply to naval warplanes. Gray was called to Washington, D.C., in June 1918 and ordered to France, again as an aircraft inspector, to help determine the perceived poor airworthiness of Allied planes. In October, during a break in his busy schedule, George crossed the English Channel in a Bristol fighter, thereby logging his last recorded flight.

Gray completed his tour abroad, returned to the States, and was on the verge of returning to France, when the Armistice was signed. He remained in the army, in its procurement section, until December 1, 1920, when he resigned to act as Washington representative of the Pioneer Instrument Company. With an office in the Star Building, the former captain supervised all of his firm's dealings with the army and navy, a huge volume of business. His leisure hours were spent with family at their Chevy Chase, Maryland, home. In 1931 Edith "Jack" Stearns Gray published "*UP*," a memoir of her husband's exhibition flying and the couple's demonstration and intercity flights together. Gray remained in the vicinity of the nation's capital for the remainder of his life. George Alphonso Gray passed away on February 1, 1956, at 74, and was buried near the North Gate of Arlington Cemetery. A beautiful spray of flowers from the Early Birds organization adorned his grave. Although a *Washington Post* obituary listed the Grays as having four children and three grandchildren, George's 1942 *Who's Who* questionnaire, at age 59, gave only three surviving direct heirs: George A. Gray, Jr., Newcombe Stearns Gray, and Jacquelin Stearns Gray. Six months later, in a moving tribute to his deceased friend, Paul Edward Garber, curator of Washington's National Air and Space Museum and secretary of the Early Birds, wrote:

> George's last days were spent in his apartment in Rockville, Md. He had experienced a brain injury, but enjoyed visits from his friends. In company with Alfred Verville, the noted airplane designer, and friend of George's, I drove out to see George a few weeks before he died. We went through our little custom, something like a ritual, to gather up all of the empty Coke bottles in his apartment, and then drove over to the drug store where George replenished his Coke supply, and laid in a fresh stock of cigars. Then we went for a little ride and chatted about the good old days before closed cockpits and jet engines. George had a badly damaged scale model of his Wright "B" which I had once repaired for him so it could be shown in a school. He wanted it fixed up again so it could go into the Early Bird models case in the National Air Museum. I received it from him and will work at it, to put it in good condition, with his name on the blinkers. When we left George, he asked to be remembered to all of his friends. Fred Verville and I attended George's burial in Arlington Cemetery.... His mortal remains lie near the North Gate of that National Shrine, but his heart and soul and his happy smile are his living heritage to us all, as he flies on above us.

George A. Gray as a captain, U.S. Air Service, and itinerant barnstormer ("Jack" Stearns Gray, "*UP*": *A True History of Aviation*).

On October 19, 1961, "Jack," at seventy, was laid to rest beside George in Arlington Cemetery. A Culpeper newspaper stated that she had died "after a brief illness in a Bethesda, Maryland, hospital following a longer illness at home." For many, it seemed fitting that one of American aviation's more illustrious husband and wife teams were together again.

HOWARD RINEHART

Orville's Favorite

On a summer afternoon in 1912 a large crowd gathered on the outskirts of Manaus, Brazil, to see the country's celebrated aviator, Alberto Santos-Dumont, perform in his Blériot monoplane. Among the gaping spectators was a tall, rangy twenty-seven-year-old American adventurer named Howard Max Rinehart. For nearly a decade, Brazilian and U.S. newspapers had piqued Rinehart's interest with accounts of the extraordinary aerial achievements of native son Santos-Dumont and the Ohio brothers Orville and Wilbur Wright, who were involved in aircraft manufacture and flight research. Family contacts had notified him of Wilbur's death on May 30, and of the continuation of the Wright Company under Orville's presidency. Since the Wrights had been practically neighbors back in Dayton, and since their celebrated Flyers had brought international acclaim and lucrative patent contracts from Europe, Rinehart now felt a bond with Orville's enterprise, derived from a common geographical association and a fascination for the work done there. It was at the Manaus air show that he decided to return home and lend his oar to this great adventure.

Howard Rinehart was born on March 16, 1885, to Franklin B. and Alma Rinehart, in Eaton, Ohio, a few miles west of Dayton. A graduate of Eaton High School, the teenager spent his afternoons and weekends as a stationary engineer in his father's planing mill. On June 16, 1902, he (still a minor) enlisted in the United States Navy as landsman for training. Rinehart completed the year at the Portsmouth Navy Yard, Norfolk, Virginia, followed by a six-month cruise on the U.S.S. *Lancaster*, a square-rigged vessel, moving through the ranks from ordinary to able-bodied seaman. Early in 1903, he was transferred to the U.S.S. *Barry*, of the first flotilla of destroyers, and served aboard through southern and northern maneuvers.

Following his 1903 tour, Howard entered the U.S. Naval Electrical School at the Washington Navy Yard, enrolling as one of the first pupils in the Naval Wireless School. After graduation he served two years of detached duty as a wireless operator and constructor, building and maintaining stations at the Norfolk and New York Navy Yards, as well as the Cape Hatteras Lightship. Rinehart received his severance pay as chief electrician at the Norfolk Navy Yard in 1906. Once again in civilian life, he worked briefly for the United Wireless Company of New York, installing equipment in steamers and stations along the Atlantic seaboard.

Late in 1906 Rinehart took employment with the National Electrical Signalling Company (NESC) of Brant Rock, Massachusetts. Under the direction of Professor R.A. Fessenden his group was instrumental in the development of the electrolytic detector and several receiving circuits. After the conclusion of his laboratory assignments, Rinehart sailed for Brazil with NESC instructions to supervise the construction of commercial wireless stations along the Amazon River for the Amazon Wireless Telegraph Company.

When his vessel docked at Bahai, Rinehart disembarked into the aftermath of a yellow fever epidemic. His subsequent inspection of Bahai revealed that city lacked electricity and that most of its newly hired electrical engineers were too ill to complete a partially constructed municipal light plant. With remarkable chutzpah, Rinehart volunteered his services (and NESC resources) toward completion of this project. During the ensuing two years he supervised the building and operation of four wireless centers located at Para, Breves, Santarém, and Manaus. In 1910, with these stations fully operational, the NESC dispatched him to Rio de Janeiro, where he spent a year equipping forty Lloyd-Brazileiro steamers with wireless. The following year he returned to Manaus, becoming manager of operations for the Amazon River Wireless Company. For relaxation Rinehart joined two separate expeditions into the Brazilian

Howard Rinehart in the Manaus office of the Amazon Wireless Telegraph Company (Rob Grant).

interior for the purpose of exploration. Back from the hinterland in time to read of his hometown's many contributions as the "cradle of aviation," the buckeye expatriate took the first available ship for Dayton via New Orleans.

On September 1, 1913, Howard enrolled in the Wright School of Aviation, receiving his technical instruction from veteran aviator Oscar Brindley, and his encouragement from Orville Wright, the latter being appreciative of his dedication. Rinehart soon discovered that his term there would be both grueling and a trifle dangerous. The Wright flying school avoided the problem of excessive air turbulence by scheduling early morning and late afternoon training flights. During those hours, Rinehart found himself either seated beside his trainer or solo aboard a Flyer Model B pusher, attempting to counterbalance a single wheezing, water-

Miriam Dove Rinehart (Rob Grant).

cooled engine that drove two propellers through a chain reduction drive, mustering thirty-five horsepower. The top speed of his Model B was fifty miles per hour, the landing speed was twenty-five, and its ceiling around 14,000 feet. Since the biplane's motor lacked a carburetor, its fuel being mixed in a pipe valve on the intake manifold, Howard had to master the technique of altering the craft's power range in retarding and advancing the magneto. From his exposed perch, he learned to control the throttle with his right foot; the wing warp and rudder by a stick to his right; and the elevator by a stick near his left knee. His ship was equipped with an angle of incidence indicator which gave the angle of the plane in relation to the wind. The gas tank held ten gallons of fuel, which was carried to the motor through a rubber hose. Howard quickly learned that one constant source of trouble was the chain drive from the engine to the two propellers. When a chain snapped, as they did frequently, it was tantamount to the loss of a motor.

In three weeks time, Rinehart flew for his license (no. 266) at Simms Station, Dayton, Ohio. After graduation Howard spent the winter with the J.S. Berger exhibition flying company giving performances on a Wright Model B, together with dare-

(From left) Miriam, Miriam's sister Mabel, and Howard Rinehart, doing the dishes back home in Ohio (Rob Grant).

devils H. Roy Waite and George Gray, at various fairs throughout the southeast. When the Wright school convened in the spring of 1914, he was appointed temporary instructor of a May 15 class which included many Canadians who would make their mark in World War I. During the summer, Rinehart took Orville's celebrity guests on skyrides and flew random exhibitions for the company in southwestern Ohio. In September he collaborated with the Elton Aviation Company of Youngstown for a few weeks, flying exhibition in a Model B and single propeller Model E pusher machine.

That summer, Rinehart married his sweetheart, Miriam Dove, between flying engagements. Long absences and related domestic issues took a toll, however, and the childless marriage was officially dissolved after seven turbulent years. Accepting his addiction to wanderlust, he never remarried.

On October 9, Howard, having rejoined the Berger aerial show, experienced a close call while flying at Lynchburg, Virginia. His craft fell out of control from 1,800 feet, turning completely over twice on the way down; this time he walked away uninjured. While flying a "date" in Columbia, South Carolina, he stalled the B and was literally catapulted from his seat. Howard dangled from a wing strut while the plane continued its descent and landed in a nearby cemetery. After this misadventure, he spent a few days in the hospital. Unfazed, Rinehart again toured the South with Berger's flying circus in the late fall.

Miriam Rinehart (left) and sister Ruth aboard Howard's Model B (Rob Grant).

Rinehart, Jack Berger, and William Conover in Mexico (Rob Grant).

Unfortunately for Berger's star attraction, the wily promoter had more than exhibition work on his calendar. In March 1915, Berger arrived in Dayton as the special envoy of Doroteo Arango — aka General Francisco "Pancho" Villa — empowered to purchase several aircraft for the Villistas in northern Mexico. Wright pilots, including Waite, Gray, and Arch Freeman, had flown for Berger on exhibition dates across the South. Due to their rather checkered relationship with him, they were dubious of his claims until he laid down cash for one Wright B to be used for instructional purposes in Mexico, and one Model HS pusher for combat use. Lured on by promises of generous expense accounts and salaries, Howard, now back in Wright employment, and mechanician Bill Conover agreed to deliver the planes.

On their arrival in El Paso, Texas, the men met Hipolito Arango, Pancho's brother, who served as the general's treasurer, purchasing agent, and representative to the United States. Rinehart and Conover were told to convey the aircraft to Juarez, Mexico, where they were to assemble the B for test flights calculated to sell the potential of airpower to the Villista military brass. The Americans spent two weeks putting the Flyer together, and on the appointed day a large gallery of officials appeared on the field. Howard made final adjustments to the engine. Right before he started the motor, a squall swept across the field and completely smashed the fragile machine, but not before it dragged a bruised and battered Conover at the other end of the tether line. Despite this setback, Berger persuaded the Villa High Command to proceed to the battlefront with the HS and to ship the wrecked B back to Dayton for repairs.

Within days, Rinehart's train left the Juarez railway yards bound for Villa's head-

Howard Rinehart (left) and unidentified student (courtesy Dr. Mary Anne Whelan).

quarters at Monterrey. From the start, plans began to unravel. When Conover under-took a side trip into Juarez in search of better cuisine, the train pulled out without him, and Howard would not see his mechanician again until he returned to Dayton. The trip to Monterrey seemed endless to Rinehart, who spent his time trying to wan-gle a portion of his pay from Berger: "It was just like the old exhibition days with Berger. There was food to keep the pilots and mechanics working but talk of salaries was met by promises and conversation. I still had hopes, however, as there was plenty of money in sight. I was rather suspicious that Berger was getting the salaries and that the money remained in his possession." Howard knew little of his boss's back-ground, only that the promoter was "a Jewish-American who was formerly a politi-cian in Chicago."

Villa's train consisted of approximately twenty box and flat cars, including a machine-shop car, a sleeping car, a supply car, a magazine car for aerial bombs, flat cars for assembled aircraft and automobiles with large gas tanks, and an armored rail-car. The train was painted a vivid green and the name on the side of the cars read: "Aviation Division of the North." The troops aboard ranged in age from teenagers to middle-age infantry accompanied by their families and assorted pets. Most of the weapons carried by these soldiers complemented the randomness of the bearers, and from windows and atop cars they fired at game and livestock indiscriminately. Camp fires were lit at each major stop and time allowed for the preparation of meals.

General Villa's headquarters were two Pullman cars located in the Monterrey train yards. In a handsomely appointed car nearby, Howard met Floyd Gibbons of the *Chicago Tribune* and George C. Carothers, a personal representative of President Woodrow Wilson. He renewed an old friendship with Jack Knight, a veteran Wright mechanician, and met Lester Barlow, who managed the general's repair shops. Villa himself impressed Howard with his sincerity and devotion to his peons. Every morn-ing he watched the revolutionary leader stand in the rail yards with bags of looted money, doling out pesos to the poor of Monterrey. At first, Rinehart could only guess at the source of Pancho's largess:

> We learned how he came by much of this money when we asked and obtained permis-sion to attend a meeting of the Chamber of Commerce of Monterrey that had been called by Villa. After all the members and merchants were assembled in the Chamber, the place was closed and surrounded by his bodyguard. Then Villa in person demanded that certain supplies of food, clothing, and money be donated at once, lest every store be seized by his army. In less than 30 minutes the quota was subscribed. Incidentally, Villa's personal guard consisted of about 300 men and boys, the majority being under 16.

When the HS was assembled Rinehart flew several test flights over and around the city. Villa always rode out to the field to observe but declined to go up. He insisted, however, that Howard take along an officer on every sortie as a precaution, lest the Carranzistas bribe him to fly the plane into their territory. As his first assign-ment Rinehart carried a dispatch to one of Villa's regiments camped at a railroad junc-tion 50 miles south of Monterrey. After landing the HS near the train depot, Howard and his escort came under murderous fire from the general's own men and were nearly killed. Matters worsened when Villa upbraided his gringo aviator on several occasions for not flying in fog. Pancho reasoned that since he could ride his horse in fog he could not comprehend why Rinehart would not or could not fly in it. When not in the air, Howard pestered the paymaster who, in turn, referred him to the evasive Berger.

On his second courier mission of March 31, Howard flew from Reynosa to Matamoras with orders for General José E. Roderíguez' siege troops to attack the city. With only the Rio Grande between himself and Brownsville, Texas, he pondered the option of escape, but decided to remain and pursue his unpaid salary. After an hour's flying time, Rinehart began to notice small puffs of white smoke as his HS passed over a rail line parallel to the border. A casual glance at his left wing revealed scores of holes in the fabric. It suddenly occurred to him that he and his chaperon had been subjected to a steady fire for thirty minutes. The men covered the 160 miles to Matamoros in 2 hours and 30 minutes, and once over the city they could see a pitched battle in progress but could not distinguish one army from another. Finally, Rinehart landed about fifteen miles from the city, near the small village of Las Rucias. In the act of alighting from the HS, he nearly stepped on a coiled rattlesnake. For several hours the men hid in brush and in a scum-covered pond, driven to their latter concealment by the approach of troops. In desperation, Howard's Mexican shadow gave him his guns and papers and strolled to the village cantina to learn their whereabouts. An hour passed before the Villista colonel returned with the welcome news that they were among friends.

By 11:00 P.M. the twosome had been taken to General Rodríguez' headquarters, where they were cheered, bathed, fed, and clothed. General Rodríguez then ordered his messengers to return to Villa with a response to his original communication. Rinehart stalled for several hours, however, on the pretense of reconditioning the HS's engine, meanwhile spending every available moment to recover a portion of his pay. When all hope for compensation had vanished, Rinehart tried to wreck the $7,000 plane in a bad landing, but only managed to collapse a wheel. He realized that without a spare, General Rodríguez would have to send him to Brownsville to have the wheel repaired. Howard crossed the Rio Grande, ditched the wheel before reaching Brownsville, spent an hour being debriefed by U.S. Major General Frederick Funston, and headed for Dayton. Amazingly, telegrams from the Villa camp followed Rinehart to his home at 38 West Shaw Avenue. The general promised his erstwhile pilot new terms if he would return to Brownsville and fly the HS back to his headquarters: a salary of $100 per day; a ministership of finances or custodian of mines and natural resources; and even lucrative gambling concessions in some political subdivision of Mexico. Howard declined the offer. Shortly thereafter another former Wright pilot and Villa mercenary, Farnum T. Fish, collected the abandoned HS at Brownsville and returned the machine to its rightful owner. Happy to be home and alive, Howard teamed with Walter Brookins in the spring of 1915 to conduct one of the Wright Company's largest classes, including Canadian, British, and Japanese students.

In mid–August Rinehart was assigned to New York to assist A.B. Gaines, Jr., a former Wright graduate, in beginning the Hudson-Wright School using the new Wright Aeroboat. Once the training facility had been established, he returned to Dayton, where he and Roderick Wright (no relation), his assistant instructor, remained busy during the Wright School's fall term. Up to now, Howard's more celebrated students included Eddie Stinson and sister Marjorie, who later founded the Stinson Aircraft Company; Griffith Brewer, who went on to become an authority on aviation in England; Captain Kenneth Whiting, U.S. Navy; and A. Roy Brown, the Canadian subsequently credited with downing Germany's leading World War I ace, Baron Manfred von Richthofen. In October 1915 Orville sold his original company to an eastern financial group, but Howard continued as one of the organization's instructors at Mineola, Long Island, New York. In addition to his regular schedule he also began to hire out as an experimental test pilot for various companies.

During his free time at Mineola, Howard converted a stock Wright B he had brought with him from Dayton. Originally the machine carried a conventional Wright 4-cylinder motor, but Rinehart replaced the anemic power plant with a peppier Rausenberger 8-cylinder 75 horsepower engine. He also substituted ailerons for warping in controlling the biplane. This radical conversion allowed him to cover the wings with lightweight linen instead of the rubber fabric formerly used on the wings as necessary for warping. Since Howard owned this craft, he eventually flew it back home when the Dayton-Wright Company was incorporated.

The Wright Winter School opened in Augusta, Georgia, on December 20, 1915, with Rinehart as chief flying instructor and William B. Atwater as his assistant. With an enrollment of 25 students, A.B. Gaines, Jr., was called south from the Hudson-Wright School to lend support. While in Augusta, Howard worked closely with an especially gifted pupil, Charles August Koch, a Hoboken, New Jersey, native and University of Georgia horticultural student. Benefiting from Rinehart's lessons and personal guidance, Koch would go on to serve as a World War I flight instructor, a combat fighter pilot (2 victories) for the Republican government in the Spanish Civil War, and a successful aeronautical engineer in civilian life.

The Augusta term closed on May 1, 1916, and the Wright Summer School opened ten days later at Hampstead Plains Flying Field, Long Island, New York, with Rinehart again in charge. It was during this program that he himself earned his "expert pilot" license (no. 50). In July Howard conducted the first flight tests on two Wright machines, the new single propeller tractor fuselage Model L and the twin-propeller, short-span fuselage pusher Model HS. Several months later, the Wright Company merged with the Glenn-Martin Company to become the Wright-Martin Aircraft Corporation, with Rinehart continuing as chief instructor and Arch Freeman as his assistant. Burdened with a large brood of students to train, the pair remained at their posts until late fall.

Following his summer school stint in Long Island, Rinehart returned to Dayton and persuaded industrialist Charles F. Kettering to enter the aircraft business. Kettering was forty years old, a celebrated inventor with nearly one hundred patents,

Howard Rinehart poses before his deHavilland DH-4 at South Field, Dayton, Ohio (Dr. Mary Anne Whelan).

Edward A. Deeds (Isaac F. Marcosson, *Colonel Deeds: Industrial Builder*).

a productive entrepreneur at the helm of two corporations, and a millionaire. It was agreed that Kettering would league with five Dayton businessmen, including his chief business counsel, Edward A. Deeds, in the creation of a syndicate for aircraft production. The Dayton-Wright Airplane Company was capitalized at $500,000, with Deeds as president and Kettering as vice president and technical adviser.

In the meantime, Howard also cajoled his prospective bosses into establishing a flying school and building a new trainer in the bargain. The Wright Field Company was formed, land procured, and North Field laid out on the site which later became McCook Field. This group convinced Orville Wright and some of the old Dayton staff to assist in the design and construction of the first training plane and, designated as Model FS (First Shot), two machines were ready in ten weeks. Utilizing these craft, Howard and Arch Freeman conducted a flying school at North Field during the spring and summer of 1917, training huge classes, including many war-bound Canadians sent there under contract with the United States government. When time permitted, Rinehart continued his custom of test flying new aircraft for Dayton-Wright's competitors, including the Wright-Martin Model V in March 1917.

As the war took its toll on Allied aircraft, Kettering and Deeds announced that well over 3,000 warplanes could be produced by the end of 1917, a phenomenal achievement anticipated as the result of a hefty congressional appropriation. Following extended deliberations between U.S.

and British aviation specialists, the delegates chose the Royal Air Force's deHavilland DH-4 bomber/reconnaissance aircraft as the model most adaptable to American production. Winning the deHavilland bid, Kettering assigned his Delco-Light plant as the new production center. With time and space at a premium, the company moved into the facility section by section, a day behind the wet cement.

When Dayton-Wright was formed in April 1917, Rinehart was named head experimental test pilot and given a flight staff. Factory facilities were not completed until August, at which time the firm began building Standard J-1 trainers. Six months later the government leased the North Field facility as a central engineering post and experimental flying depot called McCook Field. During this move, Rinehart and instructors Freeman and Bernard L. Whelan permanently relocated to the Experimental Station at South Field near the main Dayton-Wright plant.

There the crew conducted the first flight tests of the J-1 trainers, and in early November Howard flew the first Dayton-Wright built DH-4. Reports of the initial flight of the U.S. deHavilland prototype were breathtaking by any standard. According to eyewitnesses, Rinehart nearly lost Freeman, who was occupying the rear gunner's bay during inverted flight. In another potentially disastrous incident Wright mechanicians had been working all day on the carburetor of a Standard J-1 trainer. That evening Kettering climbed into the ship's cockpit with the intention of contin-

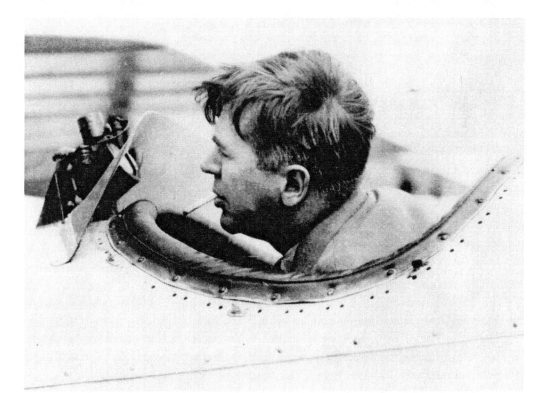

Howard Rinehart in the cockpit of his deHavilland DH-4 (Dr. Mary Anne Whelan).

uing work where the crewmen left off. The engine backfired, setting the plane on fire. As Kettering leaped from the burning ship, Howard and others pushed the destroyed craft out of the hangar and extinguished the flames.

Dayton-Wright encountered innumerable obstacles in Congress. Kettering's plan for an electric air-speed indicator only got built into the DH-4 after intensive lobbying efforts, and his nonexploding fuel tank was killed in committee. His plane, with Rinehart at the controls, crashed near Loudonville, Ohio, on the return flight from a conference with army engineers concerning the tank issue. Acting as navigator in the rear cockpit, Kettering made a poor selection of fields; when Howard touched down, the wheels hit a hummock that sheared off the landing gear and the plane tipped over. Free of injury, Rinehart jumped out and, fearing fire, quickly dragged his passenger from the craft. To his surprise, Kettering showed no concern for his well-being or apprehension about getting airborne again. Engineer Roland V. Hutchinson recalled that Kettering's machine "stubbed its toe, turned over, and the Boss bit the instrument panel, losing some teeth."

Changes were indicated in DH-4 features, such as armament and instrumentation, all of which took time to agree upon, draft and release drawings, and then produce the parts. The deHavillands were assembled in batches, with necessary adjustments noted and incorporated into the next consignment. The original British DH-4 radiator was designed for engines in the 250 to 300 hp range, and the deHavilland's American-made Liberty engine was half again as large. Howard discovered that not only was the original radiator undersized, but that there was also a mismatch in the water flow rate set by the engine coolant pump and the radiator's ability to handle it. Improper air recirculation in the area swept by the propeller also added to overheating. Rinehart's protracted radiator trials resulted in a radiator four times larger than before, with a different internal circulation system. His initial recommended solution consisted of an overhead surge tank and a pipe connection to the header tank of the radiator. The army vetoed this proposed cooling system as being too dangerous if holed in combat.

At South Field, Rinehart participated in the first demonstration of aerial radio telephone. On an appointed day a huge gallery of officers assembled on Route 25 to witness the trial. Howard was in one plane and Dr. Frank J. Jewett, then chief engineer of the Western Electric Company, piloted the other. Once aloft, the flyers began to talk back and forth between themselves. The show was successful. Apparently Jewett did not know or had forgotten that the officers on the ground could eavesdrop on the aviators' conversation and he would make some very pointed remarks about the assembled brass from time to time. Automobile magnate Henry Ford, who was in Dayton to consult with Kettering on matters pertaining to the DH-4s' Liberty engines, stood among the spectators convulsed in laughter, despite the widespread apprehension at what Jewett might say next. Rinehart ignored his partner's rambling and kept to business.

The search for a synthetic fuel was another Dayton-Wright project. Kettering's findings persuaded him that fuel structure held the key to engine behavior. When

Miriam Rinehart, Howard Rinehart, Arch Freeman, and an unidentified British flying officer pose for the camera (Rob Grant).

government reports indicated that the Germans were using a cyclic cyclohexane fuel, he refocused his research. One alternative was to synthesize cyclohexane from benzene. The freezing point of cyclohexane was 40°F, far too high a temperature for aviation use. Dayton-Wright researchers discovered a mixture of cyclohexane and benzol, with a freezing point of minus 40°F that they named "Hecter." This fuel interacted beautifully with the DH-4's Liberty engines. Regrettably, "Hecter" could not be produced in sufficient quantities. Plodding ahead, Kettering increased the cyclohexane output to twenty-eight gallons per day by the end of November 1917. At this time, Dayton-Wright had stockpiled enough cyclohexane to begin flight testing, with Rinehart at the controls.

On Howard's maiden flight with "Hecter" in his tank, he reported: "There was a very perceptible increase of power, both on the ground and at all altitudes reached in our tests (max 22,000 ft.) and the pickup was greatly improved. It was found to be exceptionally free from vibration.... In short it could almost be said that by the use of 'Hecter' a new sensation in flying had been created." Despite this optimistic report, it proved impossible to produce enough of the synthetic fuel to continuously power even a single pursuit.

Tragedy befell two of Rinehart's fellow flyers during this hectic period. Since leaving Dayton in December 1913, Howard's former instructor, Oscar Brindley, had been detached by the Wright Company as a civilian flight instructor to the army. He received a commission following the declaration of war, and his experience qualified him to evaluate the fitness of new experimental aircraft. On May 2, 1918, Major Brindley and an accompanying colonel arrived at South Field to test a DH-4. After a round of greetings with Rinehart and other former pupils, the major began his evaluation of the deHavilland. On his second flight, the plane's engine seized, and Brindley plunged to his death. Within the month, Arch Freeman forfeited his life under precisely the same circumstances.

When the deHavilland project was a year old, the Dayton-Wright management elected to promote its production efforts in a motion picture. A contract was drawn with Universal Film Company, and Carlyle Ellis, director of industrial subjects, was assigned the task. With his cameraman in tow, Ellis filmed the completion of five DH-4s and their subsequent trials. Howard strapped Ellis's assistant into the biplane's rear cockpit, climbed to 5000 feet, and threw the craft into a spin. The intrepid cameraman shut his eyes and started cranking. He kept cranking until the ship leveled off at 1000 feet. Ellis's man was horribly sick, but his shooting proved to be the first film record made from a spinning plane. After his nausea passed, the hapless filmer climbed back into his rear bay and went up again, this time to record Rinehart's entire repertoire of stunts.

During an interview with Orville, Ellis learned that an old Flyer B was being stored in a nearby hangar. "Will you fly it for us, Mr. Wright?" Ellis pleaded. "Why not?" Orville responded simply. Following a delay of several days for overhauling, the fragile machine was brought out to South Field on May 13, 1918. Orville arrived garbed in a leather jacket and helmet. As an enthusiastic crowd gathered, he performed a quick spin over the field. No sooner had Wright landed than Ellis set the Flyer on a line with a deHavilland, both engines warmed and idling. He manned a camera behind the planes, while his assistant took his camera far down the field so as to frame the aircraft head on and follow them up. Ellis asked Orville and Howard to start together on signal and to lift off and climb as rapidly as possible. The Flyer attained altitude first, but the deHavilland zoomed ahead and was hundreds of feet up before the Wright craft cleared a telephone wire downfield. Ellis had made his point. He recalled "Orv's" final solo in minute detail:

> He was headed straight for the camera. He came floating down steadily and gracefully, and hit the ground smoothly not 100 feet from where we stood. His ship rolled lightly forward until it was no more than ten feet from the bus. He stepped nonchalantly to the ground and turned questioningly to us in exactly the right position for a semi close-up portrait — a piece of unconscious action that could not have been better if it had been rehearsed many times…. We waved, of course, and our thanks were as profuse as we could make them. Mr. Wright was like a pleased, but bashful little boy. He thanked us with that wry and short-lived smile and quick wave of the hand.

Howard coaxed Orville into going aloft again, this time as his passenger in the powerful DH-4. No sooner had the deHavilland touched down than an appreciative

Orville Wright (left) and Howard Rinehart stand for a commemorative photograph of Wright's final solo flight, May 1918 (Diana Good Cornelisse, *Remarkable Journey: The Wright Field Heritage in Photographs*).

crowd circled the biplane and compelled both mentor and protégé to stand for a commemorative photograph of Orville's final solo flight.

The production work completed, Rinehart finally took Ellis up and treated him to the experience of climbing through a thick cloudbank. It had been an extraordinary day for everyone. At a show in Madison Square Garden several years later, Ellis ran into Howard. Said Rinehart, pointing to the familiar canary yellow DH-4 in the corner, "The old crate's over there."

In December 1917, the army contracted for an aerial torpedo. Kettering headed three teams assigned to the pilotless bomb's body, engine, and guidance system. The biplane missile was constructed of wood on a chassis ten feet long with a wingspan of fifteen feet. The device was gyroscopically controlled and launched from a track. Its distance mechanism could be set for a specific number of miles, fifty at most. At the end of the range set for the craft a time mechanism tripped, the wings jettisoned, and the torpedo fell, exploding a single bomb containing 400 lbs. of TNT. Kettering's "Bug" was powered by a 2-cycle, 4-cylinder V engine. A code name was assigned the device and misinformation spread about its use to supplement motorcycle riders behind the lines of communication in Europe.

In September 1918, Dayton-Wright assembled for flight-testing a somewhat larger version than the original prototype. Howard, who had recently flight-tested "Hecter," checked out the midget biplane christened the "Messenger." The enlarged aerial torpedo performed flawlessly under Rinehart's control, so perfectly, in fact, that Howard asked to be allowed to fly it into New York City's Madison Square Garden as a company sponsored stunt. His request seemed reasonable to mechanician William Conover, who had great confidence in Rinehart's flying ability: "Rinehart could fly anything. It didn't make no difference what kind of control it had. It could just be the reverse of anything that he ever flew. The minute that thing was off the ground, he had it. He was just that type." Dayton-Wright stalwart Roland Hutchinson attributed Howard's greatness as a flyer to his never-ending quest for perfection and his obsessive/compulsive personality: "He was extremely skillful, of a very inquiring turn of mind, and had a strongly developed imagination. Some of the funny landings he made exhibited remarkable control. They were all simulated emergency landings. He would practice and practice this sort of thing, which apparently had been conducive to reasonable longevity." Fellow test pilot H.T. "Slim" Lewis recalled Dayton-Wright's confidence in its premiere flyer:

> I was a great admirer of Howard Rinehart's ability, and in my aviation experience I never knew a pilot anywhere near as good as Howard. The late Chance Vought (famous aeronautical engineer and aircraft manufacturer) explained my thoughts about him in a very few words one afternoon in the late fall of 1918 in the old Miami Hotel in Dayton. A number of aviation men had gathered around talking shop and Howard's name came up. Chance remarked that there might be, in the future, a few pilots who would be as good as Howard, but he did not think any of us would ever see a better pilot than Howard. We all agreed. Howard not only was an excellent pilot but also he had the engineering ability to go with it, which, as you know, makes a hard combination to beat.

Orville put it best: "He is the one pilot who knows exactly what happens and is able to make a scrupulously honest report of it."

Despite Rinehart's confidence in the midget aircraft, the Messenger had serious shortcomings. The engine seized without warning and proved to be seriously out of balance — on one occasion three out of the four motor bolts were discovered missing after a flight. In testing the Messenger's engine shortly thereafter, Boss Kettering cranked the motor with the propeller, and it backfired and for some reason blew the head off of the motor. The head flew just past Kettering and nearly hit him in the face. Rinehart sat frozen at the controls. In addition, the rear wing spars were seen to flex upward when flying level at top speed. During one Liberty Loan drive, a party of Signal Corps officers rendezvoused at South Field to perform an air show over Dayton. Howard, who was disliked by one of the army flyers, did not get word of the event. His feelings bruised, he planned to take the Messenger aloft. Colonel Deeds learned of Howard's intentions and drove over from his nearby home, threatening to "saw the damn wings off with a handsaw before allowing anyone to fly that thing anymore." The Messenger was known around South Field as Orville's "cute little suicide kite." Toward wars' end, the flying deathtrap was wheeled out and a flight attempted. The engine quit on takeoff and it crashed — no appreciable damage to Howard beyond his pride.

Throughout the fall of 1918, the "Bug" underwent numerous trials with mixed results. Finally, in September 1919, the army transported the missile to Carlstrom Field, Florida, to match it against Elmer Sperry's navy competitor. Dayton-Wright representatives subsequently witnessed crash after crash of its prototype in a state of mortification. On November 25, the army adopted the Sperry-Curtiss JNH version. Undaunted, Kettering continued to develop his "Bug" until company cutbacks killed the project in the late 1920s.

As much a promoter as accomplished pilot, Howard believed that Kettering's public association with flying would benefit the aviation industry. At first, he piloted his boss in a Wright FS to destinations relatively close to Dayton, eventually extending his range in more sophisticated machines. Kettering commissioned Rinehart to fly him to Indianapolis, Indiana, on many occasions in his repeated attempts to have his Delco ignition products installed and used on cars in the Memorial Day races there. In doing so, Kettering was trying to counter the claim that battery ignition was not as effective as ignition by magneto at high speeds. Howard packed supplies, even complete ignition sets, and landed right in the Speedway Park. There Kettering hawked his merchandise, stopping just long enough to argue with some of the contestants. To guarantee that his equipment was correctly installed and that it would perform at maximum efficiency, Kettering impressed Howard to work with him at the track and in the pits both before the race and during the contest.

Armistice Day brought thousands of celebrants into Dayton's street in what the *Dayton Daily News* described as "a shouting, good-natured, jellifying throng." Schools and saloons closed and at McCook Field most of the civilian workers walked off their jobs and formed a victory parade of their own making. The South Field workers marched to Dayton with Howard flying over them a long way in a continuous series of loops. In the downtown district many of the revelers gazed skyward as Rinehart performed a fifteen-minute aerial extravaganza over the intersection of Third and Main streets with a program of "the most daring and novel stunts." Buzzing rooftops filled with waving spectators, he avoided crashing into the city's tallest buildings with a last-minute uplift of his DH-4's nose, and climaxed his routine by flying edgewise between the twin spires of the Catholic Church just south of the railroad station.

Throughout the Great War, and thereafter, Rinehart worked as test pilot and advisor to both the Dayton-Wright Company and the government concerning new aircraft and equipment. Howard and the late Arch Freeman had orchestrated a much publicized aerial program for the Society of Automotive Engineers' summer conclave held in Dayton on June 17 and 18, 1918. For the remainder of that year and the postwar period, Rinehart recorded several notable flights: on November 2, 1918, with Milton Baumann as a passenger, he set a new 2-man altitude mark of 22,400 feet in a deHavilland DH-4 at South Field; on November 30 he piloted Kettering from Dayton to Mineola, Long Island, nonstop in 4 hours, 10 minutes, also in a D-H; on June 17, 1919, he flew Harold E. Talbott from Dayton to Mineola nonstop in 4 hours, again in a deHavilland; and on July 19 he winged Kettering from Wichita, Kansas, to Dayton nonstop in 7 hours, 45 minutes. All of these distance flights were done with the aid of extra fuel tanks and homemade maps prepared by Howard and his crew.

In late May 1919, Rinehart raised his sights with plans to fly the Atlantic Ocean. He read that a U.S. Navy NC-4 flying boat had accomplished this feat only days before, winging its way from Rockaway, New York, to Lisbon, Portugal, in twenty-five hours' flying time (May 16–27). Could he capture the solo record? As Dayton-Wright's chief test pilot, however, he required the permission of management. Howard meant to equip a stripped deHavilland DH-4 with extra fuel tanks and detachable landing gear designed to be jettisoned after takeoff, and to retrace the course (Newfoundland to England) taken a week earlier by Australian Harry George Hawker in his unsuccessful bid. Rinehart's strengths were his navigational skills and record of high-altitude and long-distance flights. Although he obtained the blessings of President H.E. Talbott, Jr., and Kettering in time, E.A. Deeds vetoed the undertaking. The colonel subsequently lamented his decision: "It is one of the regrets of my life that I did not yield to his [Rinehart's] repeated requests. Every time I get out my kicking machine I give myself a few extra thumps on account of it. I think he would have made it, too."

The General Motors Corporation purchased the Dayton-Wright Company in 1920, but continued with design and construction of experimental aircraft. In January of that year telegrams soliciting entrants for the Gordon Bennett International Aviation Cup Race went out from the Aero Club of America. A return wire from Rinehart was received by Aero Club officials in February, declaring Dayton-Wright's plans to build a competitor. Howard guardedly admitted that the projected race was "frankly an experiment," and that he never promised to win, only put up a "damn good show." Dayton-Wright management quickly wrapped the project in a shroud of secrecy, and not even officers of the Army Air Service were allowed to see the racer until August 17, 1920.

The initials given to the craft, RB, suggest that Rinehart and Milton C. Baumann were the two principal designers under Orville Wright's general direction. Other individuals involved with the racer's layout and construction included W.N. Conover, E.F. Longchamps, George Montague Williams, general manager of Dayton-Wright, and H.E. Talbott, Jr., company president. A final unsung member of the team, Charles Hampton Grant, also made a lasting contribution to the RB's creation. A graduate of Princeton and Massachusetts Institute of Technology engineering schools, Grant had built sophisticated hang gliders and worked in a number of engineering positions in the aviation industry. His great passion, however, was model airplanes and their flight characteristics. A longtime friend of Rinehart, Grant now served as a fellow engineer at Dayton-Wright. Howard knew of Grant's research into airfoil behavior under the influence of movable leading and trailing edge devices, and persuaded him the RB's chances of success would be enhanced if the racer's wing curve could be varied while in the air to both fast and slow speed flight.

The RB design reflected both practical and innovative features: a variable camber wing to permit reasonable landing speeds yet achieve the 200 miles per hour necessary to win and stowable landing gear. A streamline fuselage for minimum resistance was sketched which would completely encapsulate the pilot, making him blind forward, above, and below. Access to the cockpit would be through a sliding trap door on top or alternatively through one of large cutouts on the side which accommodated celluloid windows, which once in place, Howard could bulge outward with his head to afford some visibility. The fuselage would be fashioned by binding thin strips of wood tightly with strips of fabric laid in glue, the strips crisscrossing the underlayer each time a layer of wood was added. The final finish was smooth and flawless.

The RB prototype's wings measured 21 feet from tip to tip and the fuselage was 22 feet 8 inches in length. It was assembled with oversize, constant-chord, strut-braced wings which permitted slow takeoff and landing speeds in order to test landing gear feasibility. Each big wheel was mounted on a steel tube V, hinged at its points of contact with the fuselage. Another thick tube extended inside, passing through a phosphor-bronze casting on which was wrapped the shock absorber cords and which itself was threaded to travel along a threaded shaft mounted vertically inside the body. This in turn, could be rotated by the pilot's crank through an arrangement of bevel gears. As the pilot turned the crank, which took between twelve and twenty seconds, the wheels were pulled flush into large, porthole recesses in the fuselage sides. The absence of the standard cross axle allowed the RB to operate easily from fields with high grass. This feature would prove a godsend in France.

Eventually the bulky flight-test wing and struts were removed and a sleek cantilever racing wing put in its place. For lightness and rigidity the wing was constructed from solid chunks of balsa wood. These sections were covered with a three-ply veneer skin which was then painted silver and polished. The operating mechanism for its moveable leading and trailing edge flaps was basic: a large shaft which ran spanwise to bellcranks. One on each side to move the flaps was connected internally by bevel gears to the same pilots' crank that operated the landing gear, thus the gear and flaps always worked in unison. To simplify matters, however, the push-pull shafts were all mounted externally in the wind above the wing.

As the date of the race drew closer, the pressure on the Dayton-Wright crew to complete its work intensified. A particularly thorny problem was the complicated mechanism for actuating the wing flaps on the RB. One evening while Rinehart and company were attempting to correct these bugs in the control system, Kettering and his wife drove up on their way to the theater. The Boss routinely came by to inspect his boys' progress. He sported a tuxedo and contrasted sharply with the disheveled laborers. Some were up on the wing, their shoes removed to avoid damage to the RB's surface, adjusting the contrary mechanism. Kettering kicked off his shoes and climbed aboard to inspect the apparatus and to see what, if anything, he could contribute. Soon he shed his coat and dropped it over the wing. A little later, he reached into his vest pocket, extracted the theater tickets, and said to Mrs. Kettering, "Here, Mother, you had better take these tickets. Ernest will drive you to the theater. I'll have to stay here." On the eve of the RB's transatlantic voyage to Le Havre, France, Howard and Kettering spent the entire night crating the experimental racer for shipment.

The RB was not without critics, even at Dayton-Wright. It was noted that external flap controls would cause great drag, and thereby nullify much of the benefit realized from a flattened wing for high speed. The racer's power plant, a Hall-Scott L-6a, a tall, blocky engine, accounted for the RB's deep fuselage, and the large, flat radiator out front added to drag. In addition, even when wound up at top rpm, the L-6a produced only 250 hp, significantly below the engines of its competitors. Rinehart hoped to achieve high speed through aerodynamic finesse. Unfortunately, the deep fuselage, by placing nearly as much vertical surface area ahead of the craft's center of gravity as the small tail provided behind, added to the plane's poor directional stability. The RB tended to "wallow." Thus, just before his arrival in France, Howard screwed two extra fins onto the tailplane. These additions helped matters somewhat, even though the RB still tended to "wander" through the sky.

Despite the machine's perceived shortcomings, on September 25, three days prior to cup day, Rinehart flew one lap of the 300 kilometer course, throttling back at 165 miles per hour. Although the RB was capable of higher performance, Howard's directional stability degraded at higher speeds, and even with its extra tail fins the racer weaved and hunted alarmingly, compelling him to throttle down. The plane's lack of forward visibility forced Rinehart to fly a zigzag course.

The competition was held at Etampes, France, about forty miles from Paris, on September 28, 1920. In attendance were reporters from the United States, France, Great Britain, Italy, Spain, and Portugal; in addition, military observers from the U.S. and practically every European country, and Japan, were there. Celebrities from the world of aviation drove out from Paris to witness the event: Henry Farman, Louis Blériot, Louis Bréguet, René Caudron, Robert Morane, Marcel Hanriot, and Delage and Barzaine of the Nieuport Company, as well as former Gordon Bennett competitors.

The race covered a 300 kilometer course consisting of three circuits from Villesauvage airdrome to a farm near Gidy and back. The contestants were allowed to take off in handicap order at intervals between 7:00 A.M. and 6:00 P.M. The first to go was the French aviator Georges Kirsch, in his Nieuport 29 V, at 1:25 P.M. He was followed at 1:30 P.M. by fellow countryman Bernard de Romanet in his Spad S.20 bis. At 2:13 P.M. the last French contestant, Sadi Lecointe, took off in another Nieuport 29V, and two minutes later Rinehart started in his RB racer. The other American challenger, Rudolph W. Schroeder, flying a Verville VCP-R which had the most powerful engine (638hp) of any of the competing aircraft, lifted off and was followed at 4:30 P.M. by the only British entrant left in the race, Freddie Raynham in the Martinsyde Semiquaver. Only two flyers completed the course and they were both French: Sadi Lecointe and Bernard de Romanet, only the former having a successful flight, in one hour, six minutes and seventeen seconds, crossing the finish line at an average speed of 168.5 mph; his fastest lap was flown at 172.522 miles per hour.

On cup day, Rinehart was the first U.S. contestant airborne. He cranked up the landing gear and headed south. To many in the crowd the RB resembled a "huge flying mackerel." In twenty minutes Howard reappeared with his gear down and landed. A control cable had failed, jamming his leading edge flap, preventing it from fully retracting. Rinehart calculated that he had no chance to place, unaware that other mishaps would plague most of his competitors, and that had he continued he would surely have come in second. A dejected Frenchman who liked the RB team sadly commented, "Personally, I wish he had won." When Rinehart extricated himself from the plane's cockpit, his usually cheerful smile had surrendered to an expression of sorrow and tears. Groundless charges immediately circulated that sabotage had been the cause of Rinehart's undoing. Of course, these dark rumors went nowhere.

Despite Sadi Lecointe's victory and France's third win and permanent capture of the Gordon Bennett Cup, Dayton-Wright issued an optimistic statement that the

Helen Cox Maloney, daughter of Ohio governor James M. Cox, congratulates Howard Rinehart during the RB's christening ceremony (Rob Grant).

novel features of retractable landing gear and variable camber wings would be used on new commercial and sport aircraft. Regrettably, these advanced features would not be employed for some time. As for Rinehart's RB racer, it would never compete again, although it is now on display at the Ford Museum near Detroit.

At this juncture, both Rinehart and his best friend, Benny Whelan, served as Dayton-Wright pilots. Soon thereafter Whelan was notified that Dayton-Wright could retain only one flyer (Howard) and that Whelan must be laid off. Company management assured him of a job with the parent company, General Motors, but that it would not be flying. In the meantime, Howard had agreed to serve as European observer and representative for the Wright Aeronautical Corporation headquartered in Patterson, New Jersey. On a lunch time visit to the Miami Hotel one afternoon, Monty Williams, general manager at Dayton-Wright, learned from several sources that Howard was planning to leave Dayton-Wright and work for the German aircraft company Dornier in Switzerland, but indirectly through Wright Aeronautical. Williams asked Howard about it, and getting confirmation, he fired Rinehart on the spot and rehired Whelan in his place. Howard, nevertheless, continued as test pilot and development engineer for Dayton-Wright on an irregular basis until June 1, 1923, when General Motors sold the assets of the organization to the Consolidated Aircraft Corporation.

The Versailles Treaty forbade Germany an air force. German aircraft manufacturers such as Albatros, Rumpler, Junkers, and Dornier therefore formulated plans to covertly rebuild the nation's civil aircraft industry as a means to eventual military use. A few companies focused on building commercial designs, while pretending to accept the Allied-imposed ceiling of 13,200 feet. Others developed new prototypes on paper in Germany that were to be constructed at branch plants in other countries. The Dornier Company chose the latter course when it launched a bold initiative to produce the Fatherland's first postwar single-seat fighter, the Falke (Falcon).

Claude Dornier's design was sent to his plant in Rorschach, Switzerland, on the banks of Lake Constance. Wright-Aeronautical sent Howard there to supervise the Falke's production, an assignment that would last nearly a year and a half.

The combination of cantilever monoplane configuration and all-metal construction in a single-seat fighter was regarded as a revolutionary design at a time when fabric and wooden-spar wings that could shred and collapse in a steep dive were still endangering the lives of aviators. Wright-Aeronautical's licensed Hispano-Suiza 300 hp engine was chosen as its power plant, partially through Howard's effective lobbying efforts. Twin machine guns in the nose, a unique underbelly radiator, oxygen equipment, cameras, and radio devices were all standard features. On November 1, 1922, the Falke was unveiled at Dübenhof, Switzerland.

Wright-Aeronautical instructed Rinehart to return with two of the machines, as the U.S. departments of the navy and army had shown an interest in the Falke. The company upgraded the fighters' engines and renamed them the WP-1, Wright Pursuit. One of the planes eventually participated in a fighter aircraft competition held in Dayton in April 1923, where it performed well. The other chaser was turned over to Howard's temporary custody for still more trials at Mitchell Field, Long Island, New York.

When General William "Billy" Mitchell of the Army Air Corps happened to stop over there, Rinehart's superiors insisted that the general test fly their new product. Howard argued that the plane was not ready for "military" trials, but the company overruled him, hoping to sway air corps brass through Mitchell's good report. The Falke was a fast craft and landed at great speed. Mitchell flew and when he touched down he badly damaged the landing gear and one wing. Rinehart, angry and embarrassed over the company's lack of confidence in his judgment, stalked away and never came back, muttering to himself that the heat-treated duralumin repair parts would have to be shipped from Switzerland. He would eventually return to Dayton.

The salvaged Falke was turned over to the U.S. Navy, which entered the fighter in its 1923 pursuit contest. Poor engine performance compromised its standing and, as a result, the United States War Department placed no orders for the Dornier entry. Perhaps Howard felt a degree of culpability in the fact that the Falke's sole weakness was a Wright-Aero product.

Back in Dayton, Howard and fellow pilot Bernard L. "Benny" Whelan would form a most unusual business partnership. Whelan was born in Cincinnati, Ohio, on

Howard Rinehart beaming following a successful flight in his speedy Model L (Rob Grant).

November 19, 1890. He attended the University of Dayton and worked for the National Cash Register Company before pursuing aviation. At twenty-three he enrolled in the Wright Flying School, making his first solo flight just eight days after beginning his instruction and earning his pilot's license no. 247 on July 16, 1913.

Benny continued flying as an avocation at Simms Station until the spring of 1916, when he became a Wright instructor. When the Dayton-Wright Company was formed in the summer of 1917, Whelan joined the staff of test pilots and remained until the end of World War I. He spent the next five years in flight-testing new Wright aircraft, in instruction work, and in cross-country flying as a company pilot for executives Kettering and Deeds. Whelan remained with Dayton-Wright until its parent organization, General Motors, discontinued aeronautical pursuits in 1923.

Even in its commercial death throes, Dayton-Wright possessed an attractive array of aircraft to a budding entrepreneur. Designed by Orville Wright in the winter of 1918-1919, the "OW Aerial Coupe" was the world's first enclosed passenger plane. The biplane accommodated a pilot and three passengers, plus baggage. It could fly nonstop from Dayton to New York City, Washington, D.C., Detroit, Buffalo, and other cities of a comparable distance. Whelan's interest was also drawn to an enlarged DH-4 cargo plane called the KT (Kettering-Talbott) and two Standard J-1 trainers. Dayton-Wright agreed to sell Whelan the OW, a $50,000 craft, for $540.00, an offer he readily accepted, along with the bargain-priced Standards.

Benny worked alone for a month before Howard joined him, thereby officially beginning operations of the Rinehart-Whelan Company on June 10, 1923. The men needed a field and some hangars, so they paid Colonel Deeds a visit. Howard explained to Deeds that they hoped to establish a "passenger-carrying business" and solicited his help, more particularly the use of South Field. The colonel pondered their request, then responded: "You boys have done so much for me, it's high time I did something for you. Of course, it will cost you money — it will cost you one dollar per year."

The new owners hired mechanicians Arthur Horton and Bill Whitman, as well as engineers Frank Whipp and Charlie Furnas. Rinehart-Whelan also acquired a fourth plane, the "KT," together with a complimentary store of spares for its Liberty and Hispano-Suiza engines. Howard instructed his mechanicians to remove the anemic Hall-Scott motors from the Standards and replace them with smooth-running 150 hp Hispano-Suiza power plants. His engineers modified the J-1s' airframe by removing the fuel tank from the fuselage, fashioning a new one, and locating it in the upper wing center section. This alteration made room for two seats, each accommodating two passengers. The pilot cockpit remained unchanged. An imbalance problem with the J-1s, caused by an increase in the weight of a new engine, radiator, propeller, and added passengers, was offset by a reconfiguration of the machine's original sweptback wings. To further improve the Standards, the deHavilland's more durable landing gear was exchanged for each trainer's original undercarriage. With these modifications done, Howard and Benny completed their aerial fleet with the purchase of a 300 hp Fiat Ansaldo Cabin plane.

Each morning the Rinehart-Whelan team would taxi two or more planes across

South Field from the hangars to the west side, which put them near the Dixie Highway. Rinehart stationed a mechanician there to crank engines and otherwise serve as needed. Weekends and holidays brought the locals in droves. Company employees and their families and friends hawked the prospective thrills of a flight with only the promise of dinner as reward for a day's work. Benny recalled one memorable exchange: "C'mon mister, it will make you feel young again; it will take years off your life." Replied the farmer, "Off which end?"

Besides sightseeing flying, there were aerial photography engagements and cross-country flights for business and professional people who remembered Rinehart and Whelan from the Dayton-Wright days and before. Their regular customers included the Inland Manufacturing Company, a division of General Motors whose personnel worked with Dayton-Wright during the war; the Rike Kumber department store; and such organizations as the Civitan Club, the Junior Chamber of Commerce, and the Optimist Club, groups which used the airplane as an effective public relations tool.

The Talbotts employed Howard's flying service for commercial and pleasure flights, either cross-country or locally for aerial joyriding. Harold Talbott, Jr., brought out to South Field as many as thirty-two customers at one time. When Jack Dempsey and Gene Tunney were in training for their championship fight, they both passed through Dayton on publicity tours. Tunney first had a flight with Nelson Talbott, and Howard flew the plane. When Dempsey arrived several weeks later, he went up with another Talbott and Benny was at the controls. During a Ziegfield Follies engagement, twenty attractive high-steppers came to South Field for a lark. A number of "Stage Door Johnnies" swelled ticket sales even more. On September 15, 1924, Rinehart and Whelan shuttled fairgoers to and from Delphos, Ohio, seventy-five miles north of Dayton, for the annual event. Aerobatic flying and parachute jumps were performed with both pilots flying Standards.

The Rinehart-Whelan Company profited from its ties to the Newspaper Enterprise Association (NEA). The airmen's standing assignment was to courier pictures of late-breaking news stories, sporting events, and catastrophes. Immediately following the crash of the navy dirigible *Shenandoah* near Cambridge, Ohio, on September 23, 1925, both Howard and Whelan flew to the site. Working their way through the carnage, they collected negatives from the press and raced to NEA headquarters in Cleveland to deliver them and claim a $1,000 payment.

As early as April 22, 1924, Rinehart had decided that a more lucrative area for flying lay in California. Acting on impulse, he took the company's best plane with him, much to his partner's dismay. Howard's argument had been persuasive, at least to himself: that covering three fixed fields would be no more difficult than their current two airstrips in Dayton and Columbus; that the California venture would be seasonal in nature; and that the two of them (Rinehart and Whelan) would be available at all three sites on a routine basis. Once there, he concluded that flying payroll shipments, usually in gold, to Americans working in Ensenada, Mexico, would prove sufficiently rewarding. U.S. corporations and businesses were ready customers as there were too many "holdups" south of the border.

Howard Rinehart (left) and business partner Bernard L. Whelan (courtesy Dr. Mary Anne Whelan).

Howard and a new mechanician, Charlie Roberts, established a makeshift airport right on the dry Los Angeles riverbed. From this border location they flew passengers and payrolls to Ensenada. When time permitted, they also sold airplane rides in Tijuana. Howard and Roberts were regulars in Tijuana's huge "Mexicali Bar," and they became friendly with the proprietor of "The Golden Jackass Bar and Restaurant" in Ensenada. The manager of the latter saloon owned a burro of a golden color and Howard, as a joke, consented to fly the animal to the "Mexicali Bar, "experiencing only minimal damage to his OW's cabin.

Rinehart's anticipated business opportunities failed to meet his lofty expectations, so he then prepared to return to Dayton. Unfortunately, the OW experienced engine trouble on his flight home and he crash-landed in eastern Indiana. Howard walked away from the wreck, but the plane's loss depressed Whelan for weeks.

Finally home in the fall of 1926, Howard found that his business was faced with an immediate demand for Liberty engine crankcases and other parts. A search revealed a source of supply in San Diego, California. Whelan flew down, located the junk dealer, bought and crated the engine parts, and shipped them to Dayton. Unbeknownst to Rinehart and Whelan these spares, destined for Detroit markets, would eventually power bootlegger's boats used in ferrying liquor across the St. Lawrence River from Canada into "dry" America.

Soon after his arrival, Howard began the financially risky project of converting Le Rhone (French rotary) engines, of which there were large quantities in war surplus, into the simpler and more efficient radial type. His plan required the services of a mechanical engineer for the design and fabrication of necessary parts. Milton Baumann joined the team, but over time, following tests and finally flight tests in a "Jenny" JN-4D, the trials did not succeed, because of which, company resources had been greatly depleted. As a result, it became necessary to sacrifice the Ansaldo Cabin plane to a locally prominent bootlegger. Still in debt, however, Howard and Benny had to also place the KT cargo carrier on the auction block. This loss brought the flight inventory down to two modified Standards.

Meanwhile, business continued as before, placing greater demands on the remaining machines. Harold Talbott, Jr., convinced Howard to fly in a large supply of whiskey from an Ontario distributor for his daughter's wedding. In no time his engineers had altered the appearance of the J-1s to resemble single-seat pursuit aircraft. A cowling was provided extending all the way from the motor cowls over the two passenger seats, obscuring them completely. The fake cowling was piano-hinged on both sides with a rod passing through for access or secure closure as needed. With this modification, the space originally meant for four passengers was made available for crates of booze. On the appointed day, Howard and Benny flew to La Salle, Ontario. After dinner they met with the distributor and left him Talbott's order. They planned delivery the following day. The consignment was transported to their idling planes in a delivery truck with an accompanying car to thwart any intruders. The airmen flew two trips of fifteen cases per plane to fill the orders of the Talbott clan.

Rinehart-Whelan Company promotional flyer (Ruth M. Reinhold, *Sky Pioneering: Arizona in Aviation History*).

In September 1927, Howard suggested to Benny that they fly the two remaining Standards to Phoenix, Arizona. Their mechanician, Bert Van Dellen, Jr., remained at his home in the South Field hangars, supplied with a list of chores and his check. Howard and mechanician Charlie Roberts went ahead, and Benny followed in a few days. When Whelan arrived in Phoenix, he discovered that his partner had built a structure of wood and chicken wire, large enough to overhaul engines. Howard subsequently hired a "mechanician's helper," a Swede named Nels, who lived in this shack.

Rinehart, Whelan, and his wife, Blanche, resided with a friend, Claude Law, at his combination home and "Rio Grande Filling Station." It was through Law's influence that his boarders were able to rent the area used as their airport. Law's good standing with the Rio Grande Oil Company also helped in another way. With his recommendation, the company agreed to furnish the Ohioans motor oil and gasoline on a "no charge" basis. In return, Howard allowed its representatives to paint their logo and name on the side of each plane.

Rinehart-Whelan's clientele included wealthy sportsmen, ranchers, itinerant cowboys, and even "ladies of the evening." A half dozen of these local entrepreneurs came out to Van Buren airport one afternoon, enjoyed their flights, and on leaving presented business cards. The flying routine never varied for sightseers. Taking off toward the west (the wind always blew from that direction), Howard or Benny was generally about 1,500 feet high in minutes and over the outskirts of Phoenix. Then, veering to the right, they headed toward Camel Back Mountain, which offered their clients a great panoramic view of the area. On the return leg to the airstrip, and just before throttling the engine to glide in for a landing, Rinehart or Whelan would point out the location of Four Peaks, the four mountains that encircle Phoenix as guardian sentinels.

The flyers had brought a parachute from Dayton, and they soon located a candidate who would jump every Sunday for $25.00. Blanche Whelan passed the hat among the spectators and added the collection to the promised sum. The jumper's name was Bernhardt, so Howard affixed the nickname of "Sarah" after the famous theatrical figure. The jumps were made between four and five P.M., with Howard taking three passengers along with the featured attraction. Whelan flew alongside Rinehart's Standard with four passengers aboard. All eyes were on "Sarah" as he leaped from the converted trainer.

On one occasion some of Bernhardt's parachute shrouds overlapped the main canopy, thereby accelerating his descent and causing both ankles to be sprained in landing. When "Sarah" had to forego his jump the next week, the company's Swedish handyman, Nels, offered to "yump," but Howard declined his services.

During the winter of 1927-1928, Rinehart-Whelan welcomed an aerial photographer named E.D. Newcomer. Initially, Newcomer's business flourished, but by 1928 commissions had fallen off alarmingly. Dreading the prospect of a layoff, he contacted W.W. "Weiss" Knorpp, the business manager of the *Arizona Republican*, proposing that his company be engaged to shoot a series of aerial photographs of the states' mines, resorts, and other commercial establishments for the newspaper. Knorpp warmed to the idea and plans were drawn for Arizona's first airborne pictorial survey. The Rinehart-Whelan/*Arizona Republican* project began on May 28, 1928, and lasted nearly three weeks, covering 3,160 miles and adding 203 pictures to Newcomer's portfolio. Included in the collection were shots of thirty-five cities, in excess of twenty mining complexes, fifteen industrial plants, a host of resorts, public buildings, agricultural developments, ranches, dams, and airports. A combination of burdensome goggles, bone chilling winds, bulky camera equipment, and bucking cockpit hampered Newcomer's work, and yet he produced photographs of amazing clarity.

In his time away from the flying service, Howard relished networking in his favorite organizations, the Association of Old Time Airmen and the Early Birds of America. For his inclusion in the Early Birds, Rinehart backdated the time of his first solo by a full year. Benny would later observe, "The record shows his license number 266, dated October 1, 1913, several months following mine which is number 247 dated July 13, 1913, although I often heard Howard tell people he was trained in 1912, reflecting a trait Howard had of slight misrepresentation if it added something to the length of his flying career." When the Early Birds sponsored its collection of vintage aircraft for the Edison Institute Museum in Dearborn, Michigan, Howard responded to an appeal with his usual levity:

> Can't find a Wright "B" either — I really believe an original one does not exist. I have a real "Honest to Gawd" Wright motor, one I used to train in here (Dayton) and at N.Y. — will take seven million dollars for same — or — will give it to the Early Birds if they will put it in an "Honest to Gawd" exhibit of EB and title it honestly, mebby.

Both groups had a terrible time keeping track of Rinehart's whereabouts. The Early Birds' membership rosters placed him at numerous points in the western hemisphere, even giving his ancient address at the American Consulate in Belem (Para), Brazil.

Before the end of the winter's flying, Whelan received a letter from Colonel Deeds telling him of the creation of the Pratt & Whitney Aircraft Company, its objective to build a 400 hp air-cooled engine, and its need for a competent test pilot. Benny was advised to report to P & W's headquarters in Hartford, Connecticut, on May 1, 1928. Howard confided that they would never become wealthy in their present enterprise, and that Whelan should seize the opportunity. Besides, the partners were about to lose their facility in Dayton, and Rinehart seemed more engrossed in working on a small plane design with Milt Baumann. Howard sold one of the Standards to a local pilot, as they still had two planes and an automobile to get back to Dayton.

Bernard Whelan remained with P & W's parent organization, United Aircraft Corporation, until 1931. At this juncture, Hartford was building a new municipal airport and Whelan became manager there until 1943, when he secured the position of general manager of Sikorsky Aircraft, another United Aircraft subsidiary, retiring as vice president in 1959. Rinehart continued to manage the remnants of the flying service in partnership with H.P. Williamson, a prominent Dayton attorney, and abandoned the business in 1932.

That same year, Rinehart developed the Zapp flap, installing it on an Aristocrat plane and demonstrating it to the Ford Company and United Aircraft, this being the first auxiliary control flap ever used. He also developed and built a small metal plane he called the Rambler, powered by a 4 cylinder, air-cooled inverted type engine. His marketing activities were discontinued, however, due to global financial conditions. This business reversal represented Rinehart's last active involvement in aviation.

Seeking a change in his life and fortune, Howard returned to the Amazon Valley in 1933, where he operated a rubber plantation at Santarém, Brazil. For six years he divided his time prospecting, cruising timber, rubber, and other tropical products down the Amazon River, and exploring. Howard organized his own expedition into the little-known Mato Grosso region, spending a year on the unexplored Rio des Mortes in prospecting ventures, and another year in the interior of British Guiana. He was familiar with all conditions of life in the tropics, as well as the customs and spoken idioms of most of the Indian tribes.

During his first year in the Amazon, Howard led an unsuccessful expedition into the Mato Grosso region in search of the celebrated English explorer, Percy Harrison Fawcett, who had disappeared on May 30, 1925, in his quest for the fabled pre–Andean lost city of "Z." In a subsequent letter to Nelson Talbott (brother of Harold E. Talbott, Jr. (see p. 71), Walter Camp, All-American tackle at Yale (1913–15), coach of the Dayton Triangles professional football team, 1916–21, and president of the N.S. Talbott Company) back in Dayton, Rinehart vividly described his life on the edge:

Dear Bud: December 30 [1933]

No reason for this letter except that I met an old acquaintance of yours from Philadelphia, a young man by the name of E.F. Buckley, who is down here shooting jaguars or attempting to. This is the poorest hunting country [British Guiana] in South America and I sent him on down to the Amazon for his sport.

Have become a regular explorer and something of a prospector. In the last year [1933] I have worked down here from Sao Paulo, Brazil, in mostly little known lands and a great deal of it unknown. Have had a wonderful time starving, mucking through swamps, drowning, dying of thirst and being eaten up by insects. Funny thing this human nature — have actually enjoyed most of it.

Last year [1933] was back in Mato Grosso state in Brazil on the trail of the lost Englishman Fawcett. Made a much better attempt than any of the big financed expeditions and found a wonderful garden of Eden up there. Am returning as soon as I work out three claims that I have up in the back of this colony.

Buckley came to see me in the hospital here [Georgetown, BG]. Had just been shipped down from the hinterland 400 miles and a three week trip by canoe with peritonitis, a result of acute appendicitis. [I] was four weeks in the savannahs alone sick before a white man found me and shipped me down here to the hospital. Okay now.

Am leaving here for up country this week and so will not have any mail service. I will be back here during March. Won't you write me at that time, care of Nottingham House, and tell me all the local news?

This Demarara rum is, I think, the best. It costs about 60 cents an imperial gallon. Give my regards to all.

Sincerely hope you and all your friends had the season's best.

Yours,
Howard Rinehart

On a return trip to the United States in 1940-1941, Rinehart tried unsuccessfully to establish a government-sponsored flying school in the South. Harry D. Geyer, a former plant superintendent of the old Dayton-Wright Airplane Company, hosted Howard during this visit. He remembered his guest's animated sales pitch for a new vegetable-type rubber emulsifier he claimed to have discovered in the Brazilian jungle. What entertained the Geyer household more than Rinehart's feats as a trailblazer and self-professed jungle botanist, however, was his remarkable fluency in the Portuguese language. After America's entry into World War II, he freelanced for the Rubber Development Corporation, a subsidiary of the Reconstruction Finance Corporation in South America. His objective was the location of large rubber tree stands in the interior.

With the Japanese seizure of East Asian rubber plantations in 1942, the United States government looked to Brazil as an alternate supplier. To reach the best trees on the high plateaus, Rinehart and a horde of U.S. rubber men, boat builders, oil experts, engineers, pilots, mechanicians, telegraphers, accountants, and doctors journeyed 1,100 miles up the Amazon to a godforsaken outpost named Higinio's. In the midst of this huge effort, Howard no doubt realized that the RDC's chances of replenishing a 600,000 ton deficit in America's rubber stockpile would be sorely tested by a number of factors: the lingering effects of a global depression; a primitive transportation system; rampant disease among a prospective labor force; an acute shortage of supplies; governmental greed and a cumbersome Brazilian bureaucracy; and chronic labor shortages.

Perhaps Rinehart recalled rubber's heyday in the Amazon before he left his adopted land for Dayton, when thousands of seringueiros, or rubber gatherers, flocked to the Basin for work. Many did not leave the region alive due to starvation and employer maltreatment. The fortunes were amassed by the middlemen and the executives of large companies who exploited the seringueiros while destroying smaller rubber producers. In the early thirties Howard's own modest plantation had succumbed to both a weak market and this cutthroat monopoly system. The RDC now faced the same callous unwillingness of the rubber interests to cooperate on its terms, which stipulated that the companies turn over U.S. supplies at cost to the laborers. The companies, accustomed to making at least 50 percent profit on everything sold to the seringueiros, continued to fleece the gatherers. When RDC officials complained, many of the merchants allowed their collectors to do without rather than reform their policies. Such institutionalized fraud benefited local German agents who never tired of reminding the workers of their historical expendability. Small wonder that of the 50,000 seringueiros needed by the RDC, only 7,000 left their homes in the central provinces to go to the Amazon. By early 1945, with ultimate victory over the Axis finally assured and the success of synthetic rubber production a recent reality, the RDC began to downsize its "rubber army," and Rinehart chose to move on.

Back in the United States in 1947, Howard renounced his life's passion for aviation during a January 16 press conference sponsored by the Early Birds association and held at the Shoreham Hotel in Washington, D.C. He conceded that although he had made a living in aviation for most of his life, he now believed it "too bad that the airplane was ever invented." Ignoring the technological progress made in the field and his own contributions toward that advancement, he concluded that the airplane "gives little saving in time, and that its use is still too highly dependent upon the weather to be thoroughly practical." Before abandoning his native land yet again for Brazil, he tried his hand at avocado farming in Homestead, Florida, and operating a hunters' retreat in Clinton, Virginia, but without success.

When Howard returned to the U.S. in March 1949, he tarried in Miami long enough to have his will drawn and to sit for an interview. In a March 21 meeting with a *Miami Daily News* reporter, he gave a highly subjective perspective on this most recent phase of his life, lamenting that civilization (American society) had become "too contentious and restrictive," bound by "too many tangled laws." Following the Rinehart-Whelan business venture in 1932, he "forgot about aviation" and became the owner of an Amazonian plantation, but "lost out in the famous bubble-bursting of the rubber industry there." He subsequently "bought into" an avocado grove near Miami, but changed his mind after the area became "crowded with too many people." He told the journalist that he planned to return to South America and settle down near Campo Grande in the Mato Grosso, acquire a homestead of 1,000 acres, and live "without too much confusion ... with the best people in the world." His concessions to civilization would be a kerosene-driven refrigerator for game, a radio, and a new pair of bifocal glasses. Howard next proceeded to Washington, D.C., to visit an old comrade and fellow Early Bird, Ernest L. Jones. From there, he started to New Orleans to prepare for his trip back to Brazil. On July 18, he wrote Whelan from Hattiesburg, Mississippi:

> Was all ready to sail from N.O., but had to turn it down — the "capital" was too much gangster type — couldn't take it — then I am not as young as I once was — strange!
>
> Have no plans — just about fresh run out — my ulcer and I are having a little armistice here.
>
> Am thinking of going on a strike — seems the modern idea. Now, I have to concentrate on what to strike against and about — only have myself left as a grievance — but that figures out quite an ample reason.

On July 29, 1949, Rinehart's body, with a .32 caliber pistol clutched in his right hand, was discovered beside his jeep outside a Hattiesburg apartment house where he had resided for nearly a month. In his suicide note, the sixty-four-year-old adventurer asked that Whelan and his Miami attorneys be notified of his death, and that there be no funeral ceremony whatsoever. His note included thirty dollars with instructions that the money be spent for expenses, "and if there was any change left that it be used to 'turn down the glass.'" Casual neighborhood acquaintances recalled him saying that he did nothing for a living, referring to himself as "just a wanderer."

Howard was returned to Dayton, where he was buried in Memorial Park Cemetery, which is between Dayton and Troy, Ohio. Only two cars comprised the funeral procession of one of the city's most colorful aviation pioneers. Three funeral home employees, Whelan, and his sister, Anna, were the mourners at graveside. Two years later his body was exhumed from the Rinehart family plot and reinterred at another location in the cemetery. On June 17, 1951, a granite monument was erected over Howard's grave. Those responsible for placing the shaft were Messers. Kettering, Deeds, and Whelan. The monument stands seven feet, ten inches high on a six-foot base. Under a reproduction of a Wright Flyer B is this inscription:

> Howard M. Rinehart—1885–1949—Pioneer American aviator whose natural courage and interest in the new and untried made him an ideal test pilot. His ability to analyze plane performance and accurately report his findings contributed much to the advancement of aviation during the early years of its development.

Bernard J. Losh, staff writer for *Camerica* magazine, wrote of the occasion:

> The three men (all pioneers in aviation) were grateful because Howard M. Rinehart had lived and they were now being permitted to bestow on him, in death, the affection he would have been too modest to receive in life. It has been said of Rinehart that he was a soldier of fortune whose restless mind denied him almost every conventional viewpoint. He was fascinated by achievement but not in the exercise of accomplishment. As quickly as he mastered a problem he was through with it and turned to the next one. In reinterring his remains in the plot they bought and providing the monument, his three closest friends were actuated solely toward making amends to a man who seems to have been overlooked by his times.

EPILOGUE

For the casual reader, the lives and careers of the six civilian aerial pathfinders profiled in this book may seem to be maddeningly disparate, and not offered collectively as a neatly packaged archetype of Wright alumni. On further reflection, however, one will perhaps concede that they did share, in their own way, personal and professional traits both common to them and necessary to anyone in their line of work: extraordinary courage; aeronautical savvy regarding the flying and maintenance of their own and other aircraft; a restless temperament which pushed them to levels of accomplishment in competition and technological discovery even they found difficult to believe; and an indomitable spirit which placed them remarkably close to pioneer aviation's inner circle of the renowned. In truth, one finally comes to the realization that these airmen, in the aggregate, represented essential everymen, acceptably reflective of the 119 graduates of Wilbur and Orville Wright's profoundly influential flying academy.

The foregoing is not to contend that these airmen were equally talented, or that they did not bring their own peculiar gifts, interests, and personal commitment to bear on one assignment or private undertaking over another. As Wright employees Rinehart, Freeman, Welsh, and Gill made exhibition, instructional, demonstration, test, and acceptance flights, with Gill's brief stint devoted to exhibition work, and Rinehart's Johnny-come-lately appearance in Dayton excluding him from their recently defunct team. Rinehart showed near genius as an aeronautical engineer and design specialist under Orville's supervision, while Gill proved equally innovative on his own. Although a mediocre exhibition flyer by instinct and belief, Welsh displayed the patience and level-headedness which made him perhaps Orville's best flying instructor. Bergdoll and Gill flew basically as independents, the former as a high-rolling amateur pilot and the latter as a self-sustaining competition flyer. Wealth and social position allowed both men to assume the mantle of patrons to the burgeoning culture of aviation. In terms of the promotion of this culture, these same individuals did as much as any of the six birdmen in bringing the spectacle of flight to the general public. Only Gray formerly served in the army's Aviation Section, enlisting as an aircraft inspector and rising to the rank of captain. Equally impressive were the roles of Rinehart, Welsh, and Freeman, who enjoyed the army's confidence as aviators and consultants, working as they did for the military's leading aircraft contractor. Finally, the contributions of Freeman and Gray regarding the application of airpower in combat situations are significant and praiseworthy, for clearly these fellows were not preaching to the converted.

By most accounts, all six Simms Station graduates lionized the Wrights, although most were closest to Orville, and Rinehart knew "Orv's" late brother, Wilbur, only through reputation. Rinehart never forgot Orville's benign intervention in the summer of 1913, when factory manager Grover Loening would have barred him from flying instruction. In his 1935 memoir, *Our Wings Grow Faster,* Loening suggested that Orville favored Howard from that fateful meeting until their deaths only a year apart.

> A very simple, unprepossessing-looking young man came in to enroll in the school. He knew nothing about motors, he didn't drive a car, he could not ride a bicycle, he had never taken up any sport, he did not even ride a horse.... He had saved up the money and now wanted to learn to fly. If ever there was an obviously unsuitable and unlikely pupil it was this one, and I did not hesitate a moment to tell him the school was full and we could not enroll him. I even tried to discourage him from wanting to take up flying. But he insisted on waiting out in the hall to see Mr. Wright and left my office. Hours passed and he still waited outside. Finally Orville arrived and talked to him in the hall for about five minutes and then burst into my office saying, "What do you mean by turning down as promising a candidate as this?" "But Mr. Wright," I replied, "he has absolutely no qualifications whatever." "Not at all," said Orville. "He will make an excellent flyer." Orville was right.... In no time he became a sensationally good pilot, teacher at the school, test pilot, stunt flyer, and famous for his skill and technique all over the United States. Orville's judgment was based on this: he had good eyes, a total absence of any nervous temperament, and persistence. Of course, it must be admitted that Orville from then on took more interest in Rinehart's training than he did in that of the other pupils at the school, and although as a rule pupils were mostly trained by [Oscar] Brindley, Rinehart had much personal training from Orville himself.

It was no accident that Howard flew alongside Wright during Orville's last official flight at South Field on May 13, 1918, "Orv" in a Model B, and Rinehart in a Dayton-Wright converted DH-4.

In the same vein, Al Welsh's desperate attempt to master Orville's unstable Model C "Mankiller" at College Park suggests that he was acutely mindful of what its sale to the army would mean to his boss, the Wright organization, and his own sense of obligation to the man who had helped raise him from obscurity and presented him with an enviable career and the means to hobnob with America's most notable persons of wealth and social position, political influence, and military standing. One may recall that Orville had retained Al's services when he dissolved his exhibition team in the fall of 1911, seeing Welsh's "safe and sane" approach to flying as reflective of his own views on the subject. Al felt comfortable with his boss's danger-avoidance position regarding aviation and had no qualms about conducting the Model C's trials; after all, Orville had both flown and endorsed the machine's airworthiness, despite growing concern as to its safety. Welsh's misplaced confidence in his mentor's assurances resulted in his death and a financial and public relations setback for the Wright Company. Time and additional Model C crashes would show that the findings of pilot error charged against Welsh's sterling flying record may have been inconclusive at best, a rush to judgment with other interests in the balance.

The erratic Bergdoll frequently went to Orville for both professional advice and consolation in times of trouble, perhaps seeing in him the father figure which had been missing in his turbulent youth. Wright repaid Grover's trust in full measure, even in the face of an unappreciative federal judicial system.

An incorrigible cynic might suspect that perhaps a few of these Early Birds regarded the Wrights with a more discerning eye, especially those who were handicapped by limited financial resources. No one can deny that these men benefited from Wright training, but in every respect they earned their keep at Simms Station, and their instructional fees were not insubstantial. For civilian trainees such as Gill and Bergdoll, who could purchase a Wright machine outright, entrée into the world of aviation was greatly facilitated — a far cry from Rinehart, Freeman, and Welsh who, at least in the early going, could get airborne only through their connection with the Wright organization. Who's to say, however, that these flyers were not the greater beneficiaries, exposed as they were to the steadying influence of the Wrights and a nationally recognized flying school, and backed by a phalanx of skilled aircraft engineers and designers, mechanicians, machinists, and assembly line fabricators. In sum, one might conclude that for Rinehart, Welsh, and Freeman, despite the liability of Orville's noncompetitive wages, flying proved to be a joyful vocation; whereas with Bergdoll and Gill its pursuit amounted to a no less enthralling avocation minus the discipline mandated by Wright management. Gill did mature in his role as an aviator during his brief time with the Wrights, bolstered then and later through painful trial and error and a great store of self-confidence. Although perhaps a better natural flyer than Gill, Bergdoll fell behind in this maturation process, accepting his station as a local amateur stunt pilot who, despite his ability to draw enormous crowds, nevertheless shunned most licensed meets, and failed to network with the country's foremost aviators. And yet, despite these shortcomings, Bergdoll's personally funded aerial demonstrations had a positive impact on the public's perception and reception of amateur flying as a sport, not only in Pennsylvania, but along the Atlantic seaboard as well.

Gray's career differed markedly from those of his fellow classmates in that he basically flew on his own as a full-time exhibition pilot and, aided by an attractive wife who served as his manager and publicity agent, made good money following the seasons largely between Florida and New Jersey seaside resorts until the crowds became jaded, a full six years after Orville's ill-starred team had folded. Wright had helped the financially strapped youth through flying school, going so far as allowing Gray to wreck his personal plane in preparing the novice for his pilot's license. Undoubtedly, Gray never forgot these kindnesses shown to him by Orville. Conversely, Wright had denied him employment in Dayton at the most critical period of his budding career, and his hero's stiff 20 percent daily fee for the use of Gray's own Burgess-Wright machine had helped end the freelancer's exhibition career. Orville, nonetheless, represented for Gray a living benchmark by which he would measure his own professional standards. On November 14, 1927, the Grays attended the presentation of the *National Geographic's* Hubbard medal to Charles Lindbergh in honor of his transatlantic flight. As President Calvin Coolidge was about to make the presentation, "Jack" noticed that her husband had fixed his gaze on two empty chairs in the front row of the Washington Auditorium. When she inquired as to his thoughts, Gray wistfully responded that he felt that Wilbur and Orville ought to be sitting in the vacant seats, explaining that Colonel Lindbergh's remarkable undertaking was but a natural extension of the brothers' even greater achievement of first flight. Unarguably, Gray's feelings were heartfelt, but his assumption of Orville's absence from the ceremony was misplaced, as Wright was proudly seated on stage and no doubt shared his former student's sentiment.

The logistics and everyday dangers facing these six pioneer flyers took an awful toll on extended and nuclear families alike. Parents and siblings fretted over the safety of sons and brothers out on exhibition tours or flying demonstration and acceptance flights for the Wrights, either in Dayton or on the road. Over time, neglected wives mustered little sympathy for husbands who were always away and with meager earnings to show for their alleged sacrifices. Miriam Dove Rinehart divorced Howard after a childless marriage of seven years, charging him with personal humiliation (stemming from frequent bouts of public drunkenness), nonsupport, and virtual abandonment. Freeman's first spouse left him over his reversal of a sacred promise to quit aviation, and his second wife was so ignorant of Arch's background that she could not recall for the coroner her late husband's birthday. Poor Gill did not survive long enough to marry the girl of his dreams, but he did suffer the indignity of a breach of promise suit as a result of his prolonged absenteeism from his fiancée's company. The marriages of Welsh and Gray remained intact largely because the Grays were a traveling team and the Welshes kept residences in both Dayton and Washington, with Anna accompanying Al on many of his engagements. Rich, handsome, and unattached, Bergdoll enjoyed playing the field of eligible socialites, using his Model B to attract the fairest of the fair sex.

The flyers considered in this study took life one day at a time, scarcely hagridden about their immediate safety as pilots and the prospects for their post-flying careers. They embraced the risks of flight as an acceptable liability, far preferable to succumbing to life's mundane routines as experienced by the majority of their fellow countrymen. Ironically, with the exception of Bergdoll, given his penchant for aerial daredeviltry, each of these aviators had experienced multiple smashups, so it was only reasonable for them to assume that it would always be the other fellow flying west at the critical juncture of a dangerous test flight or a highly competitive meet.

To a man, these birdmen accepted human error, rather than the intervention of blind fate, as the only acceptable cause of killed and maimed colleagues. Besides, the hectic schedules endured by these men left little time for grim introspection. Perhaps Gill did experience an unsettling premonition on the afternoon of his death at Cicero Field, but there is no record of either Welsh or Freeman meeting their tragic ends after comparable dark epiphanies. To the contrary, Al was making plans for spending more quality time with his family on the eve of his fatal crash.

Kith and kin were shocked to learn of Rinehart's suicide, given his role as a surviving elder statesman of Orville's pioneer circle. The conjecture surrounding his still unexplained action includes the absence of a stable family environment; his own volatile temperament; years of brooding over his dashed hopes for flying the Atlantic in 1919 and winning the Gordon-Bennett race the next year; the implosion of his once promising charter service; his Amazonian explorations and ancillary business projects which came to little beyond satisfying his need for wanderlust; his inability to establish a southern flying school; and, worst of all for this adventurer, the constraining effects of advancing age. Ironically, traveling salesman Ivan J. Dove, Rinehart's former father-in-law, perhaps unknowingly offered another take on Howard's final desperate act twenty-seven years earlier.

On March 1, 1922, in the aftermath of the couple's divorce, Dove wrote Miriam while staying at the Berkshire Hotel in Reading, Pennsylvania, asking her to intercede with Howard in hopes of securing several favors from him. In his missive, Dove expressed a surprisingly benevolent attitude toward the man who had caused his child so much grief, and even stated that Rinehart's seemingly unstable nature was, in his opinion, the result of an unhappy childhood. He wrote in part:

> He [Howard] needs friends who know him and he may come out all OK in future. I know him from just a kid and I know that to a certain extent he is a victim of circumstances and influences in his younger life and over which he had no control. That has brought things to where they now are. I would like to meet him again. I really do feel sorry for him. I never want you and he together again....Yet in all this I just can't feel like casting off old How [Rinehart] to the winds.

Less than three weeks later management at the Berkshire discovered Dove's body in his room, the cause of death later diagnosed as an abdominal aortic aneurysm. Regrettably, whatever the York, Pennsylvania, native knew of Howard's past, he took it with him to the grave.

As for Gray and Bergdoll, both outlasted their flying days and survived into their seventies, the former a credit to early aviation, the latter a tragic figure whose brilliant potential as one of Orville's elite airmen was wasted in a life of self-indulgence, disillusionment, and eventual alienation from the land of his birth.

Taken as a group, the diffuse contributions made to pioneer aviation by Welsh, Gill, Bergdoll, Freeman, Rinehart, and Gray were both similar and dissimilar, anomalies expressed through the shared love of flying, individual aeronautical interests, and multifaceted personalities. Their stories as privileged flying sportsmen, national and international competition pilots, barnstormers, and tinkerers dedicated to the perfectibility of heavier-than-air machines made the headlines and added immeasurably to the rich lore of old-time flight. The tragic path taken in later life by one of their number notwithstanding, the remarkable records of these men attest to the fact that the extraordinary flying school established by the Wrights proved to be an invaluable gift to early aviation in 119 fascinating and productive ways.

APPENDIX A:
WRIGHT TIMELINE

1900–1902s

The Wright Brothers fly gliders at Kitty Hawk, North Carolina, testing their wind warping control system. They also build a wind tunnel and undertake research on airfoil design.

1903

Orville Wright achieves the first manned, powered, heavier-than-air flight — 120 feet in 12 seconds, at Kill Devil Hills, North Carolina, on December 17. Three later flights on that day by Orville and brother Wilbur go 175 feet, 200 feet, and 852 feet. A competitor, Samuel Pierpont Langley of the Smithsonian Institution, also attempts to fly a manned version of his Aerodrome and fails.

1904

The Wright brothers employ Harry A. Toulmin, a patent attorney, to work on their patent case. The Wrights apply for French and German patents on their airplane. At Huffman Prairie, a large meadow near Dayton, Wilbur and Orville build a new heavier and stronger machine with a more powerful motor. They make practice flights with their new 1904 machine at Huffman Prairie — total flying time is forty-nine minutes. Wilbur makes the first turn in the air on September 15 and the first complete circle on September 20. Longest flight of the year is five minutes four seconds, 2¾ miles — almost four circles around the field.

1905

At Huffman Prairie outside Dayton, Ohio, Wilbur stays aloft in the Wright Flyer III for 39 minutes and 24 miles, longer than all of the brothers' 1903 and 1904 flights combined.

1906

U.S. Patent Office grants the Wright brothers patent no. 821,393 for their flying machine.

1907

The brothers travel to Europe to negotiate for the sale of the Wright airplane abroad. Hart O. Berg and Flint & Company are their agents.

1908

Casey Baldwin is the next person after the Wright brothers to fly in North America. His Red Wing biplane flies 319 feet near Hammondsport, New York. Charlie Furnas becomes the first airplane passenger, going up with Wilbur Wright on a 656-foot flight at Kill Devil Hills. Wilbur Wright makes his first flight in Europe, at Champs d'Auvours, France, astonishing Europeans skeptical about the brothers' aerial accomplishment. Lt. Thomas Selfridge is the first passenger killed in a plane crash, when a Wright Flyer piloted by Orville crashes during army tests at Fort Myer, Virginia. La Compagnie Générale de Navigation Aérienne, the French Wright company is organized. Wilbur wins 1908 Michelin Cup and a prize of twenty thousand francs with his flight of 123 kilometers, two hundred meters in two hours, 18 minutes, 33⅗ seconds. He extends this same flight to break a new world record in a time of two hours, 20 minutes, 23⅕ seconds over 124 kilometers, 700 meters.

1909

Congressional Medal is awarded to the Wrights by resolution of Congress (H.J. Resolution 246), "in recognition of the great service of Orville and Wilbur Wright, of Ohio, rendered the science of aerial navigation in the invention of the Wright aeroplane, and for their ability, courage, and success in navigating the air." The medal is subsequently presented to the brothers on June 18. Wilbur arrives in Rome to make demonstration flights and train two Italian pilots. Orville and Katharine arrive April 9. Wrights arrive in New York. Flugmaschine Wright Gesellschaft, the German Wright company in Berlin, is formed. Two-day celebration thrown by the city of Dayton to honor the Wright brothers. As part of the Hudson-Fulton Celebration, Wilbur flies round-trip demonstration flights from Governors Island, New York, to the Statue of Liberty and Grant's Tomb, New York City. More than one million spectators present. At College Park, Maryland, Wilbur trains first U.S. Army fliers. The Wright Company incorporates. Wilbur and Orville sell their patent rights to the Wright Company for $100,000. The brothers also initiate patent suits against Glenn Curtiss and other aircraft builders who are using their control system without permission. The U.S. Army buys a 1909 Wright Flyer and designates it Signal Corps Airplane No. 1. This is the world's first military aircraft.

1910

Groundbreaking for the Wright Company factory on Home Road in Dayton. Wright Exhibition Flying Team and School of Aviation formed as an adjunct of the Wright Company. Wright Exhibition Company team flies in its first show in Indianapolis, Indiana. Orville travels to Europe and finds both the German and French Wright companies struggling financially.

1911

Wright School of Aviation opens at Belmont Park, New York and Augusta, Georgia. The Wright exhibition flyers are disbanded due to an excessive loss of life.

1912

Wilbur Wright, company president, dies of typhoid fever at home in Dayton. Orville assumes the presidency.

1913

Miami River floods and causes considerable damage to the Wright family home and property in Dayton. The Wrights' collection of glass plate photographic negatives as well as early business and aviation records are damaged.

1914

Orville Wright purchases a controlling interest from Wright Company stockholders. U.S. courts support Orville in his suit against Curtiss and others. Curtiss prevents a final resolution of this case until 1917 through lengthy appeals and other delaying tactics. The Smithsonian Institution claims that Langley's Aerodrome was the first piloted machine "capable of flight" and opens a bitter feud with Orville Wright.

1915

The Wright Company is sold to a financial syndicate in New York for $1.5 million. Orville serves as a consulting engineer.

1916

The Wright Company merges with the Glenn L. Martin Company and Simplex Automobile Company to create the Wright-Martin Aircraft Corporation. Orville remains as a consulting engineer.

1917

Charles Kettering, Edward Deeds, Harold E. Talbott, Sr. and junior, and Orville Wright form the Dayton-Wright Airplane Company. The Wright-Curtiss patent litigation comes to an end with the beginning of World War I. With U.S. government direction, aircraft companies group together and found the Manufacturers' Aircraft Association to coordinate wartime aircraft production in the U.S. All patent litigation cease automatically. Royalties are reduced to 1 percent, and free exchange of inventions and ideas take place between all the air framers. Orville never forgave Glenn Curtiss. Orville establishes the Wright Aeronautical Laboratory in Dayton. The original Wright Company sells its factory in Dayton.

1918

Orville Wright solos in a Flyer B for the last time.

1919

The Wright-Martin Company reorganizes as the Wright Aeronautical Company.

1920

General Motors Corporation buys the Dayton-Wright Company. Orville is appointed to the National Advisory Council on Aeronautics (NACA), the forerunner of NASA. He remains an active participant for the remainder of his life.

1922

Orville develops the split flap, which is used to slow aircraft in a steep dive. It is his final aeronautical invention.

1923

Dayton-Wright Company is merged with Inland Division of General Motors.

1925

Orville is issued a patent for a mechanical toy. The toy is produced and sold by the Miami Specialty Wood Company in Dayton, of which Lorin Wright is president.

1928

Orville sends the 1903 Flyer I to an English museum to publicize the wrong he feels is being done to his name by the Smithsonian Institution.

1929

Wright Aeronautical Corporation and Curtiss Aeroplane and Motor combine to form the Curtiss-Wright Corporation, one of the largest manufacturers of aircraft and engines in America. Distinguished Flying Crosses awarded to Orville and Wilbur presented to Orville by Secretary of War Dwight F. Davis.

1932

The Wright Brothers Monument at Kitty Hawk is dedicated.

1940

1903 Wright airplane on exhibit at the Science Museum in London is dismantled and packed away for safekeeping during World War II. Wilbur and Orville Wright Memorial in Dayton, and near Huffman Prairie, is dedicated.

1943

The Smithsonian Institution finally apologizes to Orville and recognizes the Wrights as the first to make a controlled, sustained powered flight. Orville recalls the Flyer I from England, but World War II will delay its homecoming.

1944

Orville builds cipher machine for automatic selective coding of messages.

1948

Orville Wright dies of a heart attack in Dayton, Ohio, and the Wrights' first powered aircraft, the 1903 Flyer I, is enshrined at the Smithsonian Institution.

APPENDIX B: WRIGHT AIRCRAFT

Model B, 1910–1911

In 1910 the Wrights applied a fixed horizontal stabilizer to the tail of their 1909 machine. This addition was then made moveable, working in conjunction with the horizontal front rudder. Next, the horizontal front rudder was removed completely, and wheels were added to the skids, thereby doing away with the catapult launching device which had been used since September 1904. As the model underwent further improvement, the front ends of the skids were flattened and shortened, and triangular blinkers replaced the semicircular blinkers.

Span: 38 ft. 6 in. to 39 ft.
Chord: 6 ft. 2 in. to 6 ft. 6 in.
Gap: 5 ft. 4 in.
Camber: 1/20
Approximate wing area: 500 sq. ft.
Approximate elevator area: 40 sq. ft.
Approximate rudder area: 15 sq. ft.
Approximate gross weight: 1,250 lbs.

Model R, 1910

The model R, also called the "Roadster" and the "Baby Wright," was a one-seat racer built for speed and altitude competitions. A petite version, called the "Baby Grand," flew at the Belmont Park Meet in 1910. Powered by an 8-cylinder, 60 hp engine, Orville Wright reached a speed of between 70 and 80 miles per hour in the "Baby Grand." In both Model R versions, the pilot sat close to the engine with their arm wrapped around the nearest upright.

Span: 26 ft. 6 in.
Chord: 3 ft. 6 in.
Gap: 3 ft. 6 in.
Approximate wing area: 180 sq. ft.
Approximate gross weight: 750 lbs.

Model EX, 1911

The EX was a compact, one-seat version of the Model B, built for exhibition flying. It enjoyed an uncommon rate of climb. Equipped with a six-cylinder motor, the machine could attain nearly 65 mph and climb 600 feet a minute.

Model C, 1912

In 1912 the Model C was recognized as the natural successor to the Model B. The craft had slightly flatter wing surfaces than the B, with a simplified control system. Perhaps the most visible modification was the added vertical vanes to the forward ends of the skids, replacements for former B's triangular blinkers. The C boasted a more powerful engine, and was delivered to the army in 1912. Dubbed the Type CM-1, this machine was the forerunner of five "weight-carrying" craft ordered by the army. Specifications stipulated that this military variant of the C climb at the rate of 200 feet per minute, have a fuel supply adequate for a four-hour flight, and carry a load of 450 pounds, including pilot and passenger. Of the two variants sent for trials at College Park, there existed a slight difference in rate of climb and speed, attributable to differences in wing camber.

Span: 38 ft.
Chord: 6 ft.
Gap: 5 ft.
Approximate wing area: 440 ft.
Length: 29 ft. 9 in.
Weight: 1,090 lbs.

Model CH, 1913

The CH was the first Wright hydroplane. Basically, it was a stock C with pontoons added to allow it to take off and land on rivers, lakes, and inland waterways with shallow drafts. Experiments on the Miami River in the spring of 1913 included the affixing of "multiple-step" pontoons to the skid runners (16½ ft. by 1½ ft.). The results were unsatisfactory, providing for an unstable machine in the air. The final CH type, therefore, employed a single wooden 240 lb. pontoon, 10 ft. by 6 in. by 10 in. An abbreviated pontoon supported the tail.

Model D, 1912

The Model D was a lightweight, swift biplane built by the Wrights to meet the army's requirements for a "speed scout." A rugged, highly maneuverable aircraft, its only drawback was an excessive landing speed. The D differed little from the Model R with a 26 ft. span, and met army specifications with a speed of 70 mph and a climb rate of 525 ft. per minute. Again, however, its fast landing speed caused the machine to ground-loop in setting down in a freshly plowed field — a negative feature regarding military needs.

Span: 27 ft.
Chord: 3½ ft.

Model E, 1913

The E was a single-seat exhibition plane, comparable to the 1911 EX; the exception was that it had a single 7-ft. pusher propeller and was essentially a lesser variant of the C, as opposed to the Model B. The spars supporting the tail assembly were not parallel, as with other Wright machines, being farther apart at the trailing edges of the wings to accommodate the centrally located propeller. Its blinkers (vertical stabilizers) were fashioned from wood and positioned solidly to the front end of the skids, doing away with some of the wire bracing employed on the Model C. Two large wheels served in the landing gear, rather than the four smaller ones employed on Wright machines from 1910 to 1913. The E was quite popular on exhibition tours because of the speed and ease associated with its assembly and disassembly.

Span: 32 ft.
Chord: 5 ft. 1 in.
Gap: 4 ft.
Approximate wing area: 316 sq. ft.
Height: 7 ft.
Length: 27 ft. 11 in.
Weight: 730 lbs.

Model F, 1913

Built for the army in 1913, the F was the first Wright aircraft with a fuselage. It was powered with an Austro-Daimler 90 hp engine. Remarkably, only one machine of this type was ever built.

The F was a singular prototype in other ways. It was the first Wright aircraft to position the vertical rudder above the elevator; the first to utilize a tail skid; and the first in which the use of tractor, instead of pusher-type, propellers was even considered. As initially laid out, the propellers were mounted before the wing surfaces and the seats for the pilot and one passenger were arranged in tandem. On the one Model F assigned to the army in 1914, the propellers were repositioned to the rear to offer better visibility, and the seats were set side by side so as to make the instruments available to both pilot and passenger.

Span: 42 ft.
Chord: 6 ft.
Gap: 5 ft.

Model G, 1913–1914

The Model G "Aeroboat" was designed in 1913 by Grover Loening under Orville's general supervision. It was the first Deep Water hydroplane produced by the Wright Company. The hull was constructed of ash and spruce, covered with a special metal alloy treated to prevent saltwater corrosion (3 ft. deep, 18 ft. long, and 43 inches wide). Combined weight of the hull was 300 lbs., including motor bed, seats, and instrument panel. The machine was divided into six watertight compartments and was also supported by two floats approximately 7 ft. inboard from the wing tips. Loening's creation was steered in the water by two paddles located at the wing tips and maneuvered from the cockpit. The motor was located behind the pilot and passenger in the hull, between the lower wings. Also, the wing section of the "Aeroboat" was heftier than those of earlier Wright ships, the ribs being of solid I-beam construction. In the 1914 variant, the floats were located under the wing tips. In addition, the engine was relocated forward into the bow of the hull and the pilot and passenger now sat beneath the upper wing with the drive shaft to the propeller transmission passing under the seats. Following this repositioning of the power plant, the pilot was able to make minor adjustments in flight. The elevator was placed on top of the vertical rudder in this model and was of the "new Wright stability type." The elevator was affixed rigidly to the outriggers for two and a half feet of its fore-and-aft distance. Only the rear one-foot section was movable.

Span: 38 ft.
Chord: 6 ft.
Gap: 5 ft.
Wing area: 430 sq. ft.
Length: 28 ft.
Weight: 1,200 lbs.

Model H, 1914

The Model H was similar to the Model F in appearance except for the fuselage, which was continuous, there being no break between the cockpit and the tail assembly. The fuselage was of wood, veneered with canvas inside and out. Also, there was a slight dihedral to the wings. This machine was billed as a "weight-carrier," capable of a 1,000 lb. load with a speed of 56 mph, and with a large cockpit for pilot, passenger, and bombs.

Span: 38 ft.
Chord: 6 ft.
Gap: 5 ft.
Height: 9 ft.
Length: 26 ft 6 in.
Weight: 1,150 lbs.

Models I and **J** were not Wright products. The Burgess-Wright Company, licensees under the Wright patent, paid royalties on these models, even though Orville Wright considered them infringements of Wright patents in that the Burgess-Curtis Company had been licensed to build only exact copies of Wright machines.

Model HS

The HS was a smaller version of the Model H and one hundred pounds lighter. Its abbreviated wingspan gave the machine greater speed and climbing capability. With the exception of its wings, the HS bore little resemblance to earlier Wright machines. This model was also the last Wright craft with a double vertical rudder and pusher-type propellers.

Model K

A seaplane manufactured by the Wright Company for the United States Navy. On this model the customary double vertical rudders of earlier Wright machines were replaced by a single, nearly circular fin and rudder. The propellers were mounted high, with their hubs a few feet below the leading edge of the upper wing surface.

The K was the first tractor aircraft made by the Wright Company, and the last to employ the Wright "bent end" propeller. Another concession was the K's utilization of modern-type ailerons, on both upper and lower wings instead of the wing warping process.

Model L

A single-seat, light-scout biplane designed to satisfy army requirements for high-speed reconnaissance. The aircraft's speed range ran from 25 to 80 mph, and its rate of climb approximated 650 feet per minute. Its characteristics included squared wing tips, streamlined box-type fuselage, twin radiators, and enclosed spring-swivel tail-skid, plus ailerons on both upper and lower wings. The propeller used was a single, narrow-bladed, high-pitch, eight-foot type, mounted in the nose. At the time the L hit the market, Orville's direction of the original Wright Company had ended.

Span: 29 ft.
Chord: 6 ft. 6 in.
Gap: 5 ft. 9 in.
Wing area: 375 sq. ft.
Length: 24 ft.
Weight: 850 lbs.

APPENDIX C:
STUDENTS OF THE
WRIGHT FLYING SCHOOL

J.M. Alexander
C. Ando
R.J. Armor
Henry H. Arnold
Harry N. Atwood
L.B. Ault
M.S. Beal
Percy E. Beasley
E.P. Beckwith
Grover C. Bergdoll
J.R. Bibby
John A. Bixler
L.W. Bonney
W.E. Bowersox
George Breadner
Lloyd S. Breadner
A.A. Bressman
Griffith Brewer
A.W. Briggs
Oscar A. Brindley
C.G. Bronson
Walter Brookins
A. Roy Brown
Harold H. Brown
L.E. Brown
Verne Carter
Charles DeForest
   Chandler

W.H. Chisam
Frank T. Coffyn
Maurice Coombs
C. Couturier
C.J. Creery
O.A. Danielson
C. LaQ Day
Rose Dougan
Andrew Drew
M.C. Dubuc
S.T. Edwards
Ferdinand Eggena
Albert Elton
H.B. Evans
Farnum T. Fish
Robert G. Fowler
Archibald Freeman
Paul Gadbois
A.B. Gaines, Jr.
M.B. Galbraith
John Galpin
Howard W. Gill
James L. Gordon
George A. Gray
A.C. Harland
J.A. Harman
G.S. Harrower
J.C. Henning

H.V. Hills
Basil D. Hobbs
Arch Hoxsey
J.G. Ireland
Ralph Johnstone
William Kabitzke
P.S. Kennedy
Frank Kitamura
J.G. Klockler
Duval La Chappelle
Frank Lahm
Robert E. Lee
B.B. Lewis
K.G. MacDonald
G.A. Magor
N.A. Magor
C. McNicoll
J.A. McRae
A.A. Merrill
Thomas DeWitt Milling
Louis Mitchell
Goroku Moro
C.E. Neidig
L.E. Norman
W.E. Orchard
Philip W. Page
Philip O. Parmelee
T.D. Pemberton

C.J. Peterson

M.R. Priest

Leda Richberg-Hornsby

Howard Max Rinehart

W.E. Robinson

Calbraith P. Rodgers

John Rodgers

Gordon F. Ross

K.F. Saunders

M.T. Schermerhorn

Lyle H. Scott

J.A. Shaw

O.G. Simmons

George H. Simpson

J.C. Simpson

Harley Smith

F.J. Southard

Wilfred Stevens

Edward A. Stinson

Marjorie Stinson

W.J. Sussan

Harry Swan

C.A. Terrell

J.C. Turpin

C.E. Utter

Charles Wald

J.C. Watson

C.L. Webster

Robert McC. Weir

Arthur L. Welsh

Bernard L. Whelan

Kenneth Whiting

T.C. Wilkinson

A.Y. Wilks

A.G. Woodward

R.M. Wright

BIBLIOGRAPHY

A Note on Sources

Without the aviation libraries and museums across the United States this study would have died aborning. Orville Wright's association with the principal subjects of my book could not have been properly evaluated save for the Wright Papers, which are housed in the Library of Congress in Washington, D.C. Orv's interesting and often surprising interactions with these men are compelling, captured in the collection's subject and correspondence files, as well as folders relevant to the Wrights' exhibition department and school of aviation. These papers allowed me to fully appreciate the immediate needs and long-term aspirations of the early flyers in this book as well as their respective roles within and their personal perspectives on the Wright organization from the inside out. Equally helpful to my research were the archival holdings and ancillary materials found in the capital's National Air and Space Museum (NASM), Smithsonian Institution. The information discovered in its biographical folders contained not only detailed profiles of Welsh, Gill, Freeman, Bergdoll, Gray, and Rinehart, which complemented the Library of Congress's store of knowledge on these aviators, but also included limited personal papers, photographs, and vital records data. An equally treasured resource within NASM's walls is the Harold E. Morehouse Flying Pioneers Biographies Collection, a subgroup of unpublished sketches and related materials regarding not only my central protagonists but also many other birdmen who interacted with these six aviators throughout their flying careers.

Other sources of research material pertinent to these six pioneers and their related colleagues include selected transcriptions from the Columbia University Oral History Collection, New York, New York; an extensive oral history collection of America's pioneer airmen located in the University of Dayton's Roesch Library; vertical file holdings relevant to Howard Rinehart's time at Dayton-Wright, which are found both at the Special Services Division, Research Branch, of Wright-Patterson AFB, Ohio, and in the Historical Collections of Kettering University, Flint, Michigan; genealogical data on Howard Gill's family, gleaned from the papers of his uncle, Edwin Warfield, housed in the Special Collections Division, University of Maryland Library. Finally, confounding mysteries surrounding the life and death of Al Welsh were laid to rest through correspondence, archival records, and contemporary published articles obtained from the Special Collections Division of the College Park Aviation Museum, College Park, Maryland.

It may seem strange to salute many nameless newspaper reporters who have long since passed from the scene, but I am beholden to scores of writers in the print medium who practiced journalism a century ago. My book could not have succeeded without the newspapers (and popular, aeronautical, and scientific journals of the period), especially the *New York Times*, the *Los Angeles Times*, the *Dayton Daily News* and *Dayton Journal*, the *Chicago Daily Tribune*, the *Boston Daily Globe*, the *Atlanta Constitution*, and the *Philadelphia Bulletin, Inquirer*, and *Public Ledger*. Other newspapers, metropolitan and regional alike, were consulted with positive results. The journals *Literary Digest, Town & Country, World's Work*, and *Scientific American* covered my half dozen candidates randomly, and the aviation publications of the time afforded an indispensable glimpse into the trials and tribulations the pioneers encountered on a daily basis: *Fly, Aero, U.S. Air Services Magazine, Aero Club of America Bulletin*, and *Aeronautics*. The writings of such aviation enthusiasts as J. Herbert Duckworth, Jimmy Hare, and Henry Woodhouse lent a sense of drama, awe, and discovery to the field of early aeronautics.

Aside from the research materials consulted at the aforementioned repositories and the press coverage examined by this author, I would be remiss in not alluding to a few sources which proved helpful to this work. With regard to the brief history of the Wright Flying School in general and the lives of the six primary subjects of this volume in particular, they are as follows:

Wright Flying School

Lois E. Walker and Shelby E. Wickam: *From Huffman Prairie to the Moon: The History of Wright-Patterson Air Force Base*.

Henry H. Arnold: *Global Mission*.

Howard Mansfield: "Becoming a Birdman: The Wright School of Aviation," in *Timeline: A Publication of the Ohio Historical Society*.

Grover Cleveland Loening: "The Wright Aviation School at Simms Station," in *Flying*.

Quentin Wald: "Working for the Wright Brothers: What My Father Learned at the Wright Company about Hydroaeroplanes, Close Calls, and Practical Jokes," in *Air & Space*.

These secondary publications suggest the arduous regime of training laid down by the Wrights at Simms Station and the dedication, talent, camaraderie, and playfulness exhibited by its eager young pupils.

Arthur L. Welsh

Samuel H. Holland: "Arthur L. (Al) Welsh: Pioneer of American Aviation." *The Record: Publication of the Jewish Historical Society of Greater Washington*.

Falk Harmel: "First Jewish Airman," in *B'nai B'rith*.

James H. Hare: "Why We Did Not Fly Across the Panama Isthmus?" in *Aero Club of America Bulletin*.

The Duckworth/Hare articles in the *Town and Country* series.

The above citations portrayed a more complete side of Welsh's private life, his close association with some of New England's wealthiest men and prospective customers, and his involvement in perhaps the greatest failure of his otherwise remarkable career.

Howard W. Gill

David D. Hatfield: *Dominguez Air Meet*.

The Reminiscences of Hillery Beachey, Aviation Project, The Columbia University Oral History Collection.

The Hatfield title and Hillery Beachey's reminiscences were helpful to me in following Gill's early involvement in aviation.

Archibald Freeman

Howard Mansfield: *Skylarking: The Life, Lies, and Inventions of Harry Atwood*.

Melvin W. Hodgdon: "The Saga of Saugus," in *Journal: American Aviation Historical Society*.

The Mansfield biography of Atwood and student pilot Hodgdon's recollections of his time at Atwood Park were indispensable in my understanding of the dysfunctional nature of that bizarre facility and also my appreciation of poor Arch Freeman's trying stay there.

Grover Cleveland Bergdoll

The Bergdoll Family Papers (The Historical Society of Pennsylvania), which contain one oversize scrapbook, 1912–1920, clippings, correspondence and legal documents covering Bergdoll's family, youthful adventures and misadventures as a pilot and racing car driver, his years in exile, trial, imprisonment, and later life. An extraordinary source with special emphasis on Grover's flying career.

Roberta E. Dell: *The United States Against Bergdoll: How the Government Spent Twenty Years and Millions of Dollars to Capture and Punish America's Most Notorious Draft Dodger*. An entertaining account of Bergdoll's star-crossed life but with little mention of his early aeronautical accomplishments.

U.S. Congress. House: *Select Committee to Investigate Escape of General Prisoner Grover Cleveland Bergdoll from United States Disciplinary Barracks at Governors Island, NY*.

George Alphonso Gray

Edith "Jack" Stearns Gray's unique memoir *"UP": A True Story of Aviation* in which she details her exciting life with George during their exhibition flying days and thereafter.

George A. Gray's informative article "Early Barnstorming," in *U.S. Air Services*, is a wonderful supplement to Edith's memoir, in which he not only expounds on the couple's barnstorming days over the Florida, New Jersey, and New England circuit, but also elaborates on his post-exhibition days.

Ernest T. Pyle's "Seven Gallant Gentlemen, Each With a Past," in *U.S. Air Services* is an important source for Gray's role in World War I and his work for a defense contractor in subsequent years.

Howard Rinehart

The chapter on Howard Rinehart could not have been written without access to the private collections of Bernard L. Whelan (in the custody of his daughter, Dr. Mary Anne Whelan, Cooperstown, N.Y.) and Howard M. Rinehart (in the custody of his great-nephew, Rob Grant, Queensland, Australia). Rinehart's tenure in Mexico is briefly treated in his colorful article "Flying for Villa" in *The Sportsman Pilot* and in Lawrence D. Taylor's "Pancho Villa's Aerial Corps: Foreign Aviators in the División del Norte 1914–1915" in *Air Power History*, as well as in Sterling Seagrave's *Soldiers of Fortune*. Finally, Rinehart's South American years in later life can be appreciated in the newspaper articles "Adventures of Aviation Pioneer Rinehart Recalled" in the *Dayton Daily News*; "He's Had Enough of Civilization: Old-Time Aviator Going Back to Brazil" in the *Miami Daily News*; and "Life in South American Jungle Told By Daytonian" in the *Dayton Daily News*.

As useful as the foregoing resources were, my book also relied on contributory works about the subjects and topics covered for background and context. The standard biographies of the Wrights are Fred Howard, *Wilbur and Orville: A Biography of the Wright Brothers*, and Tom D. Crouch, *The Bishop's Boys: A Life of Wilbur and Orville Wright*. Of the two, Crouch affords more attention to the Wright family's history. Howard's study is a generally balanced and engaging treatment of the Wrights and their times. Elsbeth E. Freudenthal's *Flight Into History: The Wright Brothers and the Air Age* is an excellent, but rather critical, account of the brothers. Fred C. Kelly's *The Wright Brothers* was consulted, despite the fact that it is currently considered superficial, dated, and not entirely accurate. Its value stems from Orville's willingness to confide details to Kelly and to no one else. First among the Curtiss biographies is C.R. Roseberry's commanding biography, *Glenn Curtiss: Pioneer of Flight*, a superb counterbalance to the abovementioned Wright studies.

The fifty-nine websites listed in the bibliography were entertaining, informative, and largely error free, serving to both enhance and verify scholarship from more traditional sources.

Published and Unpublished Memoirs, Letters, and Biographical Files

Russell A. Alger Folders, General Correspondence Series, Container 10, 1908–1917, Wilbur and Orville Wright Papers, Library of Congress, Washington, D.C.

Harry H. "Hap" Arnold Biographical Files, MRC 322, Archives Division, Smithsonian Institution, National Air and Space Museum, Washington, D.C.

Hillery Beachey Biographical File, Harold E. Morehouse Flying Pioneers Biographies Collection. Smithsonian Institution, National Archives and Space Museum, Washington, D.C.

George W. Beatty Biographical Files, MRC 322, Archives Division, Smithsonian Institution, National Air and Space Museum, Washington, D.C.

Grover Cleveland Bergdoll Biographical Files, MRC 322, Archives Division, Smithsonian Institution, National Air and Space Museum, Washington, D.C.

Grover Cleveland Bergdoll Biographical File, Harold E. Morehouse Flying Pioneers Biographies Collection, Smithsonian Institution, National Air and Space Museum, Washington, D.C.

Bergdoll Family Papers, 1910–1970. Mss 21, Box 5, Oversize Package 1 Bergdoll Scrapbook, 1912–1920. The Historical Society of Pennsylvania.

Grover C. Bergdoll Folder, General Correspondence Series, Container 13, 1912–1913, Wilbur and Orville Wright Papers, Library of Congress, Washington, D.C.

Grover C. Bergdoll Folder, Subject File, Container 69, Wilbur and Orville Wright Papers, Library of Congress, Washington, D.C.

T.A. Boyd interview, n.d., transcript, Historical Collection, Kettering University, 2–4.

Oscar Brindley Biographical Files, MRC 322, Archives Division, Smithsonian Institution, National Air and Space Museum, Washington, D.C.

Christman interview, n.d., transcript, University Archives, Roesch Library, University of Dayton, 23 pp.

Frank T. Coffyn Biographical Files, MRC 322, Archives Division, Smithsonian Institution, National Air and Space Museum, Washington, D.C.

William Conover interview, n.d., transcript, University Archives, Roesch Library, University of Dayton, 12–30.

Farnum T. Fish Biographical Files, MRC 322, Archives Division, Smithsonian Institution, National Air and Space Museum, Washington, D.C.

Arch Freeman Biographical Files, MRC 322, Archives Division, Smithsonian Institution, National Air and Space Museum, Washington, D.C.

Howard W. Gill Biographical File, Harold E. Morehouse Flying Pioneers Biographies Collection. Smithsonian Institution, National Archives and Space Museum, Washington, D.C.

Howard Gill Early Aviation Scrapbooks, Acc. Nos. 0233 & 0253, Loc, B/9.5.5. Oversize container 4 Gill Scrapbooks 1909–1912. Suitland, Maryland, Remote Facility, Smithsonian Institution, National Archives and Space Museum, Washington, D.C.

Howard Gill Folder, General Correspondence Series, Container 31, 1911–1912. Wilbur and Orville Wright Papers, Library of Congress, Washington, D.C.

George A. Gray Biographical Files, MRC 322, Archives Division, Smithsonian Institution, National Air and Space Museum, Washington, D.C.

Gray, "Jack" Stearns. *"UP": A True Story of Aviation*. Strasburg, VA: Shenandoah Publishing House, 1931.

William E. Haupt Biographical File, Harold E. Morehouse Flying Pioneers Biographies Collection, Smithsonian Institution, National Air and Space Museum, Washington, D.C.

Hutchinson, Roland V. "Skylarking, 1917–1918: A Chronicle of a Few, Not All, of the Happenings at Dayton-Wright." Unpublished manuscript, Historical Collection, Kettering University, 1943, 2–49.

William Kabitzke Biographical File, Harold E. Morehouse Flying Pioneers Biographies Collection, Smithsonian Institution, National Air and Space Museum, Washington, D.C.

J.G. Kloeckler Biographical File, Early Birds of Aviation, Inc., Collection, Smithsonian Institution, National Air and Space Museum, Washington, D.C.

McFarland, Marvin W., ed. *The Papers of Wilbur and Orville Wright: Including the Chanute-Wright Letters, 1899–1948*. 2 vols. New York: McGraw-Hill, 2001.

John F. McGee Biographical Files, MRC 322, Archives Division, Smithsonian Institution, National Air and Space Museum, Washington, D.C.

George Mestach Biographical File, Harold E. Morehouse Flying Pioneers Biographies Collection. Smithsonian Institution, National Archives and Space Museum, Washington, D.C.

Thomas DeWitt Milling Biographical Files, MRC 322, Archives Division, Smithsonian Institution, National Air and Space Museum, Washington, D.C.

Official U.S. Navy Photos. Album 1, 1911–1912, of the Admiral Lansing Callan Collection. Glenn H. Curtiss Museum, Hammondsport, New York.

J. Chauncey Redding Biographical Files, MRC 322, Archives Division, Smithsonian Institution, National Air and Space Museum, Washington, D.C.

Howard Max Rinehart Biographical Files, MRC 322, Archives Division, Smithsonian Institution, National Air and Space Museum, Washington, D.C.

Howard Max Rinehart to B.L. Whelan, July 18, 1949. Original letter in the possession of Dr. Mary Anne Whelan, Cooperstown, New York.

Howard Max Rinehart Folders, Wright Brothers Collection, Special Collections and Archives, Wright State University, Dayton, Ohio.

Howard Rinehart Files, USAF Central Museum, Special Services Division, Research Branch, Wright-Patterson AFB, Ohio.

Interview with Howard M. Rinehart, Shoreham Hotel, Washington, D.C., January 16, 1947. Original transcription in the possession of Dr. Mary Anne Whelan, Cooperstown, New York. [T.A. Boyd]

Henry Roy Waite Biographical Files, MRC 322, Archives Division, Smithsonian Institution, National Air and Space Museum, Washington, D.C.

Charles Wald Biographical File, Harold E. Morehouse Flying Pioneers Biographies Collection. Smithsonian Institution, National Archives and Space Museum, Washington, D.C.

Edwin Warfield Papers. Series III, folder 2. Death of Martin Gillet Gill, 1908. Special Collections, University of Maryland Library.

Clifford L. Webster Biographical Files, MRC 322, Archives Division, Smithsonian Institution, National Air and Space Museum, Washington, D.C.

Arthur L. Welsh Biographical Files, MRC 322, Archives Division, Smithsonian Institution, National Air and Space Museum, Washington, D.C.

Arthur L. Welsh Folder, General Correspondence Series, Container 64, 1910–1912, Wilbur and Orville Wright Papers, Library of Congress.

Arthur L. Welsh Folders, Subject File Series, Container 107, 1912, Wilbur and Orville Wright Papers, Library of Congress, Washington, D.C.

Bernard L. Whelan Biographical Files, MRC 322, Archives Division, Smithsonian Institution, National Air and Space Museum, Washington, D.C.

Whelan, Bernard L. "Diary: My Life Is in Your Hands." Unpublished manuscript in the possession of Dr. Mary Anne Whelan, Cooperstown, New York, 230–266.

_____. "Howard Max Rinehart." Unpublished manuscript prepared by Bernard Whelan for the Early Birds. 2 p. Manuscript in the possession of Dr. Mary Anne Whelan, Cooperstown, New York.

Wright Company Exhibition Department, undated Folders, 1910. Miscellany, Subject File, Container 108, Wilbur and Orville Papers, Library of Congress, Washington, D.C.

Wright Company School of Aviation Folders, 1911–1916, Subject File, Container 108, Wilbur and Orville Wright Papers, Library of Congress, Washington, D.C.

Wright Company, undated folders, 1910–1916. Miscellany, Subject File, Container 108, Wilbur and Orville Wright Papers, Library of Congress, Washington, D.C.

Katharine Wright Folders, General Correspondence Series, Containers 4–8, Family Papers, 1881–1973, Wilbur and Orville Wright Papers, Library of Congress, Washington, D.C.

Books

Angelucci, Enzo. *World Encyclopedia of Civil Aircraft: From Leonardo Da Vinci to the Present.* New York: Crown, 1982.

Arnold, Henry H. *Global Mission.* New York: Harper & Brothers, 1949.

Boyd, T.A. *Professional Amateur: the Biography of Charles Franklin Kettering.* New York: E.P. Dutton, 1957.

Boyne, Walter J. *De Havilland DH-4: From Flaming Coffin to Living Legend.* Washington, D.C.: Smithsonian Institution Press, 1984.

_____. *Silver Wings: A History of the United States Air Force.* New York: Simon and Schuster, 1993.

Burden, Maria S. *The Life and Times of Robert G. Fowler.* Los Angeles: Borden Publishing, 1999.

Conover, Charlotte Reeve. "Dayton the Cradle of Aviation." In *Dayton, Ohio: An Intimate History.* New York: Lewis Historical Publishing, 1932.

Crouch, Tom D. *The Bishop's Boys: A Life of Wilbur and Orville Wright.* New York: W.W. Norton, 1989.

_____, and Peter L. Jakab. *The Wright Brothers and the Invention of the Aerial Age.* Washington, D.C.: Smithsonian Institution Press, 2003.

Dell, Roberta E. *The United States against Bergdoll: How the Government Spent Twenty Years and Millions of Dollars to Capture and Punish America's Most Notorious Draft Dodger.* New York: A.S. Barnes, 1977.

Delpar, Helen. *Encyclopedia of Latin America.* New York: McGraw-Hill, 1974.

Donaldson, Alfred L. *A History of the Adirondacks.* New York: Century, 1921.

Dwiggins, Don. *Famous Flyers and the Ships They Flew.* New York: Grosset & Dunlap, 1969.

Fischer, William Edward, Jr. *The Development of Military Night Aviation to 1919.* Montgomery: Air University Press, 1998.

Foxworth, Thomas G. *The Speed Seekers.* Somerset: Haynes Publishing, 1989.

Freudenthal, Elsbeth E. *Flight into History: The Wright Brothers and the Air Age.* Norman: University of Oklahoma Press, 1949.

Gardner, Lester D., ed. *Who's Who in American Aeronautics.* New York: Gardner, Moffat, 1922.

Gwynn-Jones, Terry. *The Air Racers: Aviation's Golden Era, 1909–1936.* London: Pelham Books, 1984.

_____. *Farther and Faster: Aviation's Adventuring Years, 1909–1939.* Washington, D.C.: Smithsonian Institution Press, 1991.

Hall, R.J., and R.D. Campbell. *Dictionary of Aviation.* Chicago: St. James Press, 1991.

Hallion, Richard P. *Taking Flight: Inventing the Aerial Age from Antiquity through the First World War.* New York: Oxford University Press, 2003.

_____, ed. *The Wright Brothers: Heirs of Prometheus.* Washington, D.C.: Smithsonian Institution Press, 1978.

Harris, Sherwood. *The First to Fly: Aviation's Pioneer Days.* New York: Simon and Schuster, 1970.

Hatfield, David D. *Dominguez Air Meet.* Inglewood: Northrop University Press, 1976.

Hennessy, Juliette A. *The United States Army Air Arm.* Washington, D.C.: Office of Air Force History, 1985.

Howard, Fred. *Wilbur and Orville: A Biography of the Wright Brothers.* New York: Alfred A. Knopf, 1987.

Kelly, Fred C. *The Wright Brothers: A Biography Authorized by Orville Wright.* New York: Harcourt Brace, 1943.

Lebow, Eileen F. *Before Amelia: Women Pilots in the Early Days of Aviation.* Washington, D.C.: Brassey's, 2002.

Leslie, Stuart W. *Boss Kettering.* New York: Columbia University Press, 1983.

Loening, Grover. *Our Wings Grow Faster.* New York: Doubleday, Doran, 1935.

_____. *Takeoff into Greatness: How American Aviation Grew So Big So Fast.* New York: G.P. Putnam's Sons, 1968.

Mansfield, Howard. *Skylarking: The Life, Lies, and Inventions of Harry Atwood.* Hanover: University Press of New England, 1999.

Marcosson, Issac F. *Colonel Deeds: Industrial Builder.* New York: Dodd, Mead, 1947.

McPeak, Merrill A. *Selected Works: 1990–1994.* Maxwell AFB, Montgomery: Air University Press, 1995.

Reinhold, Ruth M. *Sky Pioneering: Arizona in Aviation History.* Tucson: University of Arizona Press, 1982.

Renstrom, Arthur G. *Wilbur & Orville Wright: A Chronology.* Washington: Library of Congress, 1975.

Rich, Doris L. *The Magnificent Moisants: Champions of Early Flight.* Washington, D.C.: Smithsonian Books, 1998.

Roseberry, C.R. *Glenn Curtiss: Pioneer of Flight.* Syracuse University Press, 1991.

Rosenberg, Barry, and Catherine Macaulay. *Mavericks of the Sky: The First Daring Pilots of the U.S. Air Mail.* New York: William Morrow, 2006.

Seagrave, Sterling. *Soldiers of Fortune.* Alexandria: Time-Life Books, 1981.

Sweet, Donald H. *The Sailor Aviators: A Tale of the Men of Navy Patrol Bombing Squadron 21 in World War II.* Burnsville, N.C.: Celo Valley Books, 1997.

Villard, Henry Serrano. *Blue Ribbon of the Air: The Gordon-Bennett Races.* Washington, D.C.: Smithsonian Institution Press, 1987.

_____. *Contact!: The Story of the Early Birds.* Washington, D.C.: Smithsonian Institution Press, 1987.

Wagley, Charles. *Amazon Town: A Study of Man in the Tropics.* New York: Macmillan, 1953.

Walker, Lois E., and Shelby E. Wickam. *From Huffman Prairie to the Moon: The History of Wright-Patterson Air Force Base.* Washington, D.C.: GPO, 1986.

Walsh, John E. *One Day at Kitty Hawk: The Untold Story of the Wright Brothers and the Airplane.* New York: Crowell, 1975.

Who's Who in Aviation, 1942–43. Chicago: Illinois WPA Writer's Project, 1943.

Articles

"A.L. Welsh: Pilot Certificate No. 23." *Aeronautics*. July 1912, 39.

"Adventures of Aviation Pioneer Rinehart Recalled." *Dayton Daily News*, August 1, 1949, 17, 1–2.

Alrich, C.M. "Millionaire an Aviator: Louis Bergdoll Buys 'Blerioplane' and Will Fly for Sport." *Fly*. January 1910, 8–9.

"American Planes for the Gordon Bennett Cup." *Literary Digest* 66 (September 11, 1912): 82–86.

"At the United Hunts Meeting, Belmont Park." *Town and Country*. November 11, 1911, 21.

"B.L. Whelan, Company Pilot, a Flyer of the Old School." *The Bee-Hive* 5, no. 1 (January 1931): 10–11.

Berliner, Don. "College Park Airport." *Aviation Quarterly: Special Bicentennial Edition* 2, no. 1 (Winter 1976): 22–37.

"Bernard L. Whelan, Pilot Who Learned from Wrights, Dies." *New York Times Biographical Service* 14, no. 1 (March 1983): 402.

"Big Men of Finance Back of the Wrights." *New York Times*, November 23, 1909, 1.

Boyne, Walter J. "Guess What?" *Airline Pilot*. September 1984, 42–44.

Brookins, Walter R. "Early Days with the Wright Brothers." *Chirp* 16 (June 1936): 3–6.

Casari, Robert. "The Dayton-Wright 'First Shot.'" *American Aviation Historical Society Journal* 19, no. 4 (Fall 1974): 286.

"The Cause of Welsh's Death." *Scientific American*. June 29, 1912, 583.

Coffyn, Frank. "Flying as It Was: Early Days at the Wrights." *The Sportsman Pilot* 21, no. 5 (May 15, 1939): 14–15, 30, 32, 34.

_____. "Flying with the Wrights: When Aviation Was Not Even an Infant Industry and the Two 'Crank' Mechanics Were Emerging from Obscurity at Dayton" *World's Work* 58, no. 12 (December 1929): 80–86.

_____. "I Got Up Early." *Collier's* 94 (December 1934), 25, 55–57.

Curtiss, Glenn H. "Relationship between Auto and Aeroplane." *New York Times*, October 16, 1910, 2.

Duckworth, J. Herbert. "Aviation Happenings at Home." *Town and Country*, July 22, 1911, 26–27.

_____. "Aviation Happenings at Home." *Town and Country*. August 12, 1911, 24.

Edwards, John C. "Grover Berdoll: Pioneer Aviation's Maverick Birdman." *Logbook* 7, no. 2 (2nd Quarter 2006): 34–40.

_____. "Howard Rinehart: A Life of Adventure." *Aviation History* 13, no. 3 (January 2003): 42–48.

Ellis, Carlyle. "Flying as It Was: The Birth of American DHs." *The Sportsman Pilot* 22, no. 4 (October 15, 1939): 16, 29–30.

Ennels, Jerome A. "'The Wright Stuff': Pilot Training at America's First Civilian Flying School." *Air Power History* 49, no. 4 (Winter 2002): 22–31.

"Flying Now Serious Business: Immense Prices Gained by Aviators." *Atlanta Constitution*, August 28, 1910, E2.

"Flying Now the King of Sports: Aeronautical Meets Force the Horse, the Yacht and the Auto into Second Place." *Washington Post*, August 7, 1910, M3.

Gray, George A. "Early Barnstorming." *U.S. Air Services*. February 1929, 49–52.

Hare, James H. "Landscape Photography from an Airplane." *Town and Country*. October 28, 1911, 19.

_____. "Why We Did Not Fly Across the Panama Isthmus." *Aero Club of America Bulletin*. April 1912.

Harmel, Falk. "First Jewish Airman." *B'nai B'rith*. October 1930, 6–7.

"He's Had Enough of Civilization: Old-time Aviator Going Back to Brazil." *Miami Daily News*, March 21, 1949, 1B, 4–6.

Hinds, James R. "Bombs Over Mexico." *Aerospace Historian* 31, no. 3 (September 1984): 194–201.

Hodgdon, Melvin W. "The Saga of Saugus." *Journal: American Aviation Historical Society* 20, no. 2 (Summer 1975): 128–129.

Holland, Samuel H. "Arthur L. (Al) Welsh: Pioneer of American Aviation." *The Record: Publication of the Jewish Historical Society of Greater Washington* 4, no. 1 (May 1969): 9–20.

"In Town & Country." *Town and Country*. October 21, 1911, 13.

"In Town & Country." *Town and Country*. November 4, 1911, 48–50.

Jones, Ernest. "The Air War in Mexico." *Chirp*, no. 29 (December 1940): 2–5.

"Life in South American Jungle Told by Daytonian." *Dayton Daily News*, n.d. Original clipping in possession of Rob Grant, Queensland, Australia.

Loening, Grover Cleveland. "The Wright Aviation School at Simms Station." *Flying* 3, no. 3 (April 1914): 76–77, 94.

Mansfield, Howard. "Becoming a Birdman: The Wright School of Aviation." *Timeline: A Publication of the Ohio Historical Society* 17, no. 4 (July/August 2000): 2–13.

Maurer, Maurer. "McCook Field, 1917–1927." *The Ohio Historical Quarterly* 67, no. 1 (January 1958): 21–34.

McCombs, Holland. "War Taps Brazil's Wild Rubber." *Life* 14, no. 2 (May 24, 1943): 19–25.

Milot, Claude. "Racing & Motor: The Early Years." *Motor* (March 2003): 27–33.

Mitchell, John. "Earnings of Aviators." *The Saturday Evening Post* 183, no. 15 (October 8, 1910): 14–15, 32.

Molson, K.M., comp. "Canadians at the Wright School." *American Aviation Historical Society Journal* 8 (Spring 1963): 40–41.

Newton, Wesley Phillips. "The Origins and Early Development of Civil Aviation in Montgomery, 1910–1946." *Alabama Review* 57, no. 1 (January 2004): 6–25.

_____. "The Role of Aviation in Mexican-United States Relations, 1912–1929." In *Militarists, Merchants, and Missionaries: United States Expansion in Middle America*, edited by Eugene R. Huck and Edward H. Moseley. Tuscaloosa: University of Alabama Press, 1970.

"Notes of the Week." *Town and Country*. October 21, 1911, 12.

"Oscar A. Brindley." *American Aviation Historical Society Journal* 4, no. 3 (Fall 1959): 214–215.

Parsons, Edwin C. "Military Aviation Efforts in Mexico in 1913." *The Sportsman Pilot* 12 (October 1940): 16, 31–32.

Pyle, Ernest T. "Seven Gallant Gentlemen, Each with a Past." *U.S. Air Services.* May 1929, 34–39.

"The Recent Army Aeronautical Accident." *Scientific American.* June 22, 1912, 558.

"Recent Trial Flights in the American Army." *Scientific American*, June 1, 1912, 491.

Resor, Randolph R. "Rubber in Brazil: Dominance and Collapse, 1876–1945." *Business History Review* 51, no. 3 (Autumn 1977): 341–366.

"Rich Men Take Up the Dangerous Sport of Flying." *New York Times*, June 26, 1910, SM5.

Rinehart, Howard M. "Flying for Villa." *The Sportsman Pilot*, November 15, 1939, 16–17, 30.

"Rinehart, Howard Max." *Who's Who in American Aeronautics.* New York: Gardner, Moffat, 1922.

"A Serious Business: Flying Schools and Exhibitions." *Aviation Week & Science Technology* 157, no. 27 (December 2002): 36.

Stinson, Marjorie. "The Diary of a Country Girl at Flying School." *Aero Digest* 12, no. 2 (February 1928).

Taylor, Charles E. "My Story of the Wright Brothers." *Collier's* 122, no. 26 (December 25, 1948): 67–68, 70.

Taylor, Lawrence D. "Pancho Villa's Aerial Corps: Foreign Aviators in the División del Norte, 1914–1915." *Air Power History* 43 (Fall 1996): 32–43.

Tomlinson, Harry J. "Rubber — At a Price." *The Inter-American* 3, no. 1 (January 1944): 11–13.

Wald, Quentin. "Working for the Wright Brothers: What My Father Learned at the Wright Company about Hydroaeroplanes, Close Calls, and Practical Jokes." *Air & Space* 14, no. 4 (Oct/Nov 1999): 58–63.

"Wanamaker Death Grieves Aviators." *New York Times,* March 10, 1928, 8.

"Who the Men Are that Will Handle American Cars and What They Have Done." *New York Times*, November 22, 1908, 54.

Woodcock, Reginald D. *Benoist: Thomas W. Benoist Airplane Company, Benoist Students and Pilots* [S.I.: s.n.] 1971.

Woodhouse, Henry. "The Airscout." *Town and Country*, October 28, 1911, 18.

Newspapers and Journals

Aero, 1910–1912.
Atlanta, 1908–1912.
Atlanta Constitution, 1908–1915.
Boston Daily Globe, 1910–1956.
Chicago Daily Tribune, 1910–1912.
Christian Science Monitor, 1910–1920.
Dayton Daily News, 1910–1951.

Dayton Journal, 1911–1912.
Hattiesburg (MS) American, 1949.
Los Angeles Times, 1910–1912.
Malone Farmer, 1912.
New York Times, 1905–1956.
Philadelphia Bulletin, 1910–1915.
Philadelphia Inquirer, 1910–1915.
Philadelphia Public Ledger, 1910–1915.
Richmond News Leader, 1912–1948.
Wall Street Journal, 1910–1915.
Washington, 1912.
Washington Post, 1910–1932.
Washington Times, 1912.

Official Publications

Foreign Relations of the United States. Diplomatic Papers: The American Republics. Vols. 5, 7, 9 (1942–
    1946). Washington, D.C.: Government Printing Office, 1962–1969.
Harrigan v. Bergdoll, 270 U.S. 560. No. 181, 1926.
*Report on Audit of Reconstruction Finance Corporation and Affiliated Corporations, Rubber Reserve Com-
    pany, and Rubber Development Corporation*. H.D. no. 444, vol. 7, 80th Congress, 2nd Session.
    Washington, D.C.: Government Printing Office, 1947.
United States Congress. House. Select Committee to Investigate Escape of General Prisoner Grover
    Cleveland Bergdoll from United States Disciplinary Barracks at
Governors Island, NY: Hearings under House Resolution 12, Sixty-Seventh Congress, First Session.
    Washington: G.P.O., 1921.

Unpublished Manuscripts

Perkins, James H. "Dayton During World War I, 1914 to 1918." Master's thesis, Miami University, 1959.

Oral Histories

The Reminiscences of Hillery Beachey. Aviation Project. No. 388, vol. II, Part I, Oral History Research
    Office. New York: Columbia University, 1960.

Web Sites

A. Holland Forbes, 1863–1927. http://www.earlyaviators.com/eforbes.htm.
Arch Freeman. http://www.earlyaviators.com/efreeman.htm.
A.S. Richardson Aeroplane Corporations, Inc. Lowell, MA. Richardson Tandem Hydroplane. http://
    www.aerofiles.com/_ra.html.
Arthur Welsh, 1881–1912. http://www.earlyaviators.com/ewelsh.htm.
Arthur Welsh: The First American Jewish Aviator. http://www.jhsgw.org/exhibitions/online/arthur
    welsh/resources.html.
Blue Hill, Maine Founding Families. RootsWeb.com. http://worldconnect.rootsweb.com/cgi-bin/
    igm.cgi?op=GET&db=bluehillme&id=15700.
Chevalier, George. When Aviation Came to Panama. http://plus44.safe-order.net/pancanalsociety/
    Articles/GC/Chevalier5.html.
Clifford L. Webster,–1980. http://www.earlyaviators.com/ewebster.htm.
Conservation-Borel-Morane. http://www.aviation.technomuses.ca/collections/conservation/Borel
    Morane.shtml.
Courthouse Fire of 1914 Razed Three Blocks of St. George St. http://www.staugustine.com/100 years/
    1894_court.shtml.
Daso, Major Dik. Origins of Airpower: Hap Arnold's Early Career in Aviation Technology, 1903–1935.
    http://www.airpower.maxwell.af.mil/airchronicles/apj/apj96/win96/daso.html.
Early Civilian Aviation. College Park Aviation Museum. http://www.pgparks.com/places/historic/
    cpam/3early.html.
Farley, Brandy Station Culpeper County, Virginia. http://www.dasaonline.com/p-resdetails.html.

The First U.S. Aircraft Manufacturing Companies, U.S. Centennial of Flight Commission. http://www.centennialofflight.gov/essay/Aerospace/earlyU.S./Aero 1.htm.

Frank Stuart Patterson. http://www.ascho.wpafb.af.mil/wpinfo/patterson.htm.

Fraterrigo, Elizabeth. "Over a Herd of Cattle": The Wright Brothers and the Pursuit of Flight at Huffman Prairie Flying Field. http://www.libraries.wright.edu/special/symposium/fraterrigo.html.

Fred J. Southard, 1872–1912. http://www.earlyaviators.com/esouthar.htm.

George A. Gray, 1882–1956. http://earlyaviators.com/egray.htm.

George Alphonso Gray, 1882–1956. http://earlybirds.org/gravg.html.

George Mestach–1920. http://earlyaviators.com/emestach.htm.

George W. Beatty, 1887–1955. http://www.earlyaviators.com/ebeatty.htm.

Gray, Carroll. *Cicero Flying Field's Origin, Operation, Obscurity and Legacy, 1891 to 1916.* http://lincolnbeachey.com/cicart.html.

Harold E. Talbott. http://www.af.mil/history/personprint.asp?storyID=123006473.

Harvard-Boston Aviation Meet–1910. http://www.earlyaviators.com/emeebo10.htm.

Henry Morrison Flagler Biography. http://flaglermuseum.us/html/flager_biography.html.

Henry Roy Waite, 1884–1978. http://earlybirds.org/waite.html.

Hillery Beachey, 1885–1964. http://earlybirds.org/beachey.html.

A History of the First U.S. Battleship New Jersey (BB-16). http://www.bb62museum.org/bb16danfs.html.

Howard Gill, 1883–1912. http://www.earlyaviators.com/egill.htm.

H. Roy Waite, 1884–1978. http://earlyaviators.com/ewaite.htm.

Huffman Prairie Flying Field. http://www.ascho.wpafb.af.mil/Huffman.HTM.

In Praise of the Birdman. http://www.jewishdayton.org/contentdisplay.html?print=1&articleID+68275&page=1.

Jack McGee, 1885–1918. http://www.earlyaviators.com/emcgee.htm.

J. Chauncey Redding, __–1915. http://www.earlyaviators.com/eredding.htm.

John A.D. McCurdy, 1886–1961. http://collections.ic.gc.ca/heirloomseries/volume6/126–127.htm.

John A.D. McCurdy, 1886–1961. *Flight Deck: Great Aviators.* http://www.exn.ca/FlightDeck/Aviators/mcurdy 2.cfm.

Kandebo, Stanley W. The Wright Brothers and the Birth of an Industry: A Celebration of the 100th Anniversary of Manned, Controlled, Sustained, Powered, Heavier-Than-Air Flight. http://www.aviationnow.com/content/ncof/ncf_n93.htm.

Later Wright Activities. http://www.centennialofflight.gov/essay/Wright_Bros/Later_Years/WR13.htm.

Lenger, John. Conquest of the Air: In Aviation's Early Days, Harvard Pioneers Advanced Aeronautics and Brought Flight to the Masses. http://www.harvardmagazine.com/print/050332.html.

Lionel H. DeRemer, 1889–1962. http://www.earlyaviators.com/ederemer.htm.

Lubin Manufacturing Company. http://frvdb.bfi.org.uk/sift/organization/7674.

1912 Wright Model C. *http://www.first-to-fly.com/History/JUST%20the%20Facts/Modelc.htm.*

Old Portland Airport. http://www.scarborough.k12.me.us/high/projects/amhistory/17.htm.

Oliver G. Simmons, 1878–1948. http://www.earlyaviators.com/esimmoli.htm.

Oliver Thomas–1948. http://www.earlyaviators.com/ethomoli.htm.

Paul Garber, 1899–1992. http://www.earlyaviators.com/egarber.htm.

Preserving the Cradle of Aviation (College Park Airport). http://cf.alpa.org/internet/asp/2000/aug00 p28.htm.

Special Effects? Not Quite ...The Wrights on Film. http://www.centennialofflight.gov/wbh/wr_experience/film/hmtl/thril.

Stearns-L Archives, RootsWeb.com. http://archiver.rootsweb/th/read/Stearns/2003–06/1054569895.

Thomas, Thomas-Morse. *Aerofiles: A Century of American Aviation.* http://www.aerofiles.com/thomas.html.

Thum, Robert. The First Jewish Aviator, a Leader among Wright Brothers' Original Pilots. http://www.juf.org/newspublicaffairs/article.asp?key=4139.

Tom Benoist, 1875–1917. http://www.home.earthlink.net/~ralphcooper/biobenoi.htm.

"Twin-Hydro aka Burgess-Gill 1912. *Aerofiles: A Century of American Aviation.* http://www.aerofiles.com/burgess.html.

The U.S. Aircraft Industry during World War I. http://www.centennialofflight.gov.essay/Aerospace/wwi/Aero 5.htm.

USN Ships — USS *Rhode Island* (Battleship #17). http://www.history.navy.mil/photos/sh-usn/usnsh-r/bb17.htm.

What Dreams We Have: The Wright Brothers and Their Hometown of Dayton, Ohio. http://www.cr.nps.gov/history/online_books/daav/chap9.htm.

William T. Thomas, 1888–1966. http://www.earlyaviators.com/ethomwil.htm.

Wood, Esther E. A History of George Stevens Academy. http://georgestevensacademy.schoolwires.com/12051072712165377.

Wright Model C: End of the Line. http://www.wrightstories.com/afterwards.html.

INDEX